ALLDATA 2018

The Fourth International Conference on Big Data, Small Data, Linked Data and Open Data

KESA 2018

The International Workshop on Knowledge Extraction and Semantic Annotation

April 22 - 26, 2018

Athens, Greece

ALLDATA 2018 Editors

Gary Weckman, Ohio University, USA
Jerzy Grzymala-Busse, University of Kansas, USA

Printed from e-media with permission by:

Curran Associates, Inc.
57 Morehouse Lane
Red Hook, NY 12571

Some format issues inherent in the e-media version may also appear in this print version.

Printed by Curran Associates, Inc. (2018)

International Academy, Research, and Industry Association (IARIA)
412 Derby Way
Wilmington, DE 19810

Phone: (408) 893-6407
Fax: (408) 527-6351

petre@iaria.org

Additional copies of this publication are available from:

Curran Associates, Inc.
57 Morehouse Lane
Red Hook, NY 12571 USA
Phone: 845-758-0400
Fax: 845-758-2633
Email: curran@proceedings.com
Web: www.proceedings.com

ALLDATA 2018

Forward

The Fourth International Conference on Big Data, Small Data, Linked Data and Open Data (ALLDATA 2018), held between April 22, 2018 and April 26, 2018 in Athens, Greece, continued a series of events bridging the concepts and the communities devoted to each of data categories for a better understanding of data semantics and their use, by taking advantage from the development of Semantic Web, Deep Web, Internet, non-SQL and SQL structures, progresses in data processing, and the new tendency for acceptance of open environments.

The volume and the complexity of available information overwhelm human and computing resources. Several approaches, technologies and tools are dealing with different types of data when searching, mining, learning and managing existing and increasingly growing information. From understanding Small data, the academia and industry recently embraced Big data, Linked data, and Open data. Each of these concepts carries specific foundations, algorithms and techniques, and is suitable and successful for different kinds of application. While approaching each concept from a silo point of view allows a better understanding (and potential optimization), no application or service can be developed without considering all data types mentioned above.

The conference had the following tracks:

- Linked data
- Challenges in processing Big Data and applications
- Knowledge Extraction and Semantic Annotation
- Small data
- Big Data and Open Data

The conference also featured the following workshop:

- ***KESA 2018,*** *The International Workshop on Knowledge Extraction and Semantic Annotation*

We take here the opportunity to warmly thank all the members of the ALLDATA 2018 technical program committee, as well as all the reviewers. The creation of such a high quality conference program would not have been possible without their involvement. We also kindly thank all the authors who dedicated their time and effort to contribute to ALLDATA 2018. We truly believe that, thanks to all these efforts, the final conference program consisted of top quality contributions.

We also gratefully thank the members of the ALLDATA 2018 organizing committee for their help in handling the logistics and for their work that made this professional meeting a success.

We hope that ALLDATA 2018 was a successful international forum for the exchange of ideas and results between academia and industry and to promote further progress in the field of big data, small data, linked data and open data. We also hope that Athens, Greece, provided a pleasant environment during the conference and everyone saved some time to enjoy the historic charm of the city.

ALLDATA 2018 Chairs

ALLDATA Steering Committee
Venkat N. Gudivada, East Carolina University, USA
Sandjai Bhulai, Vrije Universiteit Amsterdam, the Netherlands
Jerzy Grzymala-Busse, University of Kansas, USA
Fabrice Mourlin, Université Paris-Est Créteil Val de Marne, France
Andrzej Skowron, Warsaw University, Poland

ALLDATA Industry/Research Advisory Committee
Stephane Puechmorel, ENAC, France
Cyril Onwubiko, Research Series Ltd., London, UK
Loganathan Ponnambalam, Institute of High Performance Computing, A*STAR, Singapore
Hanmin Jung [정 한 민], Korea Institute of Science and Technology Information, South Korea

KESA IARIA Advisory
Dumitru Roman, SINTEF/University of Oslo, Norway

KESA Chairs
Maria Pia di Buono, Faculty of Electrical Engineering and Computing, University of Zagreb, Croatia
Annibale Elia, University of Salerno, Italy
Johanna Monti, University of Naples 'L'Orientale', Italy
James C.N. Yang, National Dong Hwa University, Taiwan

ALLDATA 2018
Committee

ALLDATA Steering Committee
Venkat N. Gudivada, East Carolina University, USA
Sandjai Bhulai, Vrije Universiteit Amsterdam, the Netherlands
Jerzy Grzymala-Busse, University of Kansas, USA
Fabrice Mourlin, Université Paris-Est Créteil Val de Marne, France
Andrzej Skowron, Warsaw University, Poland

ALLDATA Industry/Research Advisory Committee
Stephane Puechmorel, ENAC, France
Cyril Onwubiko, Research Series Ltd., London, UK
Loganathan Ponnambalam, Institute of High Performance Computing, A*STAR, Singapore
Hanmin Jung [정한민], Korea Institute of Science and Technology Information, South Korea

ALLDATA 2018 Technical Program Committee
Maurizio Atzori, University of Cagliari, Italy
Akhilesh Bajaj, University of Tulsa, USA
Gábor Bella, University of Trento, Italy / University of Edinburgh, UK
Sandjai Bhulai, Vrije Universiteit Amsterdam, Netherlands
Peter T. Breuer, Birmingham City University, UK / Hecusys LLC, Atlanta, USA
Keith Chan, The Hong Kong Polytechnic University, Hong Kong
Rachid Chelouah, EISTI, France
Yue Chen, Florida State University, USA
Roger H. L. Chiang, University of Cincinnati, USA
Esma Nur Cinicioglu, Istanbul University, Turkey
Carmela Comito, National Research Council of Italy (CNR) - Institute for High Performance Computing and Networking, Italy
Cinzia Daraio, Sapienza University of Rome, Italy
Maaike de Boer, TNO, Netherlands
Maria Cristina De Cola, IRCCS Centro Neurolesi "Bonino-Pulejo", Messina, Italy
Konstantinos Demertzis, Eastern Macedonia & Thrace Institute of Technology, Greece
Christian Dirschl, Wolters Kluwer Deutschland GmbH, Germany
Süleyman Eken, Kocaeli University, Turkey
Mounîm A. El Yacoubi, Telecom SudParis, France
Nadia Essoussi, University of Carthage, Tunisia
Jolon Faichney, Griffith University, Australia
Denise Beatriz Ferrari, Instituto Tecnológico de Aeronáutica, São José dos Campos - SP, Brazil
Paola Festa, University of Napoli FEDERICO II, Italy
Sandro Fonseca de Souza, Universidade do Estado do Rio de Janeiro, Brazil / CERN - European Laboratory for Particle Physics, Swizerland

Paolo Romano, University of Lisbon / INESC-ID, Portugal
Giulio Rossetti, Istituto di Scienza e Tecnologie dell'Informazione "A. Faedo" - National Research Council, Italy
Ryan Rossi, Palo Alto Research Center, USA
Peter Ruppel, Technische Universität Berlin, Germany
Jedrzej Rybicki, Supercomputing Center Juelich, Germany
Suzanne Michelle Shontz, University of Kansas, USA
Andrzej Skowron, Warsaw University, Poland
Marek Śmieja, Jagiellonian University, Poland
Srivathsan Srinivasagopalan, Visa Inc., USA
Bela Stantic, Griffith University, Australia
Uta Störl, University of Applied Sciences Darmstadt, Germany
Maurizio Tesconi, Institute of Informatics and Telematics - CNR, Italy
Ismail Hakki Toroslu, Middle East Technical University, Turkey
Chrisa Tsinaraki, European Commission - Joint Research Centre, Italy
Stefanos Vrochidis, ITI-CERTH, Greece
Hironori Washizaki, Waseda University, Japan
Ouri Wolfson, University of Illinois, USA
Feng George Yu, Youngstown State University, USA
Roberto Yus, University of California, Irvine, USA
Fouad Zablith, American University of Beirut, Lebanon
Bo Zhang, IBM, USA
Li Zhang, Northumbria University, Newcastle, UK
Qiang Zhu, University of Michigan, USA

KESA IARIA Advisory

Dumitru Roman, SINTEF/University of Oslo, Norway

KESA Chairs

Maria Pia di Buono, Faculty of Electrical Engineering and Computing, University of Zagreb, Croatia
Annibale Elia, University of Salerno, Italy
Johanna Monti, University of Naples 'L'Orientale', Italy
James C.N. Yang, National Dong Hwa University, Taiwan

KESA 2018 Technical Program Committee

Afrand Agah, West Chester University of Pennsylvania, USA
Rodrigo Agerri, University of the Basque Country (UPV/EHU), Spain
Ahmet Aker, University of Sheffield, UK
Flora Amato, University of Naples, Italy
Mehran Asadi, Lincoln University, USA
Ozgu Can, Ege University, Turkey
Se-Hak Chun, Seoul National University of Science and Technology, South Korea
Bojana Dalbelo-Bašić, University of Zagreb, Croatia

Copyright Information

Table of Contents

Small Data: Applications and Architecture

Cheng-Kang Hsieh*, Faisal Alquaddoomi†, Fabian Okeke‡, John P. Pollak§, Lucky Gunasekara¶ and Deborah Estrin‖
* UCLA CSD; Los Angeles, CA, USA (changun@cs.ucla.edu)
† UCLA CSD; Los Angeles, CA, USA (faisal@cs.ucla.edu)
‡ Cornell CSD; Ithaca, NY, USA (fno2@cornell.edu)
§ Cornell Tech; New York, NY, USA (jpp9@cornell.edu)
¶ Cornell Tech; New York, NY, USA (llg24@cornell.edu)
‖ Cornell Tech; New York, NY, USA (destrin@cornell.edu)

Abstract—**Small data are the digital traces that individuals generate as a byproduct of their daily activities, such as: communicating through email or text; buying groceries or ordering delivery; or going to work on foot or by car. These traces can empower individuals to gain insights into their behavior, personalize their care, improve their relationships, motivate achievement of goals, and broadly improve their quality of life. As such small data are both byproducts of today's and drivers of tomorrow's ubiquitous computing applications. The contributions of this paper are twofold: we motivate the requirements for a small data ecosystem and supporting architecture, and present a critical component – Lifestreams Database (DB) – which is evaluated using three exemplar apps. Lifestreams DB extracts, processes, and models diverse traces from data silos and enables various small data applications through simple SPARQL queries. Its soft-state design provides storage-efficiency, robustness, and query performance for processing small data.**

Keywords–small data; linked data; knowledge representation.

I. Introduction

Small data are "digital traces", records of our activities that are stored as we interact with the world around us. These traces are passively produced when we use tools and services that maintain logs: credit cards, grocery receipts, websites and other streaming content services, browsers themselves, etc. They can also be intentionally produced and tracked by wearable sensors, including mobile phone applications. It is well-known that service providers derive value from this information – usage metrics and demographic information, all personal data, are routinely employed to help direct advertisement and optimize products. We argue that this data can and should provide value for the producers of this data as well. As a natural extension of prior ubiquitous computing applications, **small data apps** will emerge as an important class of ubicomp applications that concern themselves with deriving insight from personal data at the user's request and with their oversight.

For example, a small data app may promote healthier eating by coaching users to take the planning actions needed to prepare meals at home. The app would utilize grocery and online food delivery history, browser history, and Moves or Foursquare data to build a model of meal preferences. The user could then receive prompts at their desired frequency about which recipes they are likely to enjoy, and suggestions for additions to their grocery shopping list to enable them to prepare these meals at home. The app could incentivize this with informative comparisons of calorie and cost savings, or could be tied to more intentional gamification. Another small data app could allow independent living elderly to share how they are doing without sharing every detail of what they are doing. The app would make use of passively collected small data streams such as email, activities, and mobile phone usage to create a personalized model of the user's activity, well-being, and degree of social engagement. Rather than exposing the model itself, the app would expose deviations from the model to make family and friends aware of changes to a person's state without divulging detailed information. Such an app can support many types of relationships, including family and friends separated geographically, or other support-network relationships such as social workers, caregivers, and coaches. We describe these concepts in greater detail in section III.

The central role of a small data architecture is to facilitate application-level access to a person's diverse information sources on their behalf. While individual service providers, such as Google, Facebook, and Amazon each have information about many aspects of our behavior, they are limited in how specifically they personalize by the terms of their end-user licensing agreements and a need to preserve users' trust. They also do not each have access to all data of interest. Because of this, there is an opportunity in the market for providers to give users access to their individual data in various forms (application programming interfaces, downloads, email receipts), and for third-party products to emerge that integrate with that user's data in the same way that third party mobile apps make use of mobile-device data. These third party apps would serve the end user without degrading the large-service provider's position, and in fact have the potential to solidify the user's sense of the service provider's utility and trustworthiness. Note that we are promoting that users be given access to their data and not making any statement about data ownership. We are also not addressing the very important policy question regarding service providers making user data available to third parties directly.

As mentioned, service providers have difficulty providing apps that cut across multiple data sources or mine too deeply into their users' data. In contrast, a small data app leverages the user as the common denominator, and can take advantage of the trend for service providers to support application programming interfaces (APIs) for individuals to their data. The user has both the access and authority to collect and aggregate data across these providers, allowing for powerful and comprehensive insights that, by virtue of the fact that they are initiated and consumed by that same user, can be much more focused in their oversight and suggestions. We anticipate and favor broad provision and adoption of systematic programmatic access to personal data for the end users. However, the need for a small-data application architecture need not wait for, nor will it be obviated by, future developments. Already, today, users can obtain access to their data, albeit through idiosyncratic and sometimes ad-hoc channels: e-receipts, diverse APIs, browser plug-ins, etc. Even with access to these data, infrastructure is still required to process these traces into formats that are useful and actionable to the individual. Since most individual users do not develop their own software, we are targeting support for small-data app developers who will implement apps on the behalf of this growing user base; just as they have driven the development of third party apps for smartphones [1]. This approach is aligned with the emerging Social Web activities in W3C [2].

Our vision is to create a **small data ecosystem** in which small data apps can be readily developed and deployed atop an infrastructure that standardizes their inter-operation and addresses concerns that are common across apps, such as helping to ensure security and reducing redundancy in storage and computational resources, as well as resolving policy/legal questions that are outside the scope of this paper. The vision is, again, driven by the individual as the common denominator, and rightful beneficiary, of access to their data.

We describe the core components of a small data architecture using three exemplar applications, and present a specific system-design for the most central of these components – Lifestreams Database (hereafter "Lifestreams DB"). Lifestreams DB is designed to extract and process diverse digital traces from various sources and make them available to the client applications for further analysis or visualization. **Data interoperability** is an important requirement for such a system as it allows one to gain insights from the combination of data that were originally locked in their own data silos. Lifestreams DB extracts raw data from these data silos, and transforms them into a standardized Resource Description Format (RDF) that allows one to join these digital traces against each other and with external RDF data sources (e.g., fuse nutrition information with users' online shopping records.)

Unlike many enterprise settings, small data differs in the fact that most of original sources (e.g., Google, Facebook, etc.) persist users' data in their own databases and individually provide security and access control. Therefore, it may be wasteful, or even harmful to the users' security and privacy for Lifestreams DB to permanently replicate these data in one place. Motivated by this distinction, we propose a **soft-state design** that, while providing client applications with virtual access to all the data, only caches a part of it locally, and reproduces the rest on demand. Such a design introduces two important advantages in the context of small data. First, our soft-state model discourages our system from becoming a data "honeypot" that attracts attacks from malicious entities since only a limited amount of information is cached in the system at any given time. Second, it requires much less storage and allows the system to scale to serve a large number of users or integrate with more diverse information beyond its storage capacity. We also provide an encryption mechanism that encrypts the sensitive data to further protect the user.

After introducing related work in section II, we present three small data applications in III and use them to identify cross cutting application requirements. We provide a brief overview of our architecture in section IV, then go into depth on the main contribution of this work, Lifestreams Database (DB), in section V. Section VI contains the results of performance analyses for simulated workloads on a sample of simple and complex query types. Finally, section VII provides some observations and outlines future work.

II. Related Work

Small data are fueling a new genre of personalization technologies. Recommender systems have been some of the most successful applications in this domain to date as evidenced by recommendations for music in Pandora, consumer goods in Amazon [3], articles in Wikipedia [4], and locations in Foursquare [5]. These systems rely heavily on the users' application-specific histories, such as queries, clicks, ratings, and browsing data that result from interacting with their product. Small data can enable far more immersive recommender systems that take into account a larger space of user needs and constraints. In particular, they can benefit from user models derived from both more diverse and longitudinal data (e.g., features and dynamic patterns in: daily travel patterns, consumption from gaming to dining, interests and sentiment expressed in personal communication, etc.). General-purpose recommendation frameworks such as MyMediaLite [6] and LensKit [7] (to name a few) could make use of small data to learn these kinds of broad user models, but they require a front-end component to fetch user's data and drive the framework with appropriately-formatted inputs.

Small data's goal of providing individuals with transformative insights into their behavior is aligned with that of the Quantified Self (QS) movement [8]. In QS studies, individual experimenters engage in the self-tracking of biological or behavioral information using commercial devices such as Fitbit and myZero sleep trackers, or personal testing services such as 23AndMe, and many systems have been developed to help integrate and visualize QS data [9]. Even prior to QS's popularity, research projects such as Ubifit and BeWell demonstrated the potential of making personal data actionable [10][11]. More recent work, i.e., EmotionCheck [12], has demonstrated that not only QS data itself, but a user's trust in the tool, can serve as effective leverage for behavioral change. Small data, however, differs from earlier studies in its focus on harnessing data that are (a) generated as byproducts of interacting with services and (b) that are readily available, versus having to be manually collected or otherwise procured. These data can be complementary to or serve as a proxy for some of the data that QS studies collect.

Small data are also related to Personal Information Management (PIM) systems [13]. This line of work covers a broad range of environments from desktops [14][15], to connected-devices in the home [16][17], to e-learning [18] and health information management systems [19]-[22]. Our work is complementary to these systems' focus on information organization and retrieval, by providing support for third party applications that would generate additional inputs to these systems through the processing of small data streams that are not yet accessible.

Small data shares similar data input with Personal Automation Engines. For example, Atomate [23] is a system that integrates individuals' social and life-tracking feeds into a unified RDF database, and automatically carries out simple tasks (e.g., messaging) when the incoming feeds satisfy user-defined rules. The service "If-This-Then-That" (IFTTT) [24], expanding on the same idea, compiles a large set of feeds that monitor various online and offline activities and can trigger a wide set of actions when a user-defined condition on a feed is satisfied. On a more application-focused and user-local

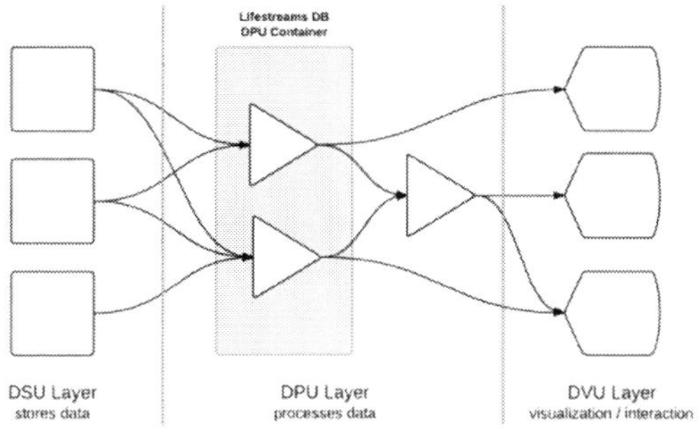

Figure 1. Small Data Architecture: illustrates the flow of data between Data Storage Units (DSUs), Data Processing Units (DPUs), and Data Visualizations Units (DVUs, e.g., apps).

level, PrefMiner [25] monitors on-device notifications from numerous sources to identify which notifications are important to the user or not. Small data differs from these services in its emphasis on providing insights that require longer-term observation, rather than performing transient event-driven actions. This fundamental distinction results in rather different system requirements, particularly in resource management and security as mentioned in the introduction. That said, our small data application architecture could enable a richer set of inputs to both of these systems.

Our aims are similar to existing systems that provide a modular computational infrastructure and mediate the release of processed personal data, such as openPDS and Virtual Individual Servers [26][27]. While these systems do provide personal data acquisition, storage, and release, they do not explicitly address the problem of normalizing and joining disparate data streams under a shared ontology. Our work complements these systems in providing data modeling and interoperability required to join multiple data streams, as opposed to simply providing analysis of individual data streams.

III. Small Data Applications

A small data application is an application that operates on multiple personal data streams, produces some kind of analysis of these streams, and presents the result to the user via an interface. Personal data can include static data, for instance the individual's genome or family lineage. We focus particularly on temporal data, either regular or episodic, that must be continually collected and analyzed. The reason for this focus is twofold: first, these information-rich data sources will be most transformative in creating detailed user models and feedback for diverse applications, and second the temporal data are the more difficult to manage since it is constantly accumulating. Of course, our focus on temporal data does not obviate the value of joining the user's data with other non-temporal data sets - e.g., summarizing nutritional exposure using temporal grocery receipts and relatively-static nutritional databases.

Below, we motivate the requirements of our software architecture using three exemplar small data apps. These applications comprise two data access modes – background and foreground. In the background mode, the application may periodically access a long history of user data to build or update the user's behavioral model. In the foreground, the user experience tends to be based on a more recent window of time, interpreted in the context of the behavioral model.

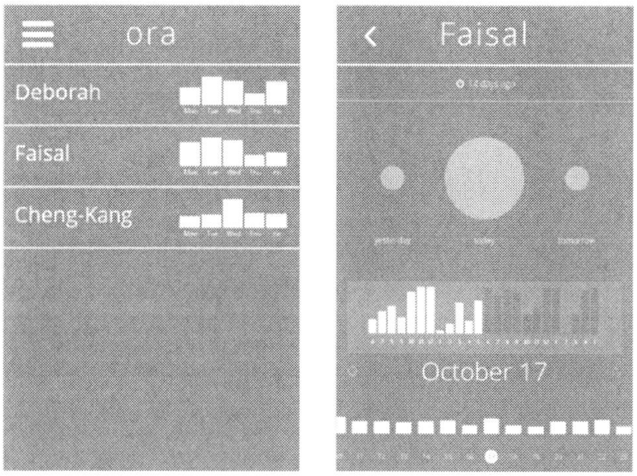

(a) Ora: List

(b) Ora: User Details

Figure 2. Ora: User List and Details View

A. *Ora*

Ora (Figure 2) is a tool for sharing how you are doing – without sharing the details of what you are doing – with family, friends, or other people who might be part of your support network (counselors, coaches, etc.) Users interact with Ora via a mobile-optimized website, where they authorize the app to connect to their Gmail and Moves accounts using an OAuth2 grant. Ora extracts descriptive numeric features from these data sources and uses them to build a baseline model that represents the user's usual values for each feature. Deviations from this model are calculated on a per-day basis and summarized into a single numeric value, referred to as a *pulse*, that acts an opaque indicator of the degree to which the user is deviating from the model.

Specifically, the pulse is computed from 20 features extracted from the users' data, including their **geodiameter** (the distance between the furthest two points in their location trace for the day), **exercise duration** (the number of minutes the user was walking or running), **time not at home** (the amount of time not spent at their primary location, typically their home), and the **number of emails sent** in a day. Then, for a set of features F, the baseline for each $f \in F$ is computed as a tuple consisting of the sample standard deviation and mean over a two-month sliding window. For a given day, the pulse (P) is then computed as the sum of the numbers of standard deviations from the mean for each feature.

B. *Pushcart*

Pushcart (Figure 3) uses receipts from services such as FreshDirect or Peapod to determine the nutritional value of the food that a household purchases. This information is provided to a "Wizard of Oz" system in which a clinician, masquerading as a learning algorithm, reviews the purchasing habits of each household and suggests substitutions of more nutritional items during future purchases.

The system's primary source of input is email – after opting in, users register the system to automatically receive a copy of their receipt email, from which the list of items is extracted and then joined against a database of nutritional information for each food item. The user interacts with the system through email as well: the user interface is a weekly "report email"

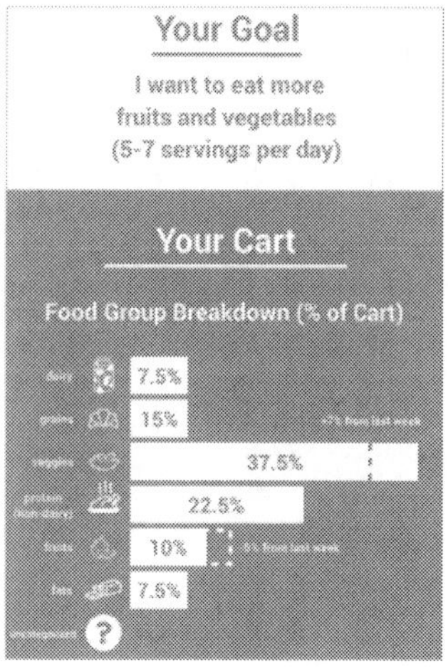

Figure 3. Pushcart: Weekly Email Report

that shows a breakdown of purchases in terms of nutritional value, and includes the nutritionist's suggestions.

C. Partner

Partner is an exploratory app designed around the hypothesis that people who spend time together tend to mimic each others' language patterns, and that the extent of this mimicry is an indicator of good relations; this is a phenomenon known as *linguistic style matching* [28]. The application uses both Gmail and Moves as its data source. After users have registered for the system, it passively collects their email and location data, building a retrospective view of the time they spend physically proximate to each other, the degree of linguistic style matching evidenced by similar values for descriptive metrics used in authorship identification, and the correlation of the two aforementioned values.

Partner relies on a few standard metrics used in authorship attribution, specifically entropy [29], stylometrics such as the percentage of personal pronouns and ratio of functional words to non-functional words (the "information density"), and the index of qualitative variation (IQV, specifically, the Gibbs M1 index) which serves as a measure of the variability of the user's vocabulary. Each of these features is computed over a categorical distribution of the user's tokens, which is produced from the concatenation of a user's emails into week-long intervals to compensate for the sparsity issues that email presents.

IV. Architecture

Our architecture is inspired by the concept of a "mashup", an application that merges multiple disparate data sources into a single interface. We started with the typical web mashup, in which data are acquired, processed, and presented solely by and at the client. We then factored out the acquisition and processing into distinct, reusable modules which can be run in the cloud and potentially consumed by multiple clients. Common concerns, such as caching, access control, and data normalization, are provided as system-wide services. While it would be feasible to implement the acquisition and processing components as tightly-coupled, one-off solutions for a single mashup, the redundancy of doing so for each additional app has lead us toward a centralized and reusable architecture.

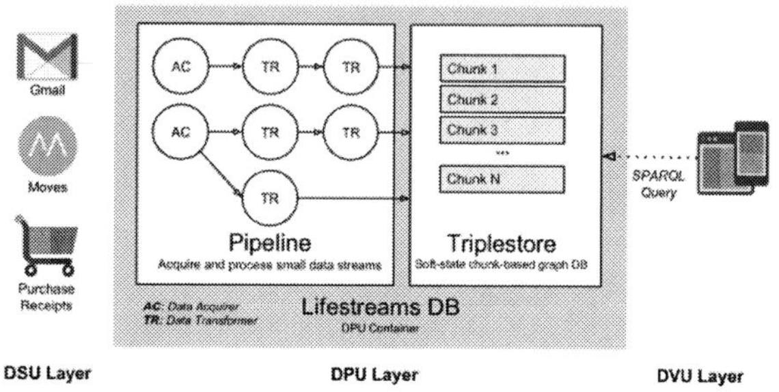

Figure 4. Lifestreams DB Pipeline: consists of a set of DPU modules that acquire and process data from various small data DSUs.

The architecture is composed of three layers, as depicted in Figure 1. There are three main entities: **Data Storage Units** (DSUs), **Data Processing Units** (DPUs), and **Data Visualization Units** (DVUs). These terms mirror the open mHealth standard [30]. DSUs include service provider APIs, e.g., Google's numerous service APIs and Facebook's Graph API. DSUs can be accessed directly from DPUs/DVUs, but are often accessed through a "transforming" DPU that converts the API's often proprietary data format into the schemas we use in small data apps. Data flows from DSUs through arbitrary compositions of DPUs – so long as their input and output types are compatible – and terminates in the DVUs. Lifestreams DB acts as a container for DPUs, and provides caching, data modeling, access control, and a unified query interface. Its outputs can be directly consumed by DVUs, or by other DPUs that provide additional data processing capability.

This modular pipeline approach is necessitated by the fact that our system will never be complete; there will always be new data sources and means of processing and displaying data, which the architecture should readily accommodate. Further, the implementation of its components is a collaborative effort and we wish to encourage developers to reuse and build upon existing components.

V. DPU Containers: Lifestreams DB

Lifestreams DB is an important component in our architecture. Positioned between data sources and small data apps, Lifestreams DB is designed to be the "narrow waist" of the small data ecosystem that provides a unified interface for querying, combining, and fusing diverse small data streams.

Lifestreams DB contains a pipeline of DPUs that Extract, Transform and Load (ETL) an individual's digital traces from different sources using common software APIs and Schemas to enable diverse small data applications. Figure 4 illustrates the architecture of Lifestreams DB. On the left is ***Lifestreams Pipeline***, a data processing pipeline that contains a set of reusable DPUs that extract raw data from different small data sources and transform raw data into structured, readily usable information. For example, raw actigraphy and geolocation sensor samples from a mobile app are transformed into structured data that describe the time, location, speed, and distance of each activity episode. These extracted data are loaded into ***Lifestreams Triplestore***, an RDF datastore built on top of Jena TDB [31], that exposes an integrated view of all the diverse RDF data for apps to query. We made two principal design decisions when designing Lifestreams DB: 1) to model data using RDF, and 2) to utilize a soft-state system design. The rationales behind these design decisions are described in the following.

a) Using RDF for interoperability: Data interoperability is key to the success of such a system. Raw data extracted from different data silos need to be transformed into a compatible form to allow one to derive knowledge from them. In Lifestreams DB, we utilize RDF to enable data interoperability. Each DPU outputs data in JavaScript Object Notation (JSON), and the DPUs at the final stage generate RDF data in the JSON-LD format, which will be transformed into RDF triples (i.e., *subject-predicate-object*) before stored in the Triplestore. The advantages of using RDF are as follow. First, it eliminates the need to define database schema, unlike, for example, in a Structured Query Language (SQL) datastore. Data generated by different DPUs are inherently interoperable if the DPUs follow the same ontology to model the data. This property is of significant benefit to a small data ecosystem, since it allows DPUs developed by different people to be plug-and-play without the need to modify the system's database schema. Also, any client application developer, given the ontology, can compose queries to filter, join, and aggregate various types of data generated by different DPUs without knowing specific implementation details such as table and column names, etc.

b) A Soft-State System Design: Architecturally, one major difference between an individuals' digital traces and an enterprise's operational data is that an individual's data are mostly persisted and protected in each original data source's databases (e.g., Google, Facebook). In many cases, there is no need, and is actually wasteful and harmful to the users' security and privacy, for Lifestreams DB to replicate all these data in one place. Thus, we propose a soft-state design that, while providing the client applications with virtual access to all the data, only caches a small portion of it in the system. Data which the user owns (e.g., sensor data from the user's phone or wearable) can be considered in the same way, except that it will reside on a personal DSU instead of in an external organization.

The advantages of this design are three-fold: First, a soft-state design requires much less storage to serve the requests, and thus allows the system to scale more effortlessly to serve a larger number of users and integrate with more diverse information beyond its storage capacity. Further, it enables elastic storage provision, where a service provider can provide the service with less storage (at consequently lower cost), and increase the storage provision only when better performance is needed. Second, it makes the system more robust, since there are less points where critical data loss can occur. If the system needs to be brought down, it can be done so without concern over maintaining important state. Third, a soft-state design inherently has better security properties. Since only a small amount of information is cached in the system at any given time, the exposure of any single data breach is limited. In addition, the fact that the data can be repopulated into the database on-the-fly allows us to encrypt sensitive data and only decrypt them when they are demanded.

These advantages do not come without a price. A soft-state system tends to incur much overhead in indexing, reproducing, and reloading data. In Lifestreams DB, we reduce these overheads by utilizing a chunk-based data management strategy that generates and manages data in chunks. Our design is particularly suitable for applications that perform timeseries-based analysis with temporal locality where subsequent accesses tend to access records that are near in time (in our scheme, in the same chunk.) Within these assumptions, we have improved Lifestreams DB's query performance by multiple factors (compared to the base Jena TDB triplestore) and made it perform even better than a hard-state system that stores all the data with only a fraction of storage space.

TABLE I. DATA MODELING TYPE ASSIGNMENTS

Data	Source	Subject Types	Object Types
Location/Mobility	Moves API [32]	Stay/Travel	Place
Email	Gmail API	Send/Receive	EmailMessage
Purchase	Gmail API	Buy	Product
Calendar	gCal API	Join	Event
Web Browse	Android API	Browse	WebPage
App Usage	Android API	Use	MobileApp
Phone Call	Android API	Call/Receive	Person
Message	Android API	Send/Receive	SMSMessage

In the following, we first describe our RDF-based data modeling approaches and demonstrate its advantages using the SPARQL queries for the real-world small data applications we are developing. Then, we describe the chunk-based management strategy and the techniques we used to realize the proposed soft-state design.

A. Data Modeling

When modeling data using RDF, one needs to follow a certain *ontology*. In small data, the concepts we come across most often are the various *actions* performed by users, such as sending emails, making purchases, etc. We chose schema.org [33] as the main ontology rather than the other competing candidates, such as Activity Streams [34], for its semantic action type system. Schema.org defines a hierarchical type system that describes different (sub)categories of actions. At the root is **Action**, a generic type that describes the common properties of an action (e.g., agent, time, etc.). It is then subclassed by more specific types, such as **MoveAction**, which, in turn, are subclassed by more specific types, such as **ArriveAction**, **DepartAction**, etc. This hierarchical structure enables one to write queries to reason across different types of actions within specific categories. For example, an app that encourages better sleep hygiene may analyze users' before-sleep routines by querying certain action categories (e.g., the ExerciseAction and all its subclasses) that occurred before the sleep period.

Table I summarizes eight different kinds of data we have extracted and modeled from four different data sources, based on schema.org's ontology. The purchase records are derived from email receipts on an opt-in basis. The phone-based data are uploaded to ohmage, a mobile sensing DSU. In the following, we demonstrate how our data modeling approaches can satisfy the requirements of the small data applications described previously with simple SPARQL queries.

Ora: Listing 5 shows a snippet of Ora Query that computes the geodiameter and the number of emails sent in a day. For brevity, the snippet omits the part that limits the time range to a single day. The first part of the snippet computes the geodiameter by selecting the maximum distance between any pairs of places at which the user stayed. The second part of the query counts the number of **SendAction**'s of which the targeted object is an email. This example is intended to

```
PREFIX schema: <http://schema.org/>
SELECT * {
  SELECT (MAX(?dist) AS ?geodiameter)
  {  ?stay_x a schema:StayAction;
             schema:location ?loc_x.
     ?stay_y a schema:StayAction;
             schema:location ?loc_y.
     BIND (
        fn:distanceInMeter(?loc_x, loc_y) AS ?dist
     ).}
  SELECT (COUNT(?send) AS ?mail_count)
  {  ?send a schema:SendAction;
           schema:object ?object.
     ?object a schema:EmailMessage.}
}
```

Figure 5. A short snippet from Ora query that computes the geodiameter and the number of emails sent.

```
PREFIX text: <http://jena.apache.org/text#>
PREFIX usda: <http://data-gov.tw.rpi.edu/vocab/p/1458/>
SELECT *
{  ?action a schema:BuyAction.
   ?action schema:object ?product.
   ?product schema:name ?product_name.
   SERVICE <http://localhost/usda/endpoint> {
    ?food_item text:query
         (usda:shrt_desc ?product_name 1).
    ?food_item usda:carbohydrt ?carbon;
               usda:protein ?protein.
   }
}
```

Figure 6. Pushcart Query joins an individual's food purchase records with the corresponding nutritional information contained in the USDA nutrient database.

demonstrate how much an application developer can achieve with Lifestreams DB using a succinct and easy to understand query. Also, this example demonstrates how heterogeneous data streams (i.e., Location/Mobility and Email) are modeled and queried in an interoperable and standardized way.

Pushcart: Listing 6 shows a snippet of the Pushcart query. It demonstrates Lifestreams DB's interoperability with an external food nutrition database. A RDF dump of the United States Department of Agriculture (USDA) nutrient database is pre-loaded into a separate triplestore [35]. The query joins the individuals' grocery purchase records with the entries contained in the USDA database using a free-text matching based on the product names, and select the amount of carbohydrates and protein contained in each of the purchased items.

Partner: Partner is an example of an app which, in addition to Lifestreams DB, requires a more domain-specific DPU. It relies on Lifestreams DB to compute the amount of time two participants spent together based on the distance between where two users stay (see Listing 7) and uses the Email Analysis Framework (EAF), a DPU for email language analysis [36], to evaluate language style matching. It is also an example where an application can query from not only one but across multiple users' data with RDF *named graphs* that refer to each user.

```
PREFIX fn: <http://lifestreams.example.org/customFn#>
PREFIX users: <http://lifestreams.example.org/users#>
SELECT (SUM(?overlap) AS ?co_present_time)
{  GRAPH <users:Bob> {
      ?stay_x a schema:StayAction;
      schema:location ?loc_x.}
   GRAPH <users:Alice> {
      ?stay_y a schema:StayAction;
      schema:location ?loc_y.}
   FILTER(fn:distanceInMeter(?loc_x, ?loc_y) < 50)
   BIND (
    fn:overlappingTime(?stay_x, ?stay_y) AS ?overlap
    )
}
```

Figure 7. Partner Query computes the time two users spent together based on their location data. Each user's data are referred to by their *named graph*.

B. Chunk-based Data Management

As mentioned, Lifestreams DB's soft-state design is made possible by a chunk-based strategy. The basic idea behind this strategy is as follows: The DPUs in Lifestreams Pipeline generate data in chunks and load them into Lifestreams Triplestore, which maintains an index to all the chunks (including the ones that are not cached in the system). When a client application submits a query, it will additionally submit a meta-query that selects the chunks it desires. If a chunk selected by the meta-query is not currently available in the system, Lifestreams Pipeline will re-run the corresponding DPUs and reproduce the chunk on the fly from the source. The chunks that contain sensitive data (determined from the data source and the user's preferences) will be encrypted and decrypted on the fly when requested by a query. The chunks are encrypted with 256-bit Advanced Encryption Standard (AES).

Our strategy allows a system to maintain only a small amount of information (i.e., the chunk index) while providing access to much larger amount of data that is beyond the system's storage capacity. In the following, we describe three major designs that realize this strategy and discuss several query optimization techniques enabled with chunking that can be utilized to provide a better user experience.

1) Chunk Index Design: The chunk index needs to be carefully designed to avoid unnecessary chunk reproduction. For each chunk of data, we extract the following features as its index:

- Distinct object types in the chunk.
- Start time and end time of the aggregate timespan.
- Geo-coordinates of a convex hull that covers all the spatial features in the chunk.

The rationales behind these choices are as follow. First, most of our applications are interested in certain types of actions or objects (e.g., CommunicationActions or ExerciseActions) so object types are a natural choice for indexing. Also, most of small data are time-tagged, and the applications we focus on tend to involve analysis of time series and aggregation based on time or location. Therefore, it is important for us to make chunk index satisfy these requirements.

2) Lifestreams Pipeline: a reproducible pipeline: We adopt a functional approach to allow Lifestreams Pipeline to reproduce arbitrary chunks of data from the original sources. The Lifestreams Pipeline consists of two types of DPUs: **Acquirers** acquire raw data from the sources while **Transformers** transform data from one form to another. These DPUs are treated as passive functions invoked by the system. Consider a simple pipeline where one Acquirer and one Transformer linked in sequence. In each iteration, the system invokes the Acquirer with a *state variable* that indicates the chunk we want the Acquirer to fetch. After fetching the corresponding chunk, the Acquirer will return the chunk along with a new state variable that indicates the subsequent chunk to be acquired in the next iteration. The system then invokes the Transformer to transform the chunk, and stores the output chunk along with the state variable. When the chunk is removed, the state variable will be preserved in the system. Therefore, when we need to reproduce the chunk, we just need to re-run the pipeline with the preserved state variable.

An assumption we make here is that the raw data are permanently persisted in the original data sources (i.e., DSUs), and can be re-acquired by the Acquirer anytime. If this is not the case, a *shim* can be implemented to transfer the data to a DSU with such properties (such as Amazon S3). Unlike some chunk-based systems where the chunk sizes are pre-determined, Lifestreams DB allows each Acquirer to decide the chunk sizes according to the characteristics of the APIs it acquires data from. A typical chunk size is daily as it is supported by most data sources. However, as the state variable is updated by the Acquirers themselves, Acquirers can have state variables with different formats or granularity (e.g., hours, weeks.). This feature is important for small data where one usually needs to work with a large variety of external data sources whose APIs it has no control over.

3) Two-Level GDS Chunk Replacement Policy: Similar to many cache systems, Lifestreams DB requires a replacement policy to select chunks for replacement when the available space is low. Our replacement policy minimizes the overall expected query latency by selecting the chunks that are of larger size and less likely to be used again, and can be reproduced in shorter time. There are two ways to make space in Lifestreams DB: (1) compress the chunk, or (2) evict the chunk entirely. Compression on average results in 7.2x size reduction and can be restored more efficiently than reproducing a chunk from the source. Considering this difference, as well as, the varying chunk sizes and cost in reproducing different kinds of chunks (see Table II), we develop a Two-level Greedy-Dual-Size (Two-Level GDS) replacement policy that is both cost- and size-aware and appropriately choose between two space reduction methods. The basic Greedy-Dual (GD) algorithm assigns each chunk a cost value H. Every time when a replacement needs to be made, the chunk with the lowest H value H_{min} will be replaced first, and all the other chunks reduce their H values by H_{min}. Only when a chunk is accessed again will its H value be restored to its initial value. Greedy-Dual-Size (GDS) incorporates the different chunk sizes by assigning H as $cost/size$ of the chunk [37]. On top of that, our Two-Level GDS algorithm additionally considers the different characteristics of compression and eviction. When a chunk is first inserted into the cache, its $cost$ is set to the estimated decompression latency, and the $size$ is the estimated space reduction after compression. When this chunk is selected for replacement, it will be compressed and re-inserted into the cache with its $cost$ increased to the estimated latency to reproduce it from the source, and the $size$ decreased to its size after compression. Only when this chunk is selected again will it be completely evicted. Similarly, after a chunk is reproduced, it will be first stored in its compressed form. When it is accessed again, it will have a certain probability to be promoted to its decompressed form. The default probability for a compressed chunk to be restored is 0.2. In this way, our algorithm uses compression as the default to make space for its efficiency, but still removes the compressed chunks to reduce cache clutter if they have not been used for long.

TABLE II. GMAIL AND MOVES DATA-SIZE AND REPRODUCTION-TIME CHARACTERISTICS

Avg. Values of 180 Chunks	Gmail	Moves
Chunk Size (KB)	20.32	392.44
Compressed Chunk Size (KB)	3.08	54.12
Required HTTP Requests	14.24	1
Reproduction Time (msec)	1423.63	182.17

4) Chunk-Assisted RDF Query Evaluation: The flexibility of RDF is not without its drawbacks: compared to many SQL datastores, a RDF datastore tends to be slower in query evaluation due mainly to the difficulty of constructing an effective data index [38]. Our chunk-based strategy has several desirable side benefits that mitigate this problem. First, chunk indexes can be utilized as a multi-column index that allows the query engine to take a short path by skipping those data that do not belong to the requested chunks. Second, chunking enables a more effective result cache, which caches the query results and returns the result when the same query is given. Unlike a record-based system, where any modification can potentially invalidate a cached result [38], a chunk-based system only needs to track the modifications of the chunks that generate a cached result to ensure the result's validity. This technique is particularly effective in our system, as most chunks won't change after they have been generated.

VI. PERFORMANCE EVALUATION

In this section, we evaluate the feasibility and performance of our system using Gmail and Moves data. Using Jena TDB as a baseline, we first evaluate the system performance in different scenarios and with different kinds of data. Then, we evaluate the overall system performance with a real-world query with a workload simulation based on an assumed application usage. The experiment was conducted on an Amazon Web Services (AWS) instance with 8 Intel Xeon E5-2680 processors and 15GB of memory.

A. Dataset

A dataset of 180 days worth of Gmail and Moves data is used to evaluate the system performance. The data are from three authors of this paper who are regular users of these services. There are in total 360 chunks in the dataset, each of which contains a single day's Gmail or Moves data. Table II summarizes the different characteristic of Gmail and Moves data. For example, while smaller in size, a Gmail chunk requires many more HTTP requests to be issued thus has longer (re)production time. A Moves chunk, on the other hand, can be (re)produced in a much shorter time, but usually is much larger in size due to the high-resolution location traces. These differences will result in different performance characteristics as shown in the following. These differences must be taken into account to achieve efficient resource utilization.

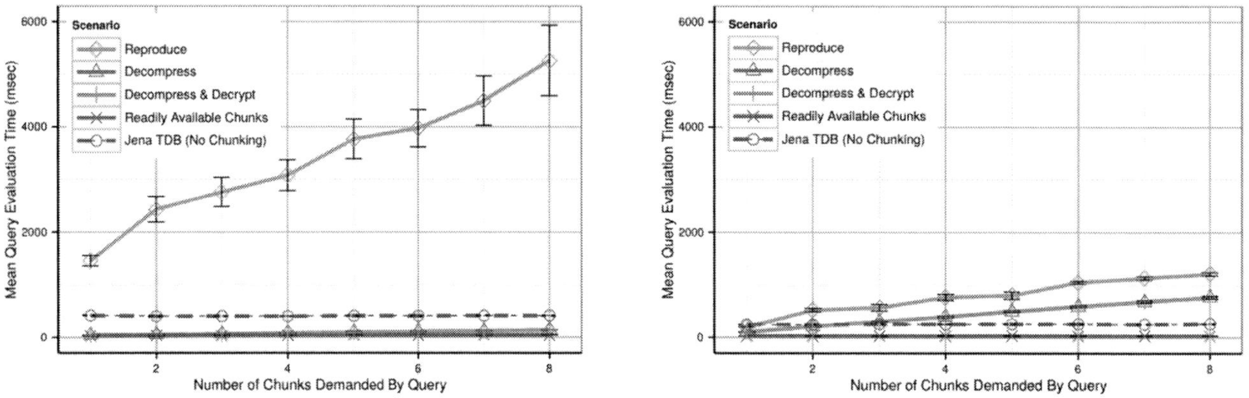

(a) Gmail Data

(b) Moves Data

Figure 8. Query Performance of Different Scenarios: our approach outperforms the Jena TDB by up to 14x when the chunks are readily available. Decompressing is much faster than reproducing a chunk, while decryption adds only negligible overhead. Gmail data requires more time to reproduce since more HTTP requests need to be made. The varying performance in different scenarios evidence the need of an cost- and size-aware chunk replacement policy.

B. *Query Performance*

We compare the query performance of our system with our baseline, Jena TDB, based on the following scenarios:

1) The demanded chunks are readily available.
2) The chunks need to be decompressed.
3) The chunks need to be decompressed and decrypted.
4) The chunks need to be reproduced from the data source.

The results suggest up to 14x performance improvement over Jena TDB for a both a simple query and a complex real-world query. The experiment was conducted with all 360 chunks pre-loaded into the triple store. Each data point presented below is an average of 30 runs of the experiment. The error bars in the figures are the 95% confidence interval.

1) Simple Query Performance: We first evaluate the performance with a simple query that counts the number of distinct Action subjects. Figure 8a and Figure 8b show the results for Gmail and Moves data respectively, where the x-axis is the number of chunks demanded in the query, and the y-axis is the mean query evaluation time. When the demanded chunks are cached in the system, our system outperforms Jena TDB by up to 14x and 10x for Gmail and Moves respectively. This performance gain is mainly attributed to the chunk-skipping optimization mentioned in the Chunk-Assisted Evaluation section. For Gmail data, decompressing shows up to 36x better performance than reproducing, and decryption adds only negligible overhead (less than 1.3%). This difference is not that significant for Moves, since Moves data can be reproduced in a relatively shorter time, but incurs larger overhead to be inserted into the triplestore in either scenario.

2) Real-World Query Performance: Next, we use a real-world query to demonstrate the system performance in a more realistic setting. A query from one of our small data applications, Ora, is used. It consists of 211 lines of SPARQL script, extracting 20 features from Gmail and Moves data (See Application section). Since this more complex query requires a larger number of scans to be made over the search space, as shown in Figure 9, the performance gain of our chunk-skipping technique becomes more evident (up to 14x improvement over Jena TDB). In addition, due to the longer overall query time, the overhead in decompression and decryption becomes less significant. Reproducing is still the slowest among the four scenarios, but it still outperforms Jena TDB by up to 1.8x.

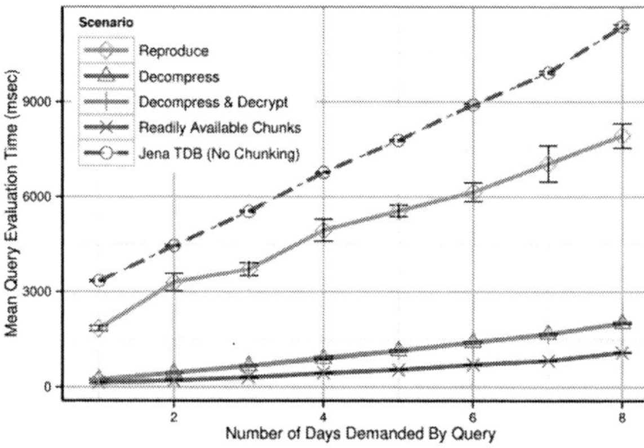

Figure 9. Real-World Query Performance: the performance gain of our chunk-skipping technique becomes more evident (up to 14x) for a complex real-world query where more scans need to be made over the search space.

C. *Performance with Simulated Workload*

The varying performance for different types of data and scenarios stresses the need for a chunk replacement policy that is able to incorporate these discrepancies. We evaluate the effectiveness of the proposed Two-Level GDS algorithm using a simulated workload of Ora. Based on the UI of Ora, we assume a binomial process usage pattern where each page shows one-week worth of data and can be browsed in a reverse chronological order. We assume the user will use the app daily, and after viewing a page, the user has a probability p to browse the next page or a probability of $1-p$ to leave the app. We set $p = 0.7$ and compare our approach with well-known Least-Recently-Used (LRU) policy, as well as the Jena TDB that

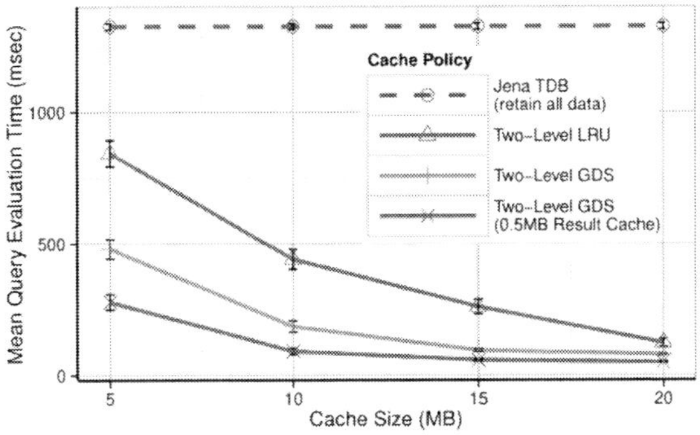

Figure 10. Query Performance with Simulated Workload: our Two-Level GDS approach shows superior performance over LRU, and outperforms Jena TDB that retains all 50.44MB of data, by up to 4.7x using only about 1/10th the storage.

retains all the data. The results suggest that overall, our system outperforms LRU and Jena TDB by up to 4.7x using only a fraction of storage.

We generate 120 days worth of data for the workload based on an assumed usage pattern of Ora. We only consider the performance of the last 60 days when the cache space has become saturated. To allow a fair comparison, we modify the traditional LRU in a way that the chunk chosen for replacement will be first compressed and re-inserted into the LRU list. Only if it is chosen again will it be entirely evicted. We refer to this variant of LRU as *Two-Level LRU*. In addition, for the baseline, Jena TDB, we assume it retains all the 120-day worth of data in the system, which is 50.44MB in size.

Figure 10 shows the performance of different approaches with cache sizes varying from 5MB to 20MB. Our Two-Level GDS shows superior performance over Two-Level LRU especially with a smaller cache size. This advantage comes from the fact the our approach takes the cost of different space reduction methods, and the size of each individual chunk into account. For example, our approach tends to evict a Moves chunk for its shorter reproduction time and larger size. On top of that, if we use 0.5MB of the cache space to cache the query results, we see another 2x of performance improvement. Overall, our approach achieves up to 4.7x performance improvement over Jena TDB, using only about 1/10th the storage. Such a performance improvement is important for small data services to be provided effectively and affordably.

VII. Conclusion and Future Work

In this work, we introduce the notion of small data apps, and the increasing opportunity of these apps to produce deeper and more comprehensive insights across the union of a user's available data, and across a wide range of ubiquitous computing applications. By virtue of the fact that these apps leverage the user as the common denominator and benefactor, there is both the potential for deeper, more personal insights, as well as the need for a robust infrastructure for accessing such intimate data. We present an architecture to support these small data apps that decouples the data sources from the processing and visualization layers, and accounts for the unique challenges presented by contending with sensitive streaming spatio-temporal data from multiple providers. We describe our implementation of a critical component of this architecture, Lifestreams DB, and several candidate applications built on top of it.

Lifestreams DB includes several improvements over existing RDF datastores in terms of storage requirements and query latency, which are likely attributable to the constraints of our domain (i.e., streaming spatio-temporal data which can be reproduced at a cost in latency from an external source.) The application of chunking to the datastore, and a cache eviction policy that leverages both the cost of reproduction/compression and the size of the data, is demonstrated to improve query latency for both a few candidate queries and in a simulated experiment modeling a user's long-term interaction with Ora, an SDA application.

While this work proposes a soft-state architecture to ameliorate the impact of a breach, there is still much work to be done in **secure data storage and distribution** so that breaches are diminished or, preferably, eliminated in the first place. On a related note, there are many improvements that can be made to ensure that the processed data does not compromise the raw data source, and to selectively control who can consume processed data in the case that it is sensitive.

Small data apps address the converse of the big data problem: rather than drawing insights about populations across broad swaths of data for purposes of similar scale (e.g., corporate, governmental, etc.), they draw insights about the individual across their own small data for personal growth and understanding. This work aspires to **foster the growth of the small data ecosystem and the role of small data in fueling ubiquitous computing applications.**

References

[1] S. Perez, "Mobile Application Stores State of Play," 2010. [Online]. Available: http://readwrite.com/2010/02/22/the_truth_about_mobile_application_stores (accessed on 2018.03.19).

[2] H. Halpin, "Social Web Working Group Charter," 2014. [Online]. Available: http://www.w3.org/2013/socialweb/social-wg-charter (accessed on 2018.03.19).

[3] G. Linden, B. Smith, and J. York, "Amazon.Com Recommendations: Item-to-Item Collaborative Filtering," IEEE Internet Computing, vol. 7, no. 1, Jan. 2003, pp. 76–80.

[4] D. Cosley, D. Frankowski, L. Terveen, and J. Riedl, "SuggestBot: Using Intelligent Task Routing to Help People Find Work in Wikipedia," in Proceedings of the 12th International Conference on Intelligent User Interfaces, ser. IUI '07. New York, NY, USA: ACM, 2007, pp. 32–41.

[5] "Foursquare." [Online]. Available: https://foursquare.com/ (accessed on 2018.03.19).

[6] Z. Gantner, S. Rendle, C. Freudenthaler, and L. Schmidt-Thieme, "Mymedialite: A free recommender system library," in Proceedings of the fifth ACM conference on Recommender systems. ACM, 2011, pp. 305–308.

[7] M. D. Ekstrand, M. Ludwig, J. Kolb, and J. T. Riedl, "Lenskit: a modular recommender framework," in Proceedings of the fifth ACM conference on Recommender systems. ACM, 2011, pp. 349–350.

[8] M. Swan, "The Quantified Self: Fundamental Disruption in Big Data Science and Biological Discovery," Big Data, vol. 1, no. 2, Jun. 2013, pp. 85–99.

[9] FitnessKeeper, Inc., "Health Graph API," 2014. [Online]. Available: http://developer.runkeeper.com/healthgraph/ (accessed on 2018.03.19).

[10] S. Consolvo, D. W. McDonald, T. Toscos, M. Y. Chen, J. Froehlich, B. Harrison, P. Klasnja, A. LaMarca, L. LeGrand, R. Libby, I. Smith, and J. A. Landay, "Activity Sensing in the Wild: A Field Trial of Ubifit Garden," in Proceedings of the SIGCHI Conference on Human Factors in Computing Systems, ser. CHI '08. New York, NY, USA: ACM, 2008, pp. 1797–1806.

[11] M. Lin, N. D. Lane, M. Mohammod, X. Yang, H. Lu, G. Cardone, S. Ali, A. Doryab, E. Berke, A. T. Campbell, and T. Choudhury,

"BeWell+: Multi-dimensional Wellbeing Monitoring with Community-guided User Feedback and Energy Optimization," in Proceedings of the Conference on Wireless Health, ser. WH '12. New York, NY, USA: ACM, 2012, pp. 10:1–10:8.

[12] J. Costa, A. T. Adams, M. F. Jung, F. Guimbetiere, and T. Choudhury, "Emotioncheck: leveraging bodily signals and false feedback to regulate our emotions," in Proceedings of the 2016 ACM International Joint Conference on Pervasive and Ubiquitous Computing. ACM, 2016, pp. 758–769.

[13] W. Jones, "Personal information management," Annual review of information science and technology, vol. 41, no. 1, 2007, pp. 453–504.

[14] L. Sauermann, G. A. Grimnes, M. Kiesel, C. Fluit, H. Maus, D. Heim, D. Nadeem, B. Horak, and A. Dengel, "Semantic Desktop 2.0: The Gnowsis Experience," in The Semantic Web - ISWC 2006, ser. Lecture Notes in Computer Science, I. Cruz, S. Decker, D. Allemang, C. Preist, D. Schwabe, P. Mika, M. Uschold, and L. M. Aroyo, Eds. Springer Berlin Heidelberg, Jan. 2006, no. 4273, pp. 887–900.

[15] Y. Cai, X. L. Dong, A. Halevy, J. M. Liu, and J. Madhavan, "Personal Information Management with SEMEX," in Proceedings of the 2005 ACM SIGMOD International Conference on Management of Data, ser. SIGMOD '05. New York, NY, USA: ACM, 2005, pp. 921–923.

[16] B. Salmon, S. W. Schlosser, L. F. Cranor, and G. R. Ganger, "Perspective: Semantic Data Management for the Home," in Proceedings of the 7th Conference on File and Storage Technologies, ser. FAST '09. Berkeley, CA, USA: USENIX Association, 2009, pp. 167–182.

[17] T. Gupta, R. P. Singh, A. Phanishayee, J. Jung, and R. Mahajan, "Bolt: Data Management for Connected Homes," in Proceedings of the 11th USENIX Conference on Networked Systems Design and Implementation, ser. NSDI'14. Berkeley, CA, USA: USENIX Association, 2014, pp. 243–256.

[18] Rustici Software, "xAPI." [Online]. Available: https://xapi.com/ (accessed on 2018.03.19).

[19] Apple Inc., "HealthKit." [Online]. Available: https://developer.apple.com/healthkit/ (accessed on 2018.03.19).

[20] Microsoft, "HealthVault." [Online]. Available: https://www.healthvault.com/ (accessed on 2018.03.19).

[21] Epic System Corp., "MyChart." [Online]. Available: https://mychart.deancare.com/mychart/ (accessed on 2018.03.19).

[22] "Google Fit." [Online]. Available: https://fit.google.com/ (accessed on 2018.03.19).

[23] M. Van Kleek, B. Moore, D. R. Karger, P. André et al., "Atomate it! end-user context-sensitive automation using heterogeneous information sources on the web," in Proceedings of the 19th international conference on World wide web. ACM, 2010, pp. 951–960.

[24] IFTTT, "IFTTT: Put the internet to work for you." 2014. [Online]. Available: https://ifttt.com/ (accessed on 2018.03.19).

[25] A. Mehrotra, R. Hendley, and M. Musolesi, "Prefminer: mining user's preferences for intelligent mobile notification management," in Proceedings of the 2016 ACM International Joint Conference on Pervasive and Ubiquitous Computing. ACM, 2016, pp. 1223–1234.

[26] Y.-A. de Montjoye, E. Shmueli, S. S. Wang, and A. S. Pentland, "openpds: Protecting the privacy of metadata through safeanswers," PloS one, vol. 9, no. 7, 2014.

[27] A. Shakimov, H. Lim, R. Cáceres, L. P. Cox, K. Li, D. Liu, and A. Varshavsky, "Vis-a-vis: Privacy-preserving online social networking via virtual individual servers," in Communication Systems and Networks (COMSNETS), 2011 Third International Conference on. IEEE, 2011, pp. 1–10.

[28] K. G. Niederhoffer and J. W. Pennebaker, "Linguistic Style Matching in Social Interaction," Journal of Language and Social Psychology, vol. 21, no. 4, Dec. 2002, pp. 337–360.

[29] M. Grabchak, Z. Zhang, and D. T. Zhang, "Authorship Attribution Using Entropy," Journal of Quantitative Linguistics, vol. 20, no. 4, Nov. 2013, pp. 301–313.

[30] Open mhealth developer wiki. (accessed on 2018.03.19). [Online]. Available: https://github.com/openmhealth/developer/wiki [retrieved: April, 2014, accessed on 2018-03-18]

[31] The Apache Software Foundation, "Apache Jena," 2014. [Online]. Available: http://jena.apache.org/ (accessed on 2018.03.19).

[32] "Moves API." [Online]. Available: https://dev.moves-app.com/ (accessed on 2018.03.19).

[33] Schema.org Community Group, "Schema.org core schema," 2018. [Online]. Available: http://schema.org/docs/schema_org_rdfa.html (accessed on 2018.03.19).

[34] J. M. Snell, "Activity Streams 2.0," 2015. [Online]. Available: http://www.w3.org/TR/activitystreams-core/ (accessed on 2018.03.19).

[35] USDA, "National Nutrient Database for Standard Reference." [Online]. Available: http://data-gov.tw.rpi.edu/wiki/Dataset_1458 (accessed on 2018.03.19).

[36] F. Alquaddoomi, C. Ketcham, and D. Estrin, "The Email Analysis Framework: Aiding the Analysis of Personal Natural Language Texts," in Hypertext 2014 Extended Proceedings, ser. CEUR Workshop Proceedings, F. Cena, A. S. d. Silva, and C. Trattner, Eds., vol. 1210. CEUR-WS.org, 2014.

[37] P. Cao and S. Irani, "Cost-Aware WWW Proxy Caching Algorithms," in Proceedings of the USENIX Symposium on Internet Technologies and SystemsMonterey, California, December 1997, 1997, pp. 193–206.

[38] M. Martin, J. Unbehauen, and S. Auer, "Improving the Performance of Semantic Web Applications with SPARQL Query Caching," in The Semantic Web: Research and Applications, ser. Lecture Notes in Computer Science, L. Aroyo, G. Antoniou, E. HyvÃűnen, A. t. Teije, H. Stuckenschmidt, L. Cabral, and T. Tudorache, Eds. Springer Berlin Heidelberg, Jan. 2010, no. 6089, pp. 304–318.

Knowledge Base L-V-C Mapping Method

Dong-Jae Lee, Yun-Hee Son, Kyu-Chul Lee
Chungnam National University
Department of Computer Science & Engineering
Daejeon, South Korea
e-mail: ehdwo115@gmail.com, {mellow211, kclee}@cnu.ac.kr

Abstract— **The defense training system uses an L (Live) system for practical training, V (Virtual) system for virtual training, and C (Constructive) system for combat command training. Recently, research to integrate the L-V-C training system has been under way to realize the same environment as an actual field. However, since the L-V-C integrated training system uses different middleware depending on the characteristics of L, V, and C, there is a problem with interoperability between middleware. The middleware used in each system is High-Level Architecture (HLA), Data Distribution Service (DDS), and Distribution Interactive Simulation (DIS). Each middleware uses a different data format: Federation Object Model (FOM), Topic, and Protocol Data Unit (PDU). In the case of FOM and PDU, there is a standard data format, but Topic does not specify a data format standard, so there is a problem with interoperability between heterogeneous middleware. In this paper, to solve the data interlocking problem of heterogeneous middleware, we constructed a knowledge base by extracting keywords based on the HLA FOM data format and extending it by ontology modeling. We also developed a knowledge base processing engine that supports interoperability between FOM and Topic using the built knowledge base and a weighted search algorithm.**

Keywords-LVC; Ontology; Knowledge Base; Keyword expansion; Keyword Extraction.

I. INTRODUCTION

The L-V-C integrated training system is a training system that integrates L (Live), V (Virtual), and C (Constructive) systems to perform various combat simulation exercises using virtual environments as real battlefields [1]. The L-system is real-life simulated training, which means it actually involves soldiers, military equipment, etc., operating in the real world rather than a virtual space. In the L system, the Data Distribution Service (DDS) is used as middleware because the real-time property is important. DDS is an OMG (Object Management Group) standard publishing / subscribing network communication middleware, and has the characteristics to support real-time [2]. V system means virtual training, which means that the soldier does not train in a real environment, but is training with real equipment in a virtual environment. The V system uses High-Level Architecture (HLA) as simulation middleware. HLA is a general-purpose architecture for distributed computer simulation systems [3]. Finally, the C system means combat command training, which means training with virtual equipment and virtual forces in a virtual environment. The C system uses Distributed Interactive Simulation (DIS), which is a middleware running in a war game. DIS is an IEEE standard for performing war games in distributed locations while transmitting and receiving data messages in real time on a distributed network [4].

Recently, research on the L-V-C integrated training system has been conducted so that it can realize the same environment as an actual field. However, when integrating the L-V-C system, since each of the systems use different middleware, there is a problem with interoperability between middleware. The DDS, HLA, DIS middleware use Topic, FOM and PDU have different data format standards [4][5]. So, there is no difficulty mapping to each other. However, since Topic does not specify a data format standard, Topic is arbitrarily defined/published by the user. Therefore, problems arise when Topic is mapping with FOM and PDU, whose data format standards are defined.

One way to solve this problem is to map the Topic based on the standard FOM. However, users who do not know how the FOM is configured will have difficulty in mapping.

We solved this problem using ontology modeling and a knowledge base. By using the ontology to analyze the semantic keywords of the FOM and building the knowledge base through synonym based extension, users can map FOM and Topic through keyword search even if they do not know the exact FOM. In addition, there is an advantage, since overhead does not increase even if the complexity increases by using the ontology.

In this paper, we developed a knowledge base processing engine for interoperability HLA and DDS among the heterogeneous middleware HLA, DDS, and DIS used in the L-V-C. The contents of this paper are as follows.

- We analyzed and extended the semantic keywords of the HLA FOM with the standard for interoperability between HLA FOM and DDS Topic. In addition, we constructed knowledge base using ontology modeling.
- We developed a weighted search algorithm that allows users to search the associated keywords in priority order using weights in the knowledge base even if they are not familiar with HLA FOM.

The composition of this paper is as follows. In Section 2, we compare the related works. In Section 3, we explain the background knowledge. In Section 4, we describe the knowledge base processing engine developed in this paper. Finally, Section 5 concludes the paper.

II. RELATED RESEARCH

The works [6][7] are studies related to this paper. [6] is a study for combining HLA and DDS into a single middleware and [7] is a study for building a system that can utilize both HLA and DDS. Both studies map only the data defined in the HLA standard and the data in the DDS specification to link HLA and DDS. This creates mapping difficulties when users add a new Topic. In this study, we support mapping between HLA FOM data and Topic, even if the user adds a new Topic.

III. BACKGROUND

A. *Ontology model*

In this paper, we used Resource Description Framework(RDF) of N-Triple format to construct the ontology model [8]. RDF is a World Wide Web Consortium(W3C) standard technology that provides interoperability between applications that exchange information that is machine understandable on the Web [9]. In addition, Simple Protocol and RDF Query Language (SPARQL) was used to query the constructed knowledge base. SPARQL is a database query language that can search and manipulate data stored in RDF. In addition, SPARQL is recognized as one of the key technologies in the Semantic Web with the standard technology established by the W3C [10]. In this paper, we employed Jena [11] to use RDF and SPARQL. Jena is a Java-based open source semantic web framework and provides a programming environment for RDF, RDF Schema(RDFS), Web Ontology Language (OWL), SPARQL, and Rule-based reasoning engines. Finally, in this paper, Jena TDB was used to store the constructed model in the knowledge base, and Jena TDB provided the function to store and manage the RDF format data [12].

B. *Keyword Extraction, Extension*

In this paper, Natural Language Processing(NLP) was used to extract nouns from the semantics of HLA FOM. OpenNLP, one of NLP's open source is a machine learning based tool for natural language text processing. It supports most common NLP tasks such as tokenization, sentence segmentation, part of speech tagging, entity extraction, and parsing, and supports advanced text processing services [13]. We also used WordNet to extend the extracted keywords. WordNet is a database in which about 150,000 words including nouns, verbs, adjectives, and adverbs are stored in a set of 115,000 synonyms [14].

C. *HLA FOM and DDS Topic*

HLA FOM is a set of federated objectives, which is an IEEE standard that contains a specification that describes the shared objects class and objects class' name, object class attributes, and interactions of the federation [5].

A data model is a description of the state of a system, including data types, processes for data transfer, and data access methods. DDS operates as defined by this data model, using the Global Data Space. DDS Topic is used to identify data in Global Data Space, and the user defines the Topic directly according to the data model [15].

D. *Interoperability*

Research on interoperability has been increasing since 1970. Interoperability is used in a variety of areas and there are 34 different definitions mentioned in research papers, standards and government documents over the past 30 years [16]. Among the various definitions, the definition that corresponds to the system we developed is "The ability of two or more systems or components to exchange and use the exchanged information in a heterogeneous network "[17].

IV. KNOWLEDGE BASE PROCESSING ENGINE

A. *Knowledge base composition diagram*

Figure 1 shows the overall structure of the LVC knowledge base processing engine. In order to map the FOM and Topic that the user arbitrarily defines, the knowledge base processing engine processes the total of two processes. One is the process of building a knowledge base. It extracts keywords from FOM through a keyword extraction process and expands extracted keywords through a keyword expansion process. The extended keyword is converted into the N-Triple format through the ontology modeling process and stored in the knowledge base (triple store).

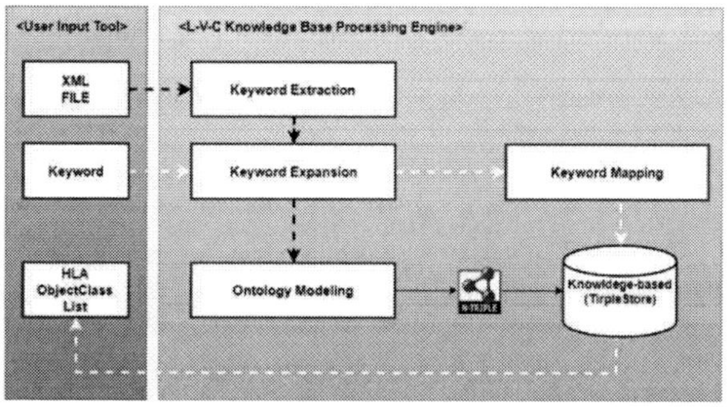

Figure 1. Overall structure of the LVC knowledge base processing engine

The other process is the keyword search process. We expanded the FOM keyword in the knowledge base building stage. However, to further increase accuracy, we also expanded the keywords that the user types and then performed the keyword search process. In the keyword search process, after querying the knowledge base using the weighted search algorithm, the extended keyword is returned and a list of the object class to which the mapping is performed is returned.

B. Knowledge base construction

Although existing HLA and DDS mapping methods can be mapped only to predefined ones, it is necessary to build a knowledge base to map the Topic and HLA that the user defined arbitrarily. We constructed the knowledge base using synonyms to support user convenience. The knowledge base construction is divided into three stages: keyword extraction, keyword expansion, and ontology modeling.

1) Keyword Extraction: In the keyword extraction process, the HLA FOM (XML) file is received through user input. It parses the semantic sentence describing the object class name and object class in the FOM and uses OpenNLP to extract nouns from object class names and semantic sentences.

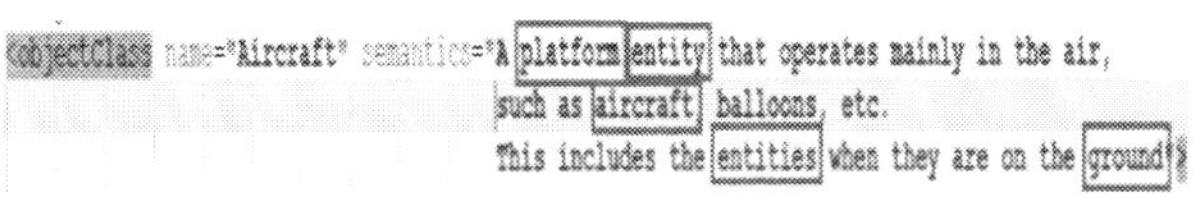

Figure 2. Example of FOM file

Figure 2 shows an example of an HLA FOM file. The name of the object class is 'Aircraft' and there is a semantic sentence describing it. The object class of HLA FOM is described in the background section.

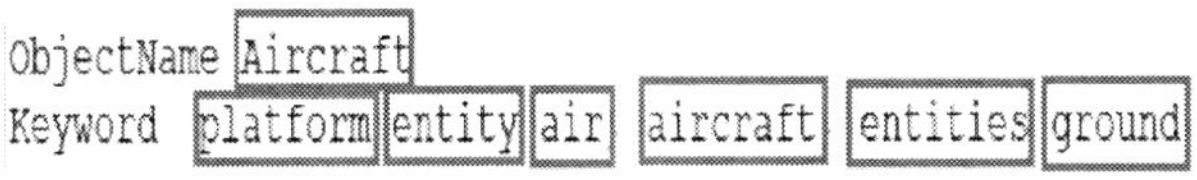

Figure 3. Aircraft extraction result

Figure 3 shows the nouns extracted from the object class names and semantic sentences in the FOM File in Figure 2 using OpenNLP. The object class name 'Aircraft' and the nouns 'platform', 'entity', 'air', 'aircraft', 'entities', and 'ground' in the semantic sentence are extracted.

2) Keyword expansion: To extract keywords based on synonyms, the extracted nouns are searched in a separate dictionary built in WordNet. When a retrieved noun is searched in the Wordnet dictionary, the synonym result for the extracted noun comes out. This result extends the data. Figure 4 shows the expanded word 'platform' extracted from Figure 3. 'Platform' expands to 'platform', 'political_platform', 'political_program', 'program', 'chopine' .

3) Ontology Modeling: Figure 5 shows the ontology model. The object class has subclasses as Keyword, and the Keywords are subclasses that have an Expansion Keyword extended through WordNet. Also, the Keyword and the Expansion Keyword have a weight indicating their priority.

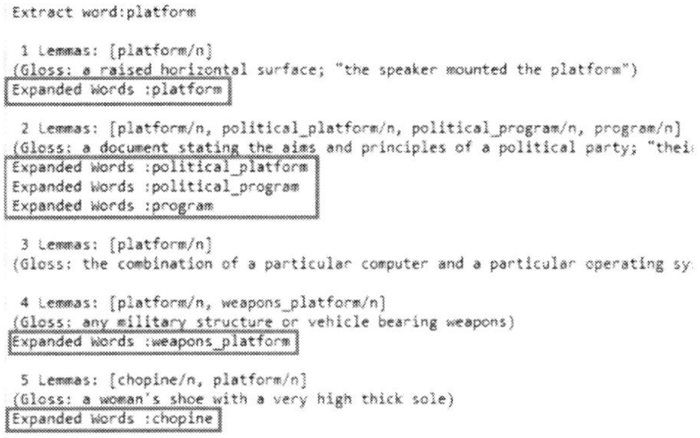

Figure 4. Example of Platform extension

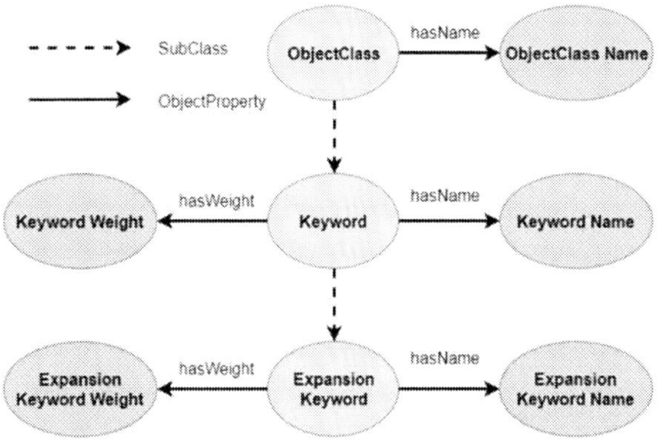

Figure 5. Knowledge base ontology model

Data generated by the ontology modeling is stored in N-Triple format and the created N-Triple is stored in the database using Jena TDB.

C. Keyword search

The Keyword search performs the SPARQL query by receiving the keywords (e.g., 'craft') necessary for the ontology query, based on the knowledge base constructed above. When performing a query, one you may not know exactly what object class name to look for. Because the knowledge base is built by synonym extension, in this case one can still retrieve the associated object class name. In addition, when the keyword alone does not produce a result, the input keyword is further expanded by synonyms to query the constructed knowledge base to derive the result. For this process, weighted search algorithms were newly implemented and used.

D. Weighted search algorithm.

In Figure 5, Keyword and Expansion Keyword have weighted properties. The method of weighting is as follows

- Keywords are extracted from the object class name are assigned a weight of 1, and keywords are extracted from a semantic sentence are assigned a weight of 2.

- In the above process, expanded keywords are re-expanded through WordNet, and the weight is incremented by one in the expanded keywords order.

The object class is organized into a tree using these weights. Figure 6 shows an example of a tree.

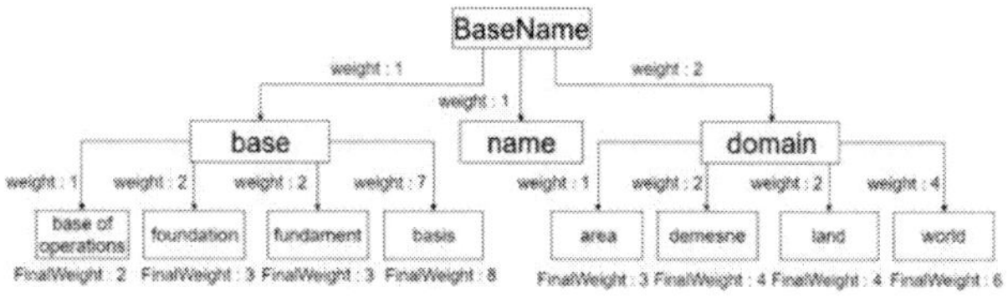

Figure 6. BaseName tree example

This tree is as large as the number of ObjectClass, and is sequentially searched in three cases using the configured tree as follows.

1) Keyword (knowledge base) and Keyword (user search) mapping: The keyword of the knowledge base is mapped to the keyword inputted by the user.

2) Expansion Keyword (knowledge base) and Keyword (user search) mapping: The expansion keyword of the knowledge base is mapped to the keyword inputted by the user.

3) Expansion keyword (knowledge base) and Expansion keyword (user search) mapping: The expansion keyword of the knowledge base is mapped to the extended keyword inputted by the user.

At each step when a result is obtained, it ends without going to the next step. If the keyword entered by the user in each search step matches the keywords stored in the plurality of *object class trees, the weighted* values are compared and the keywords of the lowest weighted value are output in ascending order from the keywords of the tree.

V. Conclusion and Future Work

In this paper, we analyzed related technologies needed to develop a knowledge base processing engine. We analyzed OpenNLP and WordNet for keyword extraction and extension of the L-V-C knowledge base processing engine. We also analyzed the ontology representation language, RDF, and the query language, SPARQL, and analyzed the Jena TDB for ontology data storage. Based on these related technologies, we developed a knowledge base processing engine that supports interoperability between heterogeneous middleware.

Through this study, it was confirmed that more flexible interoperability and expansion is possible knowledge base of ontology based . Also, the development of a knowledge base processing engine enables data interoperability through keyword-based retrieval even if there is no prior knowledge of the L-V-C system. Therefore, it is expected that users' barriers to entry will also be lowered, and the knowledge base can be utilized in various fields.

It is expected that future research plan will be able to develop a knowledge base processing engine that is not dependent on a specific field so that it can interoperate with the heterogeneous middleware of L-V-C system as well as through knowledge base in various fields.

References

[1] B. Pollock, E. Winer and S. Gilbert, "LVC interaction within a mixed-reality training system." The Engineering Reality of Virtual Reality 2012. Vol. 8289. International Society for Optics and Photonics, 2012.

[2] G. Pardo-Castellote, "Omg data-distribution service: Architectural overview," Proceedings of 23rd IEEE International Conference on Distributed Computing Systems Workshops, pp. 200-206, 2003.

[3] J. S.dahmann, "High Level Architecture for Simulation," Proceedings of the First International Workshop on Distributed Interactive Simulation and Real-Time Application, pp. 9-14, 1997.

[4] DIS Steering Committee, "IEEE standard for distributed interactive simulation-application protocols." IEEE Standard 1278, pp 1-52, 1998

[5] HLA Working Group, "IEEE standard for modeling and simulation (M&S) high level architecture (HLA)-framework and rules." IEEE Standard,1516-2000, 2000.

[6] P. Yunjung and M. Dugki, "Development of HLA-DDS wrapper API for network-controllable distributed simulation," Application of Information and Communication Technologies (AICT), 2013 7th International Conference on. IEEE, pp. 1-5, 2013.

[7] J. Rajive and G. Pardo-Castellote, "A comparison and mapping of data distribution service and high-level architecture," Technology, The Netherlands. His research interests include parallel and distributed computing, component based architectures, and embedded systems, 2006.

[8] O. Lassila and R. R. Swick, " Resource description framework (RDF) model and syntax specification,", 1999.

[9] World Wide Web Consortium. "About the World Wide Web Consortium (W3C).", 2001.

[10] E. Prud and A. Seaborne, "SPARQL query language for RDF," 2006.

[11] Jena, Apache, "semantic web framework for Java," 2007.

[12] A. Seaborne, "Jena TDB," 2011

[13] J. Baldridge and T. Morton, "OpenNLP," 2004

[14] C. Fellbaum, WordNet John Wiley & Sons, Inc., 1998

[15] G. Pardo-Castellote, "Data-Centric Programming Best Practices: Using DDS to Integrate Real-World Systems.", 2010.

[16] C. Ford-Thomas, et al., "Survey on Interoperability Measurement", AIR FORCE INST OF TECH WRIGHT-PATTERSON AFB OH, 2007.

[17] A. Geraci et al., "IEEE standard computer dictionary: Compilation of IEEE standard computer glossaries", IEEE Press, 1991.

Data Provenance Service Prototype for Collaborative Data Infrastructures

Vasily Bunakov
Science and Technology Facilities Council
Harwell Campus, United Kingdom
e-mail: vasily.bunakov@stfc.ac.uk

Javier Quinteros
GFZ German Research Centre for Geoscience
Potsdam, Germany
e-mail: javier@gfz-potsdam.de

Linda Reijnhoudt
Data Archiving and Networked Services
The Hague, Netherlands
e-mail: linda.reijnhoudt@dans.knaw.nl

Abstract—**We report on the ongoing work of augmenting the services of EUDAT Collaborative Data Infrastructure with data provenance components. These will support the progression of existing software platforms for research data management to mature solutions for accountable data curation to improve reproducibility of results and authenticity of data. The approach and technology considered may be of interest to other collaborative data infrastructures.**

Keywords – data infrastructure; data curation; provenance.

I. INTRODUCTION

EUDAT Collaborative Data Infrastructure (CDI) [1] is a European e-infrastructure that has emerged as a result of two consecutive European projects bearing the same name [2]. An e-infrastructure is comprised of a few software platforms [3] that support different cases of data management for research: individual data publishing, data sharing, large-scale (institutional) data management, data staging for computation, data annotation, and building a public service (catalogue) for research data discoverability.

The collaborative nature of the EUDAT CDI implies multiple instances of the same service being run by different organizations, and data movements across multiple human, organizational and software agents. This diversity and complexity raise questions about data origin, data traceability, and accountability for all actions performed over data through its entire lifecycle. The lifecycle spans from ingestion through movements and transformations to the eventual distribution and consumption. This group of questions can be referred to by an umbrella term *data provenance* which is an aspect of wider considerations for the selection, collection, preservation, and maintenance of data that are known as *data curation,* which is a prominent topic in EUDAT [4].

The problems of data provenance become more acute in the operation of software platforms that handle big amounts of data with high level of automation for all the actions performed over data. EUDAT B2SAFE [5] – a robust, safe and highly available service for storing large-scale data in community and institutional repositories – is a perfect example where automated and scalable data provenance is in high demand.

We consider design and implementation of data provenance components for EUDAT B2SAFE that can be considered a prototype for a distributed data provenance service spanning different locations and a variety of research communities.

The rest of the paper is structured as follows. In Section II, we describe the first implementation that was made for GEOFON Data Centre in Potsdam, Germany, that runs an instance of EUDAT B2SAFE. We outline the use case, explain design and implementation of data provenance components, and indicate future developments. In Section III, we describe Provgen software component for generation of provenance records. In Section IV, we discuss coupling of Provgen with other software components and possible routes for publishing provenance records. We conclude our work in Section V.

II. GEOFON USE CASE

GEOFON [6] is a seismological data infrastructure that consists of a number of data centres across the globe with GFZ, the German Research Centre for Geosciences, being one of the prominent data nodes. GEOFON is the earthquake information provider worldwide; it is also one of the largest nodes of the European Integrated Data Archive (EIDA) for seismological data under the ORFEUS umbrella [7].

For partner networks, GEOFON acts as a data centre that saves a replica of the original data and as a data distribution centre at the same time. Most of the data is Open Access, but there is a small amount of data under an embargo, usually for a limited period of 3 to 4 years.

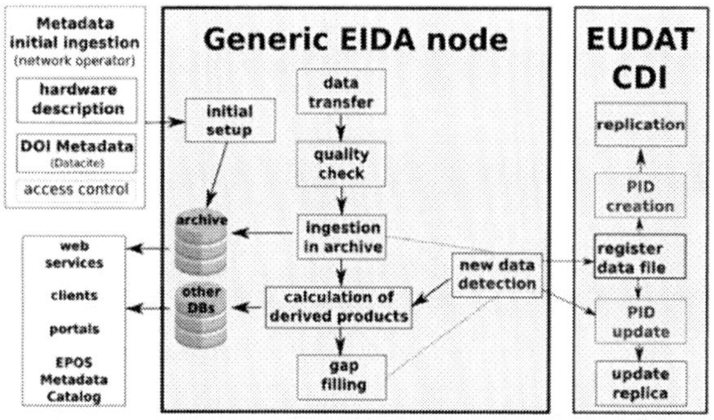

Figure 1. Data workflow in GEOFON.

Data is supplied in GEOFON along with its metadata, and data quality checks are performed upon ingestion. Also, data coming from different sources is checked for possible overlaps. The data workflow in GEOFON is illustrated in Figure 1.

Many services have been implemented by GEOFON itself, and the GFZ participation in EUDAT projects allowed to integrate two EUDAT services: B2SAFE and B2HANDLE. B2SAFE is used for data management at scale, and B2HANDLE allows minting and managing persistent identifiers (PIDs) for data [8]. Each PID is stored along with a set of key-value pairs called "PID record". This allows tracking down replicas of the file in different data centres and offers a reliable identification of not only a data asset itself but of all derived information, such as calculated checksums for data integrity checks. So, having clear provenance information for PID records, which can be considered valuable data themselves, is important and this is why it has been the focus of an initial testing for our implementation.

III. Provgen: A component for provenance data generation

One of the clearer requirements for a data provenance service is to have a high configurability to adjust to different user needs. Another requirement was that it should be decoupled from other EUDAT services, and should not have many software dependencies.

To fulfil these requirements, we designed a templating system where templates can be loaded by the operator of the system. Templates are in the Resource Description Framework (RDF) Notation3 format and each template is the result of the design of a certain Provenance record type that depends on a particular workflow.

```
@prefix prov: <http://www.w3.org/ns/prov#> .
@prefix dct: <http://purl.org/dc/terms/> .
@prefix datacite: <http://purl.org/spar/datacite/> .
@prefix provgen: <http://provgen.eudat.eu/> .
@prefix rdfs: <http://www.w3.org/2000/01/rdf-schema#> .

provgen:EUDATCreatePID_at_{EUDAT_LITERAL:timestamp}
    a prov:Activity;
    prov:endedAtTime
"{EUDAT_LITERAL:timestamp}"^^xsd:dateTime ;
    prov:wasAssociatedWith provgen:EUDATCreatePID;
    prov:generated provgen:{EUDAT_ESCAPE:PID}; .

provgen:EUDATCreatePID
    a prov:Agent;
    a prov:Type prov:SoftwareAgent;
    prov:atLocation <https://github.com/EUDAT-B2SAFE>; .

provgen:{EUDAT_LITERAL:node}:{EUDAT_ESCAPE:irods_path}
    a prov:Entity;
    rdfs:label "{EUDAT_LITERAL:irods_path}";
    prov:atLocation "{EUDAT_LITERAL:node}";
    datacite:hasIdentifier provgen:{EUDAT_ESCAPE:PID};
    prov:atLocation "{EUDAT_LITERAL:irods_path}"; .

provgen:{EUDAT_ESCAPE:PID}
    a prov:Entity;
    dct:identifier "{EUDAT_LITERAL:PID}";
    datacite:usesIdentifierScheme
          <http://purl.org/spar/datacite/handle>; .
```

Figure 2. Provenance template *createPID*

As an example, the template of a record for the creation of a PID for a data file is expressed as the RDF snippet in Figure 2. It uses the PROV ontology [9] to express relations between Agents and Entities, through Activities. The EUDATCreatePID functionality (the Agent) generated a PID (the Entity) during the Activity. Other ontologies were used to record more details, such as the actual identifier generated and the identifier scheme used. When the calling service creates a PID, it calls the Provgen with the variables required for the *createPID* template.

Figure 3 shows the completed provenance document, in which the placeholders in the template have been replaced with the actual. To facilitate the correct markup of the resulting completed document, we defined at least two different ways to do the replacement of the variables: literal or escaped.

```
@prefix prov: <http://www.w3.org/ns/prov#> .
@prefix dct: <http://purl.org/dc/terms/> .
@prefix datacite: <http://purl.org/spar/datacite/> .
@prefix provgen: <http://provgen.eudat.eu/> .
@prefix rdfs: <http://www.w3.org/2000/01/rdf-schema#> .

provgen:EUDATCreatePID_at_2017-12-02T17:29:23
    a prov:Activity;
    prov:endedAtTime "2017-12-02T17:29:23"^^xsd:dateTime;
    prov:wasAssociatedWith provgen:EUDATCreatePID;
    prov:generated provgen:PREFIX1\/PID1; .

provgen:EUDATCreatePID
    a prov:Agent;
    a prov:Type prov:SoftwareAgent;
    prov:atLocation <https://github.com/EUDAT-B2SAFE>; .

provgen:server1:\/path\/filename
    a prov:Entity;
    rdfs:label "/path/filename";
    prov:atLocation "server1";
    datacite:hasIdentifier provgen:PREFIX1\/PID1;
    prov:atLocation "/path/filename";

provgen:PREFIX1\/PID1
    a prov:Entity;
    dct:identifier "PREFIX1/PID1";
    datacite:usesIdentifierScheme
          <http://purl.org/spar/datacite/handle>; .
```

Figure 3. Completed provenance document for the creation of a PID.

It can be seen in Figure 3 that elements such as a file path which includes characters like "/", will be invalid if they are literally replaced where a subject or an object is expected in the triple. However, they should still appear without modifications in the case of being used as literals.

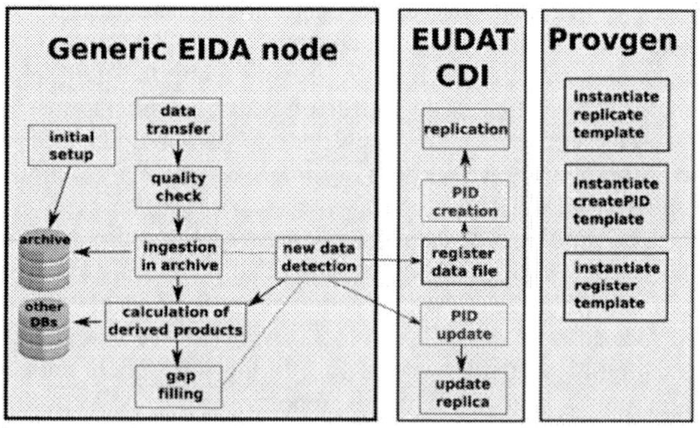

Figure 4. Calls to the Provgen service in the GEOFON work-flow

To decouple Provgen from other components of the EUDAT CDI and avoid the already mentioned dependencies, we specified an API [10] which allows the following:

- list available templates in Provgen including the specification of each template (expected variables and their description),
- instantiate a template,
- show the Provgen documentation,
- show the Provgen configuration.

Before using Provgen, a developer needs to identify points in the data workflow where provenance information should be generated.

Every call identifies the template to be used and the replacements for the placeholders in the template. If no suitable template exists, the developer needs to create a template and put it into the "templates" folder. Then, the program can make a call to the Provgen API in the respective point of a data workflow.

The template should be documented with comments on the first lines of the document, where a list of the variables to be replaced within the document is presented and explained in detail. For instance, the template in Figure 2 can be documented with the following comments to explain the parameters used:

```
# EUDAT_PARAM:timestamp - the time at which
the PID was generated
# EUDAT_PARAM:PID - the handle PID that was
generated
# EUDAT_PARAM:irods_path - the absolute path
of the file in iRODS
# EUDAT_PARAM:node - the domain name of the
server where the node resides
```

The template-based design makes Provgen quite universal: it can be used not only in the B2SAFE service where it was tested but with any other EUDAT service, or by other data infrastructures.

IV. COUPLING PROVGEN WITH OTHER COMPONENTS, AND SERVICE DESIGN CONSIDERATIONS

Provgen per se is just a flexible, configurable component for provenance records generation. It can be interacted with using its API. In the simplest and default installation, records will be stored in the free online Provenance backend storage called ProvStore [11][12]. This could cover the needs of most users, as the only technical requirement is to open a free account. The free ProvStore service includes the capability to store, share, export and visualize the documents generated by Provgen.

In the case that a considerable number of provenance records are expected (e.g. millions), we also provide the option to make the records available in files and upload them to a more powerful external backend storage (e.g. triple store). This gives also the possibility of exposing them for querying using an endpoint for RDF Query language (SPARQL).

For testing this bridge to a triple store, we used Jena TDB, a native triple store, as the backend with Fuseki server as a frontend [13]. The ingest of Provgen-generated records was straightforward, and Fuseki allowed to expose them via a SPARQL endpoint – so Jena framework allowed a persistence layer for provenance records and a decent commonly understandable API in the form of a SPARQL endpoint. As Provgen-generated records are primarily based on the popular PROV specification, it makes the service interface quite universal and self-specified, with good prospects of adoption across different data infrastructures and user communities.

We are considering further experiments on Provgen-generated records ingestion in a neo4j graph database [14] as EUDAT services, B2SAFE in particular, favour this database engine for metadata management. Provenance records then may become additional metadata in a common metadata storage, which may allow insightful inquiries into data and metadata quality and into data maintenance procedures; as an example, using provenance records in order to judge on the quality of data policy implementation. The inclusion of provenance records in a common metadata store will have its conceptual advantages, also operational advantages as one will not need additional software components (RDF triple store and a frontend for it), but can just rely on the graph database component already in use.

This approach will have its disadvantages, too, as one of the strengths of the RDF representation of provenance records is an out-of-box ability to conduct standardized machine reasoning over provenance. Provenance exposure via SPARQL endpoint will have an architectural advantage, too, as SPARQL endpoints allow building up natural service federations with simultaneous requests to multiple endpoints from the same software components and thus can support the development of a universal infrastructure-wide provenance service (which in the case of EUDAT, according to this e-infrastructure naming conventions, could be named a B2PROV service). Also, SPARQL as a query language, as well as RDF APIs for high-level programming languages are more common than specific query languages and APIs for graph databases, which is important for a favourable adoption of the data provenance service by a wider community of software developers.

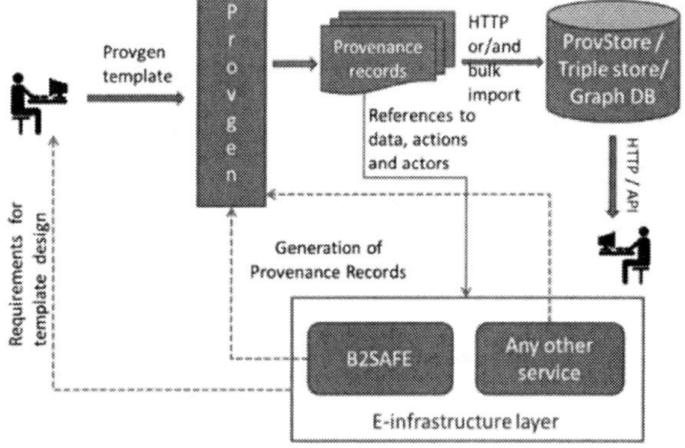

Figure 5. Provgen integration with a triple store or/and a graph database.

Which route, RDF-based or with graph databases, will prevail in EUDAT Collaborative Data Infrastructure, will depend on its operational and sustainability considerations. For other data infrastructures, especially for newly emerging ones without a burden of years-long particular implementations, we expect the RDF-based approach could be preferred for publishing provenance records and performing machine reasoning over them. Figure 3 indicates both possible routes.

V. CONCLUSION

This work reports on the progress made with design and implementation of a provenance service applied to the use case of the thematic GEOFON seismological data infrastructure [6] that interacts with the common domain-agnostic EUDAT data infrastructure [1]. The service prototype implemented [10] prepares and publishes well-structured provenance records for the GEOFON data managed by the EUDAT B2SAFE service [5]. The future work will involve further testing and promotion of the provenance component to its adoption in EUDAT B2SAFE Production. The opportunities will be explored for a wider use of the provenance component, or a generic service based on it, in other EUDAT services [3] and for other use cases beyond seismological data.

ACKNOWLEDGMENTS

This work is supported by EUDAT 2020 project that receives funding from the European Union's Horizon 2020 research and innovation program under grant agreement No. 654065. The views expressed are those of the authors and not necessarily those of the funding project or institutions.

REFERENCES

[1] EUDAT Collaborative Data Infrastructure. [Online]. Available from: https://www.eudat.eu/eudat-cdi [retrieved: March, 2018]

[2] EUDAT project. [Online]. Available from: https://www.eudat.eu/ [retrieved: March, 2018]

[3] EUDAT services. [Online]. Available from: https://www.eudat.eu/services-support [retrieved: March, 2018]

[4] V. Bunakov et al. "Data curation policies for EUDAT collaborative data infrastructure", Selected Papers of the XIX International Conference on Data Analytics and Management in Data Intensive Domains (DAMDID/RCDL 2017). CEUR Workshop Proceedings Vol-2022, 2017, urn:nbn:de:0074-2022-6, pp. 72-78

[5] EUDAT B2SAFE service. [Online]. Available from: https://www.eudat.eu/b2safe/ [retrieved: March, 2018]

[6] W. Hanka and R. Kind, The GEOFON Program. Annals of Geophysics v. 37, n. 5, Nov. 1994. ISSN 2037-416X. doi:10.4401/ag-4196 (1994)

[7] L. Trani et al. "The European seismological waveform framework EIDA". In *Geophysical Research Abstracts*, vol. 19, EGU2017-13770, Vienna, Austria, April 2017.

[8] J. Quinteros et al. "Moving towards persistent identification in the seismological community". In *Geophysical Research Abstracts*, vol. 18, EGU2016-15619-1, Vienna, Austria, Apr 2017.

[9] PROV ontology. [Online]. Available from: https://www.w3.org/TR/prov-o/ [retrieved: March, 2018]

[10] Provgen API specification. [Online]. Available from: https://raw.githubusercontent.com/javiquinte/provgen/master/swagger.yaml [retrieved: March, 2018]

[11] T. D. Huynh and L. Moreau (2014) ProvStore: a public provenance repository.At *5th International Provenance and Annotation Workshop (IPAW'14) , Cologne, Germany,09 - 13 Jun 2014.* 3pp

[12] ProvStore service. [Online]. Available from: https://provenance.ecs.soton.ac.uk/store/ [retrieved: March, 2018]

[13] Apache Jena framework. [Online]. Available from: https://jena.apache.org/ [retrieved: March, 2018]

[14] NEO4J graph platform. [Online]. Available from: https://neo4j.com/ [retrieved: March, 2018]

Design and Implementation of Candlestick Chart Retrieval Algorithm for Predicting Stock Price Trend

Yoshihisa Udagawa
Computer Science Department, Faculty of Engineering,
Tokyo Polytechnic University
Atsugi-city, Kanagawa, Japan
e-mail: udagawa@cs.t-kougei.ac.jp

Abstract—**Advances in data mining techniques are now making it possible to analyze a large amount of stock data for predicting future price trends. The candlestick charting is one of the most popular techniques used to predict short-term stock price trends, i.e., bullish, bearish, continuation. While the charting technique is popular among traders and has long history, there is still no consistent conclusion for the predictability of the technique. The trend of stock prices often continues after intervals of several days because stock prices tend to fluctuate according to announcements of important economic indicators, economic and political news, etc. To cope with this kind of stock price characteristics, this paper focuses on a dynamic programming algorithm for retrieving similar numerical sequences. To be specific, the well-known Longest Common Subsequence (LCS) algorithm is revised to retrieve numerical sequences that partially match. The proposed algorithm also handles a relative position among a stock price, 5-day moving average, and 25-day moving average to take into account where the price occurs in price zones. Experimental results on the daily data of the Nikkei stock average show that the proposed algorithm is effective to forecast short-term trends of stock prices.**

Keywords— Stock price prediction; Technical analysis; Candlestick charts; Longest common subsequence algorithm for numbers; Multi numerical attributes; Nikkei stock average.

I. INTRODUCTION

Stock market prediction techniques play a crucial role to bring more people into market and encourage markets as a whole. Fundamental analysis and technical analysis are two popular approaches to successful stock trading [1].

Fundamental analysis combines economic, industry, and company analysis to derive a stock's current fair value and forecast future value. Traders apply this approach over a long period of time, e.g., months, quarters. Because of this analyzing processes, most investors believe that fundamental analysis is mainly suitable for long-term prediction.

Technical analysis is a study of market action, primarily through the use of charts for the purpose of forecasting future price trends [2]. Technical analysis is based on the following three premises:

1. Market action discounts everything: a stock's price reflects all relevant information such as economic, fundamental and news events,
2. Prices move in trends: prices trend keep directionally, i.e., up, down, or sideways, for a certain period,
3. History repeats itself: the repetitive nature of price movements is mainly attributed to market emotions like fear or excitement that often repeat themselves.

One of the important types of technical analysis is candlestick chart patterns [2]. The candlestick chart patterns provide short-term predictions for traders to make buy or sell decisions. While most of techniques use statistics of stock prices, the candlestick charting technique focuses on patterns among several days of candlesticks formulated by opening, high, low, and closing prices within a specific time frame, such as minute, hour, day or week. Dozens of candlestick chart patterns are identified to be signals of bullish/bearish reversals and continuations. These patterns consist of a single candlestick or a combination of multiple candlesticks. In fact, the technique acts as a leading indicator with its capability to provide trading signals earlier than other technical indicators based on statistics. It is also used by some real time technical service providers [3] to provide quick signals for market's sentiments.

The candlestick charting technique probably began sometime after 1850 [2]. Despite of its long history and popularity, mixed results are obtained in the studies on candlestick charting. Negative conclusions to the predictability of candlesticks are reported [4]-[6], while positive evidences are provided for several candlestick chart patterns in experiments using the U.S. and the Asian stock markets [7]-[10].

It is also pointed out that candlestick chart pattern recognition is subjective [2][7][11]. The candlestick chart patterns are often qualitatively described using words and illustrations. The studies [6][7] adopt definitions using a series of inequalities with different parameters that specify candlestick patterns. Numerical definitions of candlestick patterns are still controversial issues.

In addition, they don't occur in time series in a strict sense because stock price fluctuation continues after intervals of several days depending on announcements of important economic indicators, economic and political news, etc. Because of these characteristics, the candlestick chart patterns are deemed to bring controversial results on predictability regarding future market trends even sort-term prediction.

The aim of the study is to estimate the predictability of candlestick patterns for future stock price trends. The proposed algorithm is applied to the daily Nikkei stock average (Nikkei 225) in the experiments. Daily historical stock prices are used because we plan to relate chart patterns to economic and political news in the future study.

The contributions of this paper are as follows:

(I) The Longest Common Substring (LCS) algorithm [12], which is a kind of dynamic programming algorithms, is improved to cope with candlestick patterns containing several intervals,

(II) The proposed model utilizes tolerances for multiple attributes that specify candlestick charts, so it can retrieve similar candlestick charts in terms of upper and lower tolerance bounds,

(III) The proposed model uses relative position among a stock price, 5-day moving average, and 25-day moving average to decide whether the price occurs in high or low price zones,

(IV) The proposed model uses slopes of the moving averages to identify their trends,

(V) The proposed model devises a graphical representation to make evaluation of the retrieval results easy to depict the predictability for short-term trends.

The remainder of the paper is organized as follows. Section II gives backgrounds of the candlestick chart. Section III describes a model for retrieving similar candlestick charts. An augmented dynamic programing technique is used to implement the proposed model. Section VI presents experimental results on both the uptrend and downtrend of stock prices. Section V gives some of the most related work. Section VI concludes the paper with our plans for future work.

II. CANDLESTICK CHART AND PATTERNS

This section introduces the formation of a candlestick. Candlestick patterns are a combination of one or more candlesticks [2]. Samples of well-known candlestick chart patterns are shown. Because the candlestick patterns are described in natural language and illustrations, there are criticisms on their use for trend prediction by a computer.

A. Formation of Candlestick

A daily candlestick line is formed with the market's opening, high, low, and closing prices of a specific trading day. Figure 1 represents the image of a typical candlestick. The candlestick has a wide part, which is called the "real body" representing the range between the opening and closing prices of that day's trading.

If the closing price is above the opening price, then a white candlestick with black border is drawn to represent a bullish candlestick. If the opening price is above the closing price, then a filled candlestick is drawn. Normally, black color is used for filling the candle to represent a bearish candlestick.

The thin lines above and below the body represent the high/low ranges. These lines and are called "shadows" and also referred to as "wicks" and "tails." The high is marked by the top of the upper shadow and the low by the bottom of the lower shadow.

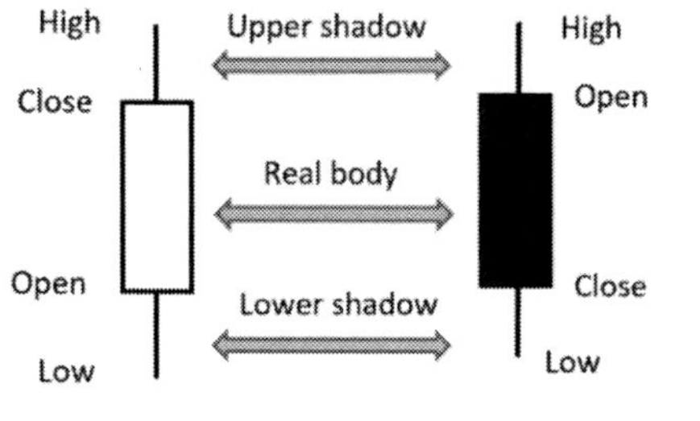

Figure 1. Candlestick formation

B. Samples of Candlestick Patterns

Dozens of candlestick patterns are identified and become popular among stock traders [2][3]. These patterns have colorful names like *morning star*, *evening star*, *three white soldiers*, and *three black crows*.

Figure 2 shows the *morning star* pattern which is considered as a major reversal signal when it appears in a low price zone or at a bottom. It consists of three candles, i.e., one short-bodied candle (black or white) between a preceding long black candle and a succeeding long white one. The pattern shows that the selling pressure that was there the day before is now subsiding. The third white candle overlaps with the body of the black candle showing a start of a bullish reversal. The larger the white and black candle, and the higher the white candle moves, the larger the potential reversal. The opposite version of the *morning star* pattern is known as the *evening star* pattern which is a reversal signal when it appears in a high price zone or at the end of an uptrend.

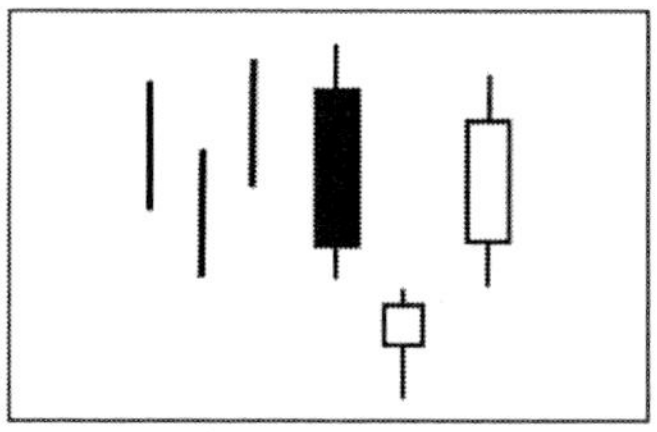

Figure 2. Morning star pattern

Figure 3 shows the *three white soldiers* pattern which is interpreted as a strong indication of a bullish market reversal when it appears in a low price zone. It consists of three long white candles that close progressively higher on each subsequent trading day. Each candle opens higher than the previous opening price and closes near the high price of the day, showing a steady advance of buying pressure. The opposite of the three white soldiers pattern is known as the *three black crows* pattern which is interpreted as a bearish signal of market trend.

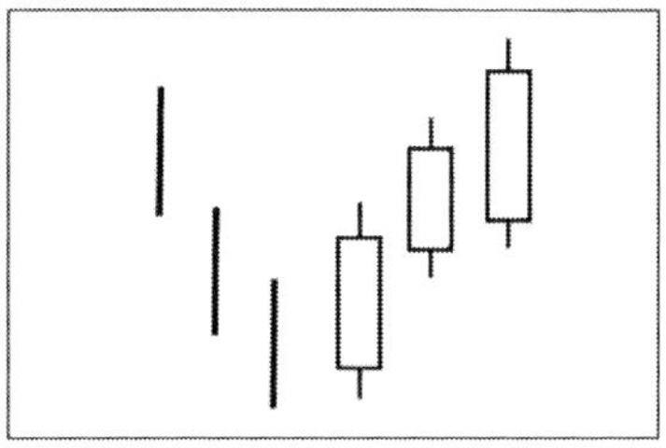

Figure 3. Three white soldiers pattern

C. *Criticism of Candlestick Patterns*

The major criticism of the candlestick chart patterns is that the patterns are qualitatively described with words, such as "long/short candlesticks," "higher/lower trading," "strong/weak signal," supported by some illustrations [2]. What percentage of price change does "long/short" mean? Without modeling the candlestick patterns in a way that a computer can process and performing experiments comprehensively, arguments on the effectiveness of chart patterns would not come to an end.

Since it is highly possible that the existence and predictability of candlestick patterns depends on stock markets, this study focuses on the Nikkei stock average (Nikkei 225) as the first stage of study. This paper proposes a model for retrieving similar candlestick charts based on a data mining algorithm using dynamic programing technique to handle candlestick patterns including several intervals that suggest unpredictable price trends.

III. Proposed Model for Retrieving Candlestick Patterns

This section describes a model for retrieving similar candlestick charts. A dynamic programing technique is used to implement the proposed model.

A. *Parameters Featuring Candlestick Patterns*

As a preliminary stage of study, experiments only using the closing prices and the length of real bodies are conducted. The experiments simply correspond to the conditions of the candlestick chart patterns [2]. The results are discouraging. Although mined stock price sequences are similar before the specified period of the reference date, trends of the sequences after the reference date are seemed to be random. Analyses of the results show that the randomness occurs due to the relative position among the stock price, the 5-day moving averages, and the 25-day moving averages.

Based on the results of the preliminary experiments, we propose the model for retrieving similar candlestick charts. Figure 4 depicts the model that consists of the six parameters as follows:

(1) Change of prices w.r.t previous closing price,
(2) Length of candlestick body,
(3) Difference from 5-day moving average,
(4) Difference from 25-day moving average,
(5) Slope of 5-day moving average,
(6) Slope of 25-day moving average.

The proposed model is unique because it uses two moving averages and their slopes, while the previous studies [4]-[12] do not deal with them. Relative position among a stock price, 5-day moving average, and 25-day moving average is significant to identify the zone where the candlestick pattern under consideration occurs, which is vital information for applying the candlestick pattern. The slopes of the moving averages are also important to identify their trends, e.g., an uptrend, a downtrend or a sideway (flat).

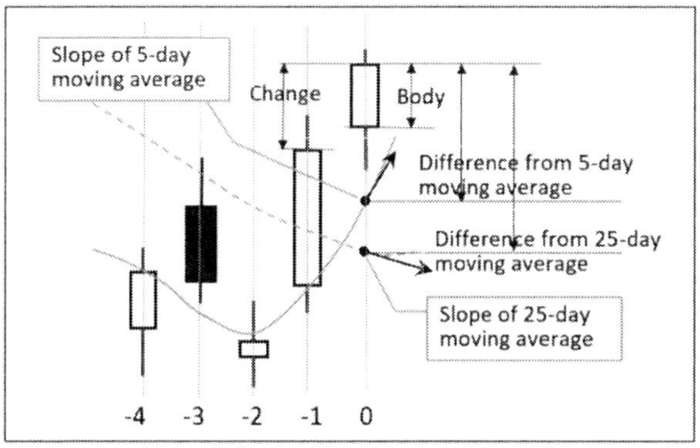

Figure 4. Candlestick pattern retrieval model

B. *nLCS: LCS for Numerical Subsequences*

Another issue of retrieving candlestick chart patterns is that stock prices can move continued after a few days of intervals because stock prices can vary according to important economic indicators, political news and actions, etc. The detection of similar candlestick chart patterns is essentially the detection of a set of numerical sequences that partially match the numerical sequences corresponding to a chart pattern under consideration.

The Longest Common Subsequence (LCS) algorithm is originally developed for character strings [12]. Finding the LCS between two strings is described as follows. Given two strings, find the longest character subsequence that presents in both of them. Characters of the subsequence appear in the same relative order, but not necessarily contiguous. Figure 5 depicts the LCS of the two strings "246612" and "3651." Since elements of sequences are interpreted as characters that require an exact match, the LCS is "61."

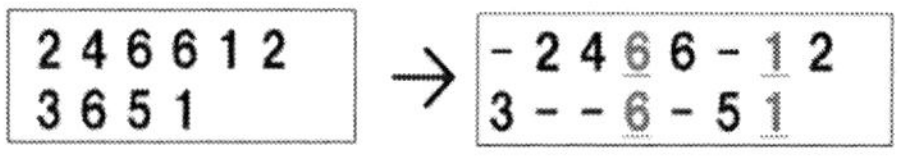

Figure 5. The LCS of two character sequences, "246612" and "3651"

It is rather easy to improve the LCS algorithm to deal with numerical sequences (nLCS) by interpreting each element as a number and using a tolerance given by a user. If the difference of two numbers is not greater than the given tolerance, then the two numbers are regarded as the same. For example, let the tolerance be set to one, and the two number sequences be "246612" and "3651." The nLCS are "2661" and "3651" as shown in Figure 6.

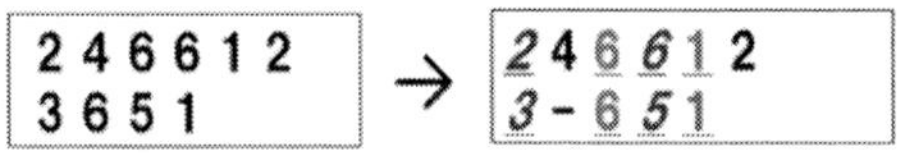

Figure 6. The nLCS of the two number sequences "246612" and "3651" for the tolerance of one

The LCS and nLCS are formally defined as follows.

LCS algorithm: Let the input sequences be X[1 … m] of length m and Y[1 … n] of length n. Let D[i, j] denote the length of the longest common subsequence of X[i] and Y[j] for $0 \leqq i \leqq m$ and $0 \leqq j \leqq n$.

A) If either sequence or both sequences are empty, then the LCS is empty, i.e., D[i, 0] = 0 and D[0, j] = 0.

B) If X[i] and Y[j] match (X[i] = Y[j]), then the LCS is become longer than the previous sequences by one, i.e., D[i, j] = D[i−1, j−1] + 1.

C) If X[i] and Y[j] do not match (X[i] ≠Y[j]), then the LCS is the maximum of the previous sequences, i.e., max(D[i−1, j], D[i, j−1]).

The value of D[m, n] is the LCS of the sequences X[1 … m] and Y[1 … n]. The actual LCS sequence can be extracted by following the matrix D[i, j].

nLCS algorithm: The nLCS algorithm is derived from the LCS algorithm by replacing the match condition (X[i] = Y[j]) with ((X[i] − Y[j]) ≦ diff) where diff is a tolerance given by a user.

C. *nLCSm: LCS for Subsequences with Multi Numerical Attributes*

The idea of deriving the nLCS from the LCS can be further extend to the multi numerical attributes to obtain the nLCS for subsequences with multi numerical attributes (nLCSm).

nLCSm algorithm: Let p ($1 \leqq p$) denote the number of numerical attributes. Let C_q ($1 \leqq q \leqq p$) denote the match conditions for the qth numerical attribute. The nLCSm is derived by replacing the match condition of the nLCS, i.e., ((X[i] − Y[j]) ≦ diff), with ($C_1 \wedge \ldots \wedge C_q \wedge \ldots \wedge C_p$).

D. *nLCSm and candlestick pattern retrieval*

Given the candlestick pattern model with six parameters as depicted in Figure 4, the nLCSm algorithm can be applied to implementing the model by assigning match conditions C_1 to C_6 for each candlestick as follows.

C_1: if a difference between closing price change of a given candlestick and that of a candidate candlestick is within the change tolerance (*change_tol*), then C_1 is true.

C_2: if a difference between body length of a given candlestick and that of a candidate candlestick is within the body tolerance (*body_tol*), then C_2 is true.

C_3: if a difference between a closing price and a 5-day moving average is within the tolerance (*av5diff_tol*), then C_3 is true.

C_4: if a difference between a closing price and a 25-day moving average is within the tolerance (*av25diff_tol*), then C_4 is true.

C_5: if a slope of a 5-day moving average is within the given tolerance (*slope5_tol*), then C_5 is true.

C_6: if a slope of a 25-day moving average is within the given tolerance (*slope25_tol*), then C_6 is true.

The 5-day moving average is calculated by the latest five days' closing prices. Because these prices are just a sample of larger population of closing prices, the sample standard deviation or *Bessel's* correction [2] is adopted as a measure of threshold to decide whether a given 5-day moving average is within an expected distribution.

The tolerance of 5-day moving average *av5diff_tol* is statistically dependent on the change tolerance *change_tol*. In the proposed retrieval model, *av5diff_tol* and *av25diff_tol* are calculated by the following formulas as defaults according to the definition of the sample standard deviation.

av5diff_tol = *change_tol* / SQRT(4)= *change_tol* / 2 (1)

av25diff_tol = *change_tol* / SQRT(24)= *change_tol* / 4.899 (2)

Thus, there are essentially four independent parameters in the proposed model, which still causes difficulties in setting parameters. Assuming that each parameter has 5 ranges of values representing, for instance, very high, high, the same level, low, and very low. The candlestick patterns of one candlestick have 5 to the power 4, i.e., 5^4= 625 cases of parameters. The patterns composed of two candlesticks have 5^(4*2)= 625*625= 390,625 cases. The patterns of tree candlesticks have 244,140,625 cases. These cases mean very wide varieties of candlestick charts leading difficulties even in setting parameters for retrieving a specific candlestick chart pattern.

IV. Experimental Results

The predictabilities of the *morning star* pattern and the *evening star* pattern are evaluated through experiments. The experiments are conducted on the daily historical stock prices of Nikkei stock average (Nikkei 225) of 2,420 business days from Jan. 4, 2008 to Nov. 15, 2017.

A. *Data Conversion*

The stock prices are converted to the ratio of closing prices to reduce the effects of highness or lowness of the stock prices. The formula below is used for calculating the ratio of prices in a percentage.

$$R_i = (CP_i - CP_{i+1})*100 / CP_i \quad (1 \leqq i \leqq n) \qquad (3)$$

CP_i indicates the closing price of the i-th business date. CP_1 means the closing price of the current date. R_1 is the ratio of the closing price of the current date CP_1 and the difference between CP_1 and CP_2, i.e., the closing price of the date before the current date. The similar calculations are performed to opening, high, and low prices. In addition, the 5-day and 25 day moving averages, and their slopes are calculated before the experiments. The number of data valid, i.e., n in effect is 2,396 (=2,420−24) because the 25-day averages can't be calculated to the last 24 days.

B. Experiments on Morning Star Pattern

Figure 7 shows the candlestick chart of the Nikkei 225 in which a strong uptrend starts on Sept. 11, 2017. The candlesticks ending on Sept. 11, 2017 form a *morning star* pattern. The first experiment is performed on the three candlesticks surrounded by a dotted rectangle in Figure 7.

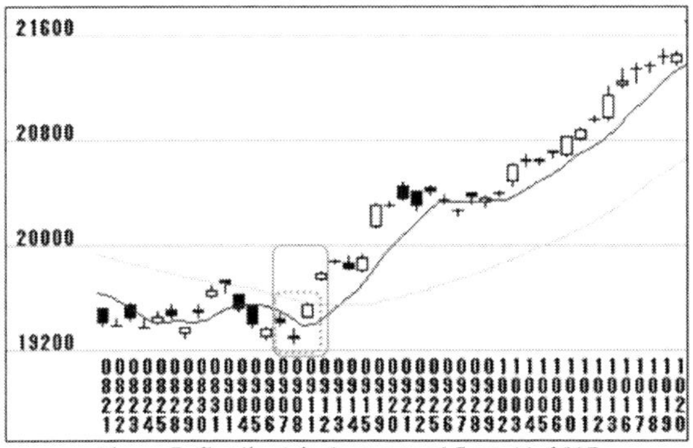

Figure 7. Candlestick chart around Sept. 11, 2017

Table I shows a list of the retrieved business dates, the number of matched days or nLCSm. The ratio of nLCSm is calculated by dividing the nLCSm by the period of three. The parameters used for the experiment are as follows: *change_tol*=1.600, *body_tol*=1.600, *av5diff_tol*=0.800, *av25diff_tol*=0.327, *slope5_tol*=0.050, *lope25_tol*=0.020.

TABLE I. RESULTS CONCERNING MORNING STAR PATTERN ON SEPT. 11, 2017

Date	Match	Ratio of nLCSm
20170911	3	1.000
20170802	2	0.667
20170726	2	0.667
20160825	2	0.667
20160525	2	0.667
20150707	2	0.667
20140502	2	0.667
20131111	3	1.000

The three candlesticks that end on Nov. 11, 2013 totally match those on Sept. 11, 2017. It is not surprising that the chart pattern on Nov. 11, 2013 in Figure 8 draws a similar trend as Sept. 11, 2017 in Figure 7.

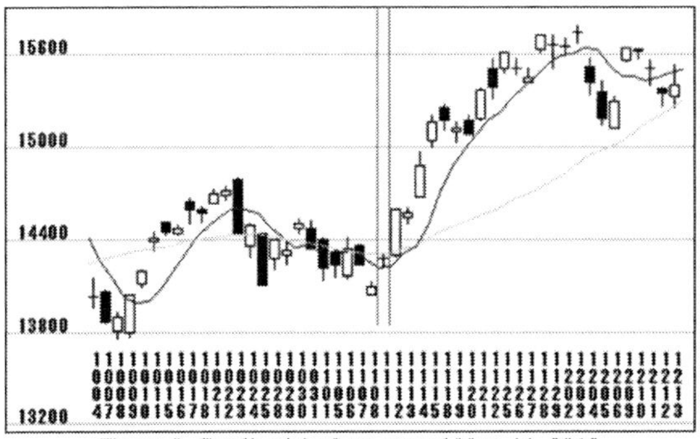

Figure 8. Candlestick chart around Nov. 11, 2013

Figure 9 shows overlapped closing prices whose business dates are listed in Table I for graphically representing the future stock trend. All reference dates are aligned on the origin to make the comparison easy. The thick black line represents the closing price sequences of the reference date, i.e., Sept. 11, 2017. Thin solid lines represent the closing price sequences of business dates listed in Table I except for the reference date. The thick light blue line indicates the average of the candlestick charts plotted by thin solid lines.

Three out of the seven closing price sequences suggest an uptrend, while two out of the seven suggest downtrend. The others suggest sideways. It can be reasonable to say that no trade judgments, i.e., indecision, should be made based on the results of retrieval.

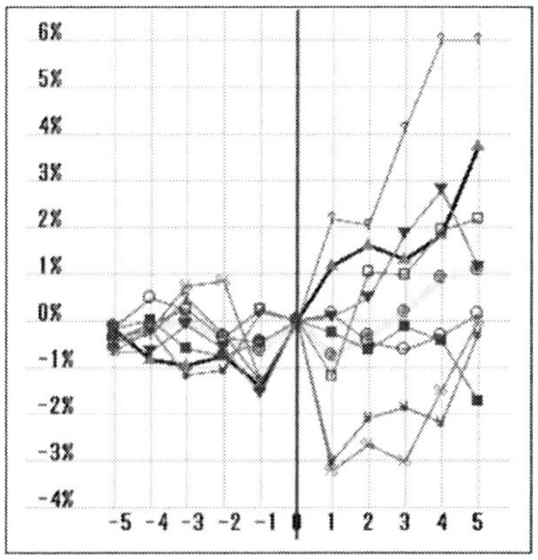

Figure 9. Overlapped closing prices representing for future stock trend

C. Experiments on Morning Star Pattern with Confirmation

Four candlesticks enclosed by a solid rectangle in Figure 7 show the *morning star* pattern plus one confirmation day. Table II summarizes the result of the experiment on four candlesticks ending on Sept. 12, 2017.

TABLE II. RESULTS CONCERNING MORNING STAR PATTERN ON SEPT. 11, 2017 PLUS ONE CONFIRMATION DAY

Date	Match	Ratio of nLCSm
20170912	4	1
20160829	3	0.75
20150519	3	0.75
20141030	4	1
20140523	3	0.75
20120118	3	0.75
20110622	4	1
20091016	3	0.75

Figure 10 shows overlapped closing prices whose business dates are listed in Table II for representing the future stock trend. Five out of seven closing price sequences suggest an uptrend, while the other two out of seven ones suggest keeping the same price level. This result may well be noteworthy for traders to identify buying opportunities with expectation of approximately 2.5% profits on average in the next five days.

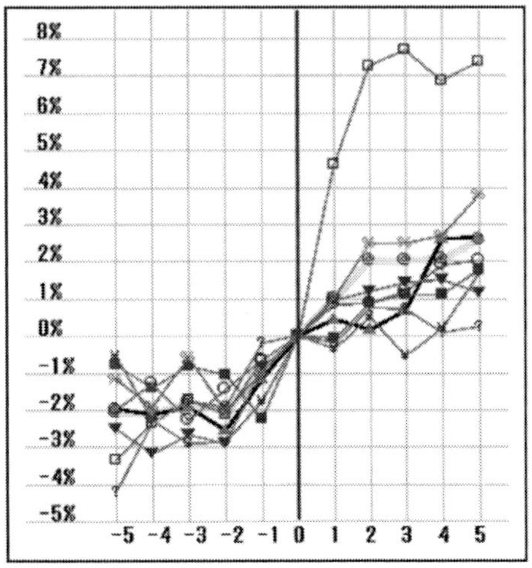

Figure 10. Overlapped closing prices for representing future stock trend

D. Experiments on Evening Star Pattern

Figure 11 shows the candlestick charts with respect to an *evening star* pattern ending on June 6, 2017. The patterns consist of four candlesticks enclosed by a solid rectangle in Figure 11.

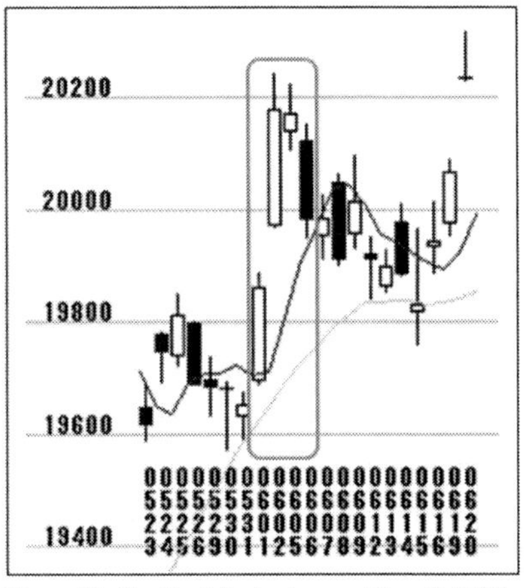

Figure 11. Candlestick chart around June 6, 2017

Table III summarizes the result of the experiment on the pattern. The parameters used for the experiment are as follows:

change_tol=1.320, body_tol=1.3200, *av5diff_tol*=0.660, *av25diff_tol*=0.269, *slope5_tol*=0.050, *slope25_tol*=0.020.

TABLE III. RESULTS CONCERNING EVENING STAR CHART PATTERN ON JUNE 6, 2017

Date	Match	Ratio of nLCSm
20170606	4	1
20170315	3	0.75
20150811	3	0.75
20150129	4	1

Figure 12 shows overlapped closing prices whose business dates are listed in Table III. Figure 12 generally suggests a downtrend of the future stock price. However, two closing price sequences and that of June 6, 2017 predict a dip in stock prices of approximately 1%.

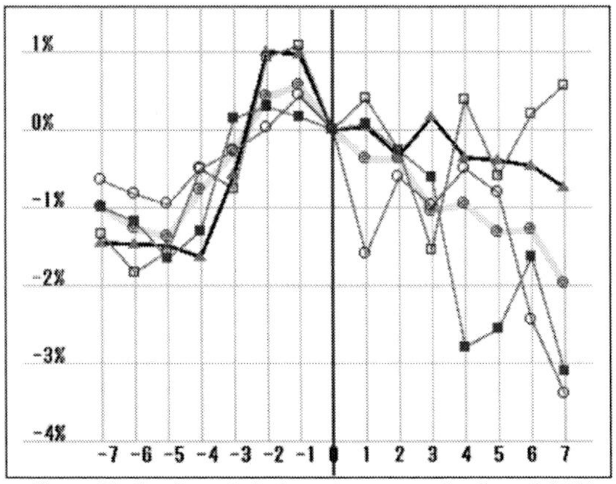

Figure 12. Overlapped closing prices concerning June 6, 2017

The closing price on June 6, 2017 (Figure 11) shows sudden drop, but is still above the 5-day and 25-day moving averages. Many traders know that there are two possible price trends at this position of prices, i.e., continuing downtrends and/or bargain-hunting after several days of stock price decline. The proposed algorithm seems to be successful in retrieving both possible price trends.

V. RELATED WORK

Some studies [4]-[6] find that the candlestick charting is useless based on the experiments using the stock exchange markets' data in the U.S., Japan and Thailand. Tharavanij, Siraprapasiri, and Rajchamaha [6] investigate the profitability of bullish and bearish candlestick patterns consisted of one-day, two-day, and three-day candle sticks. The candlestick patterns are defined by a set of inequalities defined by opening, high, low, and closing prices. These inequalities are originally proposed by Goo, Chen, and Chang [7] who report positive results in Taiwan markets. Based on experiments using stock data in the Stock Exchange of Thailand, they conclude that any candlestick patterns cannot reliably predict market directions even with filtering by well-known stochastic oscillators [2].

Other studies conclude that applying certain candlestick patterns is profitable at least for short-term trading [8]-[11]. Chootong and Sornil [8] propose a trading strategy combining price movement patterns, candlestick chart patterns, and trading indicators. A neural network is employed to determine buy and sell signals. Experimental results using stock data in the Stock Exchange of Thailand show that the proposed strategy generally outperforms the use of traditional trading methods based on indicators. Zhu, Atri, and Yegen [9] examine the effectiveness of five different candlestick reversal patterns in predicting short-term stock movements using two Chinese stock data. The results of statistical analysis suggest that the patterns perform well in predicting price trend reversals.

Lu, Chen, and Hsu [10] apply candlestick trading strategies to the U.S. market data with several trend definitions. They find three-day reversal patterns are profitable when the transaction cost is set at 0.5%.

One of the obstacles of candlestick charting is the highly subjective nature of candlestick pattern [2] since the candlestick patterns are defined using words and illustrations. Tsai and Quan [11] propose an image processing technique to analyze the similarities of the candlestick charts for stock prediction instead of using numerical inequality formulas. The experimental results using the Dow Jones Industrial Average (DJIA) show that visual extraction of contents and similarity matching of candlestick charts are suitable for predicting stock movements.

The studies [4]-[10] translate these candlestick verbal and visual descriptions into numeric formulas in order to be used in an algorithm. However, they fail to consider zones where the candlestick patterns in focus occur. The interpretation of candlestick patterns depends on the price zone, e.g., high, low, neutral. For example, the *morning star* pattern generally suggests a bullish trend when it occurs in a low price zone. However, the morning star pattern is deemed to be less bullish when it occurs in a high price zone than it occurs in a low price zone.

Most importantly, the studies [4]-[10] do not discuss neutral candlesticks or intervals that often take place in charts because stock prices depend on important economic and political news and events.

VI. Conclusions and Future Work

This paper proposes a model for retrieving similar candlestick charts with six parameters that feature candlestick charts. A numerical sequence version of the Longest Common Substring (LCS) algorithm is devised to implement the proposed model because partial matching of candlesticks plays a significant role to retrieve similar candlestick patterns. Results of experiments using the Nikkei stock average show some positive evidences regarding the prediction of future market trends.

As for the future work, we are planning to improve the proposed model by augmenting available parameters including the upper and lower shadows. The augmentation allows the model to examine various shadow sensitive patterns known as the *hammer*, *dragon fly* patterns [2]. As the current study is limited to a Japanese stock market, it is suggested that future researches may focus on different stock markets from other countries for further analyses of candle stick patterns.

Acknowledgment

This research is supported by the JSPS KAKENHI under grant number 16K00161.

References

[1] V. Drakopoulou, "A Review of Fundamental and Technical Stock Analysis Techniques," Journal of Stock & Forex Trading vol. 5, pp. 1–8, Nov. 2015.

[2] "Technical Analysis," Cambridge Univ. pp. 1–179, Available from: http://www.mrao.cam.ac.uk/~mph/TechnicalAnalysis.pdf, Feb. 2011.

[3] Fusion Media Limited., "Nikkei 225 Futures," https://www.investing.com/indices/japan-225-futures-candlestick, April, 2018.

[4] J. M. Horton, "Stars, crows, and doji: The use of candlesticks in stock selection," Quarterly Review of Economics and Finance, vol. 49, pp. 283–294, Nov. 2007.

[5] R. B. Marshall, R. M. Young, and R. Cahan, "Are candlestick technical trading strategies profitable in the Japanese equity market?" Review of Quantitative Finance and Accounting, vol. 31, pp. 191–207, August 2008.

[6] P. Tharavanij, V. Siraprapasiri, and K. Rajchamaha, "Profitability of Candlestick Charting Patterns in the Stock Exchange of Thailand," SAGE journals, pp. 1–18, Oct. 2017.

[7] Y.-J. Goo, D.-H. Chen, and Y.-W. Chang, "The application of Japanese candlestick trading strategies in Taiwan," Investment Management and Financial Innovations, vol. 4, pp. 49–79, Jan. 2007.

[8] C. Chootong and O. Sornil, "Trading Signal Generation Using A Combination of Chart Patterns and Indicators," International Journal of Computer Science Issues, vol. 9, pp 202–209, Nov. 2012.

[9] M. Zhu, S. Atri, and E. Yegen, "Are candlestick trading strategies effective in certain stocks with distinct features?" Pacific Basin Finance Journal, vol. 37, pp. 116–127, April 2016.

[10] T.-H. Lu, Y.-. Chen, and Y.-C. Hsu, "Trend definition or holding strategy: What determines the profitability of candlestick charting?" Journal of Banking & Finance, vol. 61, Dec. 2015, pp. 172–183.

[11] C.-F. Tsai and Z.-Y. Quan, "Stock Prediction by Searching for Similarities in Candlestick Charts," Journal ACM Transactions on Management Information Systems (TMIS), vol. 5, Article No. 9, July 2014.

[12] D. Mount, "Dynamic Programming Longest Common Subsequence," CMSC 451, Maryland Univ., pp. 1–5, Available from: https://www.cs.umd.edu/class/fall2010/cmsc451/lect451.pdf, Sept. 2010.

Design of Elastic Hadoop Supporting Dynamic Scaling of the Cluster

Wooseok Ryu
Dept. of Healthcare Management
Catholic University of Pusan
Busan, Republic of Korea
e-mail: wsryu@cup.ac.kr

***Abstract*—This paper discusses the problem of node management in the Hadoop cluster and presents a mechanism for managing the Hadoop cluster more elastically. The proposed mechanism supports instant removal of a slave node from the cluster and reconnection to the cluster. Using this, the cluster can be managed more elastically because slave nodes no longer need to be dedicated to the cluster. The experimental results show that the proposed mechanism can process 5 times faster than when a slave node is arbitrarily stopped.**

Keywords-Hadoop; cluster management; scalability.

I. INTRODUCTION

Big data computing is one of key issues in many areas of business domains that wish to discover breaking knowledge from massive data [1]. Apache Hadoop is the most popular open source platform that contributes to broadening the scope of big data analysis. Its distributed processing capability can be extended to thousands of nodes because it supports real-time up-scaling of the cluster [2].

However, we found that Hadoop lacks real-time down-scaling of the cluster [3]. This causes serious problems for small business domains that want to configure a Hadoop cluster with limited resources. The reason is that it would be a financial burden for small businesses to construct a cluster using a large number of dedicated systems. If dynamic up/down scaling of Hadoop is provided, the cluster can be configured more economically by using existing business computers only when necessary. Although cloud computing can be considered as an alternative, some domains, such as small-and-medium sized hospitals do not agree to it due to security reasons.

This paper presents an implementation-level mechanism to manage the Hadoop cluster more elastically by removing nodes from the cluster and adding them again to the cluster in an instant manner. This makes it possible to maintain an elastic Hadoop cluster including existing computers, which means that these computers can be used for analysis or at work in turn, depending on the circumstances at that time. The main idea of this work is initiated and partly implemented by our previous works [3][4]. This paper improves the previous studies through detailed implementation and experiments.

This paper first analyzes the Hadoop architecture with problem statements in Section 2. In Section 3, this paper presents a design and implementation of the elastic node management in Hadoop. Experimental studies are discussed in Section 4, followed by the conclusion.

II. PROBLEM STATEMENT

A Hadoop cluster consists of one master node and a set of slave nodes. The main components of the Hadoop are the Hadoop Distributed File System (HDFS) and the MapReduce framework. The former is a filesystem to store big data in a distributed manner. The latter is to process user requests on big data in parallel. Currently, the MapReduce framework is controlled by Yarn, which is a new framework for job scheduling and resource management [5]. The software architecture of Hadoop is depicted in Figure 1.

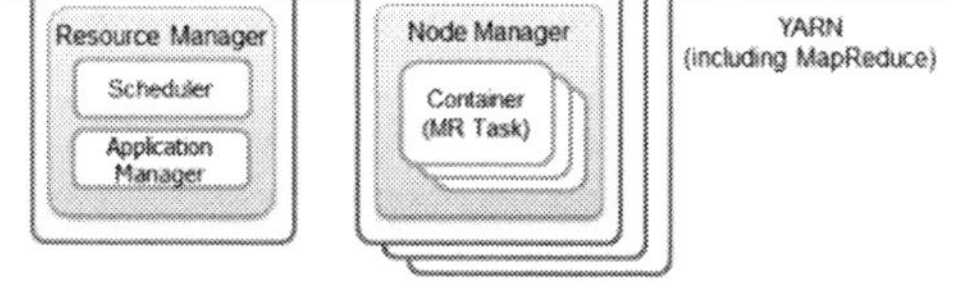

Figure 1. Software architecture of Hadoop.

If a certain slave node needs to be stopped, all the processes inside the node should of course be closed. The first problem is that the processes are handled separately even though they are tightly related to each other. The second problem is that there is no way to stop the *DataNode* process instantly. The existing decommissioning mechanism of HDFS includes moving of data blocks to other live nodes, which cannot be done in a short period of time.

III. SYSTEM DESIGN AND IMPLEMENTATION

In our implementation, we designed a single, unified interface for the Hadoop cluster, which immediately pauses or resumes all the server processes of a slave node. When a pause of a certain slave node is requested, the interface lets *NameNode* and *Resource Manager* of the master node finish the execution of related server processes running on the slave node and delegate task executions to other slave nodes. If a resumption of the node is requested, the master node automatically initiates server processes on the slave node without additional user control.

We implemented the mechanism in the Apache Hadoop version 2.7.4. We modified some source codes to support new properties and pausing/resuming procedures of HDFS and Yarn in addition to the new interface. Figure 2 shows the detailed mechanism when the cluster needs to be down-scaled. In step 1 in the figure, user requests for a pause by calling the shell command "*NodeManage.sh pause slavenode1*". This adds the node descriptor in a configuration file specified by a new server property named *dfs.host.pause* specified by *yarn.resourcemanager.nodes.pause-path*, followed by sending a *refreshNode* command to the *Resource Manager* and *NameNode*. We consider the state of the node in the configuration file as *Paused* [3][4]. The *Resource Manager* reads the configuration file and decommissions the *Node Manager* process on the specified slave node by terminating the related daemon, marks the node as unusable, and reschedules tasks to other nodes as described in steps 2 and 3. In steps 4 and 5, the *NameNode* reads the file and terminates the *DataNode* daemon when receiving a heartbeat message. This does not decommission the *DataNode*, which demands extra time for moving data blocks, which cannot be done immediately [4].

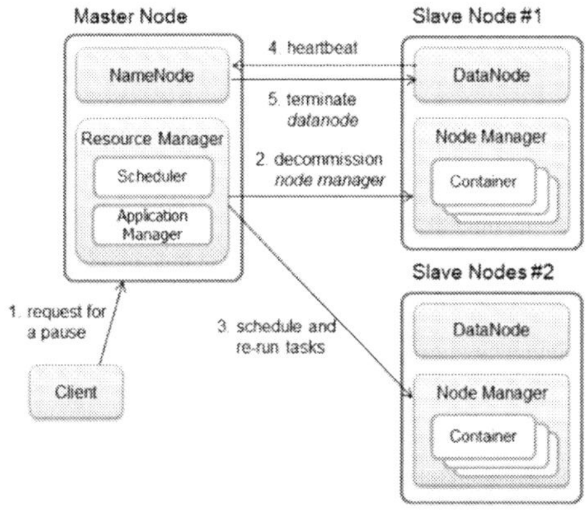

Figure 2. Processing flow for pausing a slave node.

We implemented that the resumption of the paused node can be done by calling a command "*NodeManage.sh resume slavenode1*", which initiates the *DataNode* and *Node Manager* processes in consecutive order. Once the node is resumed, it can store data blocks and execute job tasks immediately without any further work.

IV. Experimental Results

To verify feasibility of the proposed mechanism, we built a small Hadoop cluster consisting of one master node and four slave nodes. Each node is equipped with a 2-core Pentium processor and 4GB main memory. Ubuntu 14 is installed as an operating system. All the nodes are connected to each other with a 1 Giga-bit Ethernet switch.

Figure 3 shows the comparison of processing times among three evaluation cases when executing a *wordcount* program with two text datasets of which sizes are 1Gbyte and 2Gbyte, respectively. When one slave node is paused while the program is running (marked as *Pause*), its processing time was 10~20% slower than when all slave nodes are running (marked as *Normal*). If server processes of one slave node are killed during the execution (marked as *Kill*), its processing time was more than 6 times slower than that of *Normal*. The reason is that the *Resource Manager* has to wait for a timeout, 10 minutes by default, when a slave node is not reachable.

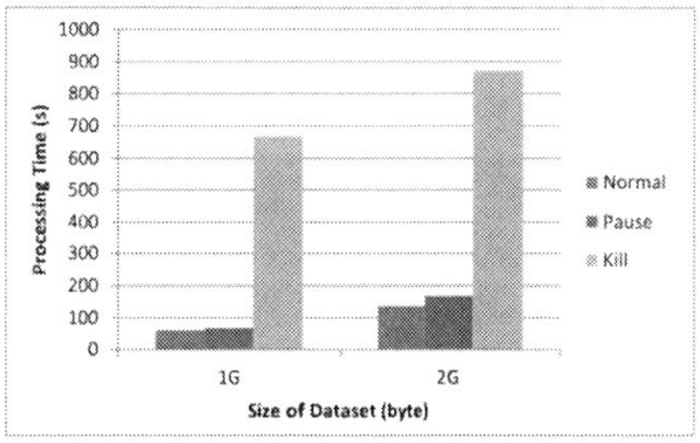

Figure 3. Performance comparison of the proposed implementation

The result shows that the proposed implementation can speed up more than 5 times faster than when the processes are killed arbitrarily in the Apache Hadoop with the default configuration.

V. Conclusion

This paper discussed problems of dynamic node management in the Hadoop cluster and proposed a new mechanism to manage slave nodes more elastically. Implementation of the proposed mechanism is also discussed, along with the experiment. The experimental results show that when a slave node is being stopped, the proposed mechanism can speed up more than 5 times compared with the Apache Hadoop. The main contribution of this paper is to provide the empirical implementation of the proposed mechanism. More comprehensive experimental studies need to be performed as future works.

Acknowledgment

This work was supported by the National Research Foundation of Korea (NRF) grant funded by the Korea government (MSIP) (No. NRF-2016R1C1B1012364).

References

[1] R. Kune, P. K. Konugurthi, A. Agarwal, R. R. Chillarige, and R. Buyya, "The anatomy of big data computing," Software: Practice and Experience, vol. 46, no. 1, pp.79–105, 2016.

[2] W. K. Lai, Y. U. Chen, and T. Y. Wu, "Towards a framework for large-scale multimedia data storage and processing on Hadoop platform," The Journal of Supercomputing, vol. 68, no. 1, pp. 488–507, 2014.

[3] W. Ryu, "Flexible management of data nodes for Hadoop Distributed File System," The Third International Conference on Big Data, Small Data, Linked Data and Open Data (ALLDATA 2017) IARIA, Apr. 2017, pp. 1–2, ISBN: 978-1-61208-070-3.

[4] W. Ryu, "Implementation of dynamic node management in Hadoop cluster," International Conference on Electronics, Information, and Communication (ICEIC 2018), Jan. 2018, pp. 814–815.

[5] V. K. Vavilapalli et al. "Apache Hadoop Yarn: Yet another Resource Negotiator," Proc. Symp. Cloud Computing, ACM, Oct. 2013, doi:10.1145/2523616.2523633.

A New Representation of Air Traffic Data Adapted to Complexity Assessment

Georges Mykoniatis†, Florence Nicol‡, Stephane Puechmorel (*)

Ecole Nationale de l'Aviation Civile
Toulouse France
Email: †georges.mykoniatis@enac.fr, ‡florence.nicol@enac.fr, (*)stephane.puechmore@enac.fr

***Abstract*—Air traffic is generally characterized by simple indicators like the number of aircraft flying over a given area or the total distance flown during a time window. As an example, these values may be used for estimating a rough number of air traffic controllers needed in a given control center or for performing economic studies. However, this approach is not adapted to more complex situations such as those encountered in airspace comparison or air traffic controllers training. An innovative representation of the traffic data, relying on a sound theoretical framework, is introduced in this work. It will pave the way to a number of tools dedicated to traffic analysis. Based on an extraction of local covariance, a grid with values in the space of symmetric positive definite matrices is obtained. It can serve as a basis of comparison or be subject to filtering and selection to obtain a digest of a traffic situation suitable for efficient complexity assessment.**

***Keywords*—Air traffic complexity; spatial data; manifold valued images; covariance function estimation; non-parametric estimation.**

I. INTRODUCTION

Key performance indicators (KPI) are of common use in air transportation. However, they are designed mainly to address global aspects of the systems and cannot address problems, where it is mandatory to be able to distinguish between traffic situations based on the structure of the trajectories. As an example, the training of air traffic controllers relies on carefully selected traffic patterns that are presented to the trainees in an order of increasing perceived complexity. Creating such scenarios is quite a lengthy process, involving hundreds of hours of works by experienced controllers. On the other hand, it is easy to start from real situations, with known flight plans, and to use a traffic simulator to put the trainees in a nearly operational setting. The drawback of this approach is the need to evaluate the traffic patterns in order to assess a complexity value for each of them. It has to be done automatically, to avoid having to resort to human experts.

In a more operational context, nearly the same question arises when trying to find the right number of controllers needed at a give time to take care of the incoming flights in their assigned airspace. Too many controllers induces an extra cost and too few put a high pressure on the operators, with possible detrimental effects on flight safety. Assessing the right level of complexity of the expected traffic may greatly improve over the current state of the art that simply estimates the number of aircraft that will be present. Once again, it is mainly a matter of finding an adequate traffic complexity indicator [1] [2].

A lot of work was dedicated to the issue of air traffic complexity measurement. Unfortunately, no really satisfactory solution exists, as the problem itself is ill posed: depending on the point of view, the complexity may be a concept roughly equivalent to the cognitive workload or, on the contrary, be based on purely structural features, without any reference to the way it will be used. One of the most widely used complexity measures is the dynamic density [3], that combines several potential indicators, like number of maneuvering aircraft, number of level changes, convergence and so on. All these values are used as inputs of a multivariate linear model, or in recent implementations, of a neural network. The tuning of the free parameters of the predictors is made using examples coming from an expertized database of traffic situations. While being quite efficient for assessing complexity values in an operational context, the method has two important drawbacks:

- The tuning procedure requires a sufficient number of expertized samples. A costly experiment involving several air traffic controllers must be set up.
- The indicator is valid only in a specific area of the airspace. Adaptation to other countries or even control centers requires a re-tuning that is almost as complicated as the first one.

The last point is a severe flaw if one wants to use dynamic complexity in the context of air traffic databases, as a world covering has to be obtained first. Even for country sized databases, some geographical tuning has to be added.

Another way to deal with complexity is through purely geometrical indicators [4] [5]. Within this frame, there is no reference to a perceived complexity but only to structural features. An obvious benefit is that the same metric may be used everywhere, without needing a specific tuning. It is also the weak point of the method as the relation with the controllers workload is not direct.

The present article introduces the theoretical material underlying a new approach to complexity assessment and more generally to traffic characterization, based on a representation of traffic situations as images whose pixels are covariance matrices. The idea underlying it is that local disorder is an indicator of complexity that captures most of the elementary metrics entering the dynamic density. This is a work in progress that will ultimately allow the use of deep learning on such pseudo-images in conjunction with an expertized database to produce a complexity metric with low tuning requirements. A by product is the ability to compute distances between traffic situations, allowing for efficient indexing in dedicated databases. The rest of the paper is structured as follows. In Section II, the traffic is modeled after a Gaussian random field, whose covariance function is estimated on two dimensional grid. In Section III, tools dedicated to the processing of such grids of symmetric positive definite matrices are introduced. Finally, in Section IV, a conclusion is drawn, introducing the next generation of algorithms able to exploit this novel representation.

II. Traffic representation

The first stage in the computation of the complexity index is the processing of traffic samples in order to summarize their local features. It is done by estimating a local covariance matrix at each point of an evenly spaced grid. While aircraft positions are actually points in $\mathbb{R}^3$, the altitude plays a special role and is not presented on controllers displays. The choice made in the present work is to use a planar representation, disregarding the altitude, which is in compliance with the operational setting. From here on, all the derivations will be made using aircraft positions in $\mathbb{R}^2$.

All samples are assumed to be dated positions (t, x) where t is the sampling time and $x \in \mathbb{R}^2$ is the sample position. Finally, a dataset is simply a sequence $(t_i, x_i)_{i=1...N}$ of samples collected in a given time interval and spatial area. Please note that samples will not be distinguished by the trajectory they belong to, so that different flight patterns may generate exactly the same dataset. This is a limitation of the present work that will be addressed in a future extension of the method.

A. A Gaussian field model

Collected samples without taking time into consideration may be viewed as realizations of an underlying spatial stochastic process X with values in $\mathbb{R}^2$. Such a process is called a Gaussian vector field when for any collection of points $(x_1, \ldots, x_p)$, the joint distribution of the random variables $(X(x_1), \ldots, X(x_p))$ is Gaussian. Such a process is characterized by its mean and covariance functions:

$$\mu(x) = E[X(x)] \tag{1}$$

$$C(x, y) = E\left[(X(x) - \mu(x))(X(y) - \mu(y))^t\right] \tag{2}$$

In practice, μ and C must be estimated from a dataset of couples $(x_i, v_i)_{i=1...N}$ where v_i is the observed vector value at position x_i. Available methods fall into two categories: parametric and non parametric. In the parametric approach, μ and C are approximated by members of a family of functions depending on a finite number of free parameters that are tuned to best match the observations. A usual choice is to use finite cubic splines expansions whose coefficients are identified by a least square fitting. The efficiency of parametric estimation is heavily dependent on the actual mean and covariance functions and may be computationally expensive for large datasets. In the non parametric approach, a different methodology is used: the samples themselves act as coefficients of an expansion involving so-called kernel functions. Apart from the obvious benefit of avoiding a costly least square procedure, most of the kernels used in practice are compactly supported, so that evaluating an approximate mean and covariance at a given location requires far less terms that the number of samples. Due to its simplicity and the previous property, a non parametric estimation was selected to process the traffic.

B. Mean and covariance matrix estimation

The key ingredient in non parametric estimation is the kernel function, that is a smooth enough mapping $K : \mathbb{R}^2 \to \mathbb{R}^+$ that integrates to 1.

It is usually more tractable to restrict kernels to a smaller class:

Definition 1. *A radial kernel is a mapping $K : \mathbb{R}^2 \to \mathbb{R}^+$ that is of the form $K(x) = K(\|x\|)$ and such that :*

$$\int_{\mathbb{R}^2} K(x)dx = 1$$

From here on, only radial kernels will be used.

Kernels are most of the time at least continuous. Furthermore, as mentioned above, compactly supported function will save a lot of computation in the evaluations and it is thus advisable to use kernels pertaining to this class. Classical examples are the multivariate Epanechnikov kernel [6] and its higher regularity versions which are widely used in the non-parametric estimation community:

$$K_e(x) = \frac{2}{\pi}\left(1 - \|x\|^2\right)_+ \tag{3}$$

$$K_2(x) = \frac{3}{\pi}\left(1 - \|x\|^2\right)_+^2 \tag{4}$$

$$K_3(x) = \frac{4}{\pi}\left(1 - \|x\|^2\right)_+^3 \tag{5}$$

Given a radial kernel K and a positive real number h, the scaled kernel K_h is defined to be:

$$K_h(x) = \frac{1}{h^2} K\left(\frac{x}{h}\right) \tag{6}$$

h is termed as the bandwidth of the kernel and controls the degree of smoothing introduced by the kernel and its support. It has to be tuned with respect to the dataset to obtain the best compromise between smoothing and accuracy. A kernel estimator of the covariance function C of a stationary stochastic process X can be found in [7]. Using a straightforward extension, a kernel estimator for the correlation function of a locally stationary random field is given in [8]. Finally, a weighed maximum likelihood approach is taken in [9], for computing at any location x the mean $\mu(x)$ and variance $C(x, x) = \Sigma(x)$ of a Gaussian random field. This last work can easily be generalized to yield an estimate for the covariance function, under normality assumption for the random field X. Given a dataset $(x_i, v_i)_{i=1...N}$, where the sampling positions x_i are assumed to be distinct, the weighted joint log likelihood of the couples $(x_i, v_i), (x_j, v_j), j \neq i$ at locations x, y is given, for a fixed kernel bandwidth h, by:

$$
\begin{aligned}
&L(x,y) = \\
&-\frac{1}{2}\sum_{i=1}^{N}\sum_{j=1}^{N} V_{ij}^t \Sigma^{-1}(x,y) V_{ij} K_h(\|x_i - x\|) K_h(\|x_j - y\|) \\
&+\frac{1}{2}\log\left(|\Sigma^{-1}|\right)\left(\sum_{i=1}^{N}\sum_{j=1^N} K_h(\|x_i - x\|) K_h(\|x_j - y\|)\right) \\
&+A
\end{aligned}
$$

where:

$$
V_{ij} = (v_i - m(x), v_j - m(y))
$$

$m(x)$ is the mean of $X(x)$ and $\Sigma(x,y)$ is the variance matrix of the Gaussian vector $(X(x), X(y))$. The term A accounts for the log of the normalizing constant occurring in the expression of the multidimensional normal distribution and will play no role in the sequel. Please note that the kernel was selected to be a product of elementary kernels.

The differential of the log likelihood with respect to the mean value can be computed as:

$$
\sum_{i,j} \operatorname{tr}\left(V_{ij}^t \Sigma^{-1}(x,y)\right) K_h(\|x_i - x\|) K_h(\|x_j - y\|) \quad (7)
$$

The first order optimality condition yields for the non-parametric estimate for the mean function:

$$
\hat{m}(x) = \frac{\sum_{i=1}^N v_i K_h(\|x - x_i\|)}{\sum_{i=1}^N K_h(\|x - x_i\|)} \quad (8)
$$

A similar derivation can be made to obtain the differential with respect to the Σ matrix, using the two identities below:

$$
d\Sigma^{-1} = -\Sigma^{-1} d\Sigma \Sigma^{-1} \quad (9)
$$

$$
d\log\left(|\Sigma^{-1}|\right) = -\operatorname{tr} d\Sigma\Sigma^{-1} \quad (10)
$$

The non-parametric estimator for $\Sigma(x,y)$ is then:

$$
\hat{\Sigma}(x,y) = \frac{\sum_{i=1}^N \sum_{j=1}^N \hat{C}_{ij}(x,y) K_h(\|x_i - x\|) K_h(\|x_j - y\|)}{\sum_{i=1}^N \sum_{j=1}^N K_h(\|x_i - x\|) K_h(\|x_j - y\|)} \quad (11)
$$

with:

$$
\hat{C}_{ij}(x,y) = \begin{pmatrix} v_i - \hat{m}(x) \\ v_j - \hat{m}(y) \end{pmatrix} \begin{pmatrix} v_i - \hat{m}(x) \\ v_j - \hat{m}(y) \end{pmatrix}^t
$$

Using the definition 8 of $\hat{m}$, it appears that $\hat{\Sigma}(x,y)$ is block diagonal:

$$
\begin{pmatrix} \hat{\Sigma(x)} & 0 \\ 0 & \hat{\Sigma(y)} \end{pmatrix} \quad (12)
$$

with:

$$
\Sigma(x) = \frac{\sum_{i=1}^N \hat{C}_{ii}(x) K_h(\|x_i - x\|)}{\sum_{i=1}^N K_h(\|x_i - x\|)} \quad (13)
$$

This estimator is similar to the one in [8], and is of Nadaraya-Watson [10] type. It enjoys asymptotic normality. The reason for the vanishing of the off diagonal blocks is a consequence of the special shape of the kernel that implicitly approximates the joint distribution of $X(x)$ and $X(y)$ by product laws.

C. Computation of the mean and covariance functions

In order to allow further treatments, mean and covariance functions will be evaluated only at points located on an evenly spaced two dimensional grid whose points are located at coordinates:

$$
\begin{aligned}
p_{nm} &= (x_0 + n\delta_x, y_0 + m\delta_y) \\
n &\in \{-L, \ldots, L\},\ m \in \{-M, \ldots, M\}
\end{aligned}
$$

where δ_x, δ_y are respective step sizes along x and y axis. In the expressions 8,13 of the mean and covariance functions evaluated at grid point p_{nm}, the kernel appears as $K_h(\|x_i - p_{nm}\|)$. If the grid is fine enough, one can approximate it by $K_h(\|p_{kl} - p_{nm}\|)$ where p_{kl} is the grid point closest to x_i. Using coordinates, we have:

$$
K_h(\|p_{kl} - p_{nm}\|) = K_h\left(\sqrt{(n-k)^2\delta_x^2 + (m-l)^2\delta_y^2}\right) \quad (14)
$$

Values depends only on the difference between the grid points indices and are thus independent on the location p_{kl}. Furthermore, since K is assumed to have compact support, the same is true for K_h so that $K_h\left(\sqrt{(n-k)^2 + (m-l)^2}\right)$ will vanish when indices differences exceed a given threshold. Gathering things together, all non-zero values of the kernel can be tabulated on a grid of size $(2P+1) \times (2Q+1)$ if the support of the kernel K_h is contained in the square $[-P\delta_x, P\delta_x] \times [-Q\delta_y, Q\delta_y]$:

$$
K_h(i,j) = K_h\left(\sqrt{n^2\delta_x^2 + (m)^2\delta_y^2}\right) \quad (15)
$$

$$
n \in \{-P, \ldots, P\}, m \in \{-Q, \ldots, Q\} \quad (16)
$$

All the entries in the equation 15 can be scaled so that they sum to 1: this saves the division by the sum of kernel values. Simultaneous evaluation of the mean at all grid points can then be made in an efficient manner using Algorithm 1. Once the mean has been computed, the covariance is estimated the same way (see Algorithm 2).

When the grid is not fine enough to replace the true sample location by a grid point, a trick based on bilinear interpolation can be used. Using again the equation 15 and the closest grid point $p_{k_1 l_1}$ to x_i, the true sample position x_i will be located within a cell as indicated in Figure 1. The kernel value can be approximated as:

$$
K_h(k_1, l_1) + \frac{dx}{\delta_x} a + \frac{dy}{\delta_y} b + \frac{dx}{\delta_x}\frac{dy}{\delta_y} c \quad (17)
$$

Algorithm 1 Mean kernel estimate

```
for i ← 0, 2L; j ← 0, 2 * M do
    m(i, j) ← 0
end for
for k ← 0, N − 1 do
    (k, l) ← ClosestGridPoint(x_i)
    for i ← −P, P; j ← −Q, Q do
        if k + i ≥ 0 ∧ k + i ≤ 2L then
            if l + j ≥ 0 ∧ l + j ≤ 2M then
                m(k + i, l + j) ← m(k + i, l + j) + K_h(i, j) v_i / N
            end if
        end if
    end for
end for
```

Algorithm 2 Covariance kernel estimate

```
for i ← 0, 2L; j ← 0, 2 * M do
    C(i, j) ← 0
end for
for k ← 0, N − 1 do
    (k, l) ← ClosestGridPoint(x_i)
    for i ← −P, P; j ← −Q, Q do
        if k + i ≥ 0 ∧ k + i ≤ 2L then
            if l + j ≥ 0 ∧ l + j ≤ 2M then
                A ← (v_i − m(k, l))(v_i − m(k, l))^t
                C(k + i, l + j) ← C(k + i, l + j) + K_h(i, j).A/N
            end if
        end if
    end for
end for
```

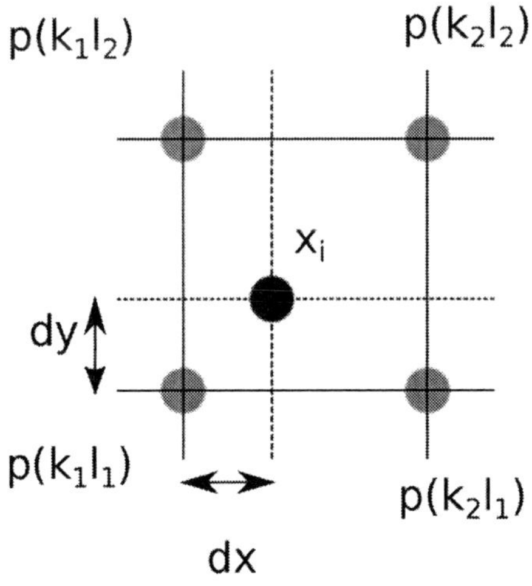

Fig. 1. Bilinear interpolation

with:

$$a = K_h(k_2, l_1) - K_h(k_1, l1)$$
$$b = K_h(k_1, l_2) - K_h(k_1, l1)$$
$$c = K_h(k_2, l_2) + K_h(k_1, l1) - K_h(k_2, l_1) - K_h(k_1, l_2)$$

Gathering terms by tabulated values yields a kernel value:

$$K_h(k_1, l_1)\left(1 - s_x - s_y + s_x s_y\right) \quad (18)$$
$$+ K_h(k_2, l_1)\left(s_x - s_x s_y\right) \quad (19)$$
$$+ K_h(k_1, l_2)\left(s_y - s_x s_y\right) \quad (20)$$
$$+ K_h(k_2, l_2) s_x s_y \quad (21)$$

where:

$$sx = \frac{dx}{\delta_x}, \; sy = \frac{dy}{\delta_y}$$

It is thus possible to compute the mean and covariance functions on a coarser grid using Algorithms 1 and 2 by applying them on the four locations $(k_1, l_1), (k_2, l_1), (k_1, l_2), (k_2, l_2)$, with an observed value multiplied by their respective coefficients $(1 - s_x - s_y + s_x s_y)$, $(s_x - s_x s_y)$,$(s_y - s_x s_y)$,$K_h(k_2, l_2) s_x s_y$.

The overall complexity of the algorithm is linear in the number of grid points and in the number of samples. It is similar to filtering an image and can be implemented the same way on modern Graphics Processing Units (GPU). Please note also that for kernels with large supports, a fast Fourier transform may be used at the expense of a slight increase in the complexity order that will be balance by the constant term due to the support size.

III. Processing Tools

The preceding phase allows the computation of a traffic pattern digest as a two dimensional grid of Symmetric Positive Definite (SPD) matrices. It may be used as is for building an index in a database, using the same procedure as for images. However, the geometry underlying the space of 2×2 positive definite matrices is not euclidean, but hyperbolic. The proposed index is an adaptation of images distances, using hyperbolic geometry.

A. The Riemannian structure of symmetric positive definite matrices

The purpose of this part is to introduce at a basic level the tools used to build the index. Results are given without proofs, the interested reader may refer to [11] for a more in-depth exposition.

Proposition 1. *The space of $n \times n$ SPD matrices, denoted by $SPD(n)$, may be endowed with a Riemannian manifold structure with metric at point A given by the differential:*

$$ds^2 = \mathrm{tr}\left(A^{-1} dA\right) \quad (22)$$

Proposition 2. *Let A, B be SPD matrices. It exists a unique minimizing geodesic joining them in $SPD(n)$. It is given in parametrized form by:*

$$\gamma : t \in [0,1] \mapsto A^{1/2} \left(\exp t \log \left(A^{-1/2} B A^{-1/2} \right) \right) A^{1/2} \tag{23}$$

Proposition 2 yields the geodesic distance between any two matrices A, B from $SPD(n)$ as $d(A,B) = \sqrt{\operatorname{tr} \log^2 (A^{-1}B}$. It can be expressed as $d(A,B) = \sqrt{\sum_{i=1}^{n} \log^2 \lambda_i}$ with $\lambda_i, i = 1 \dots n$ the eigenvalues of $A^{-1}B$.

The geodesic distance between matrices from $SPD(2)$ may be used to compute a distance between grids produced by the traffic processing phase in a very simple way, as indicated in Algorithm 3.

Algorithm 3 Distance between grids

A, B are $P \times Q$ grids of $SPD(2)$ matrices.
$dsq = 0$
for $i \leftarrow 0, P-1; j \leftarrow 0, Q-1$ **do**
    $dsq \leftarrow dsq + \operatorname{tr} \log^2 (A(i,j)^{-1} B(i,j))$
end for
$d(A,B) = \sqrt{dsq}$

Please note that this distance is based on a point-wise comparison and is very similar to the L^2 distance used for images. It has a higher cost of evaluation due to the distance computation in $SPD(2)$ that involves an matrix inverse, product and logarithm. However, it is not as critical in $SPD(2)$ than it may be in a general $SPD(n)$, since eigenvalues and eigenvectors can be computed in closed form (this is true also in $SPD(3)$ and $SPD(4)$, with more complex expressions). Furthermore, grid distance computation is easy to parallelize on modern graphics hardware since it involves independent operations on small matrices. As an example, computing the distance between two grids of size 100×100 on a TitanX pascal card from Nvidia takes around $100\mu s$.

B. Grid filtering

In the traffic processing phase, grids have sizes ranging from 100×100 to 300×300. Due to the processing cost incurred by the $SPD(2)$ setting, it is advisable in many cases, and especially if one wants to use the grids as index in a traffic database, to reduce the size of grids to more tractable dimensions, say 10×10 to 50×50. This has to be done without wiping out the salients features of the traffic captured by the original grid. In the spirit of what is done in the first layers of an image processing deep network, it is proposed to apply in sequence a filtering and a selection process on the original grid.

Definition 2. *Let $A_i, i = 1 \dots n$ be a sequence of elements of $SPD(n)$, $w_1, \dots w_n$ be a sequence of real numbers and B be an element of $SPD(n)$. The log-euclidean weighted combination (LWC) at B of the $(A_i)_{i=1 \dots n}$ with weights $(w_i)_{i=1 \dots n}$ is the matrix:*

$$B^{1/2} \exp \left(\sum_{i=1}^{n} w_i \log \left(B^{-1/2} A_i B^{-1/2} \right) \right) B^{1/2} \tag{24}$$

The LWC may be used to compute a filtered version of a grid using the same procedure as for an image. The process is given in Algorithm 4 that yields the filtered grid as B.

Algorithm 4 Grid filtering

A is a $P \times Q$ grid of $SPD(2)$ matrices.
$w_i, i = 1 \dots 9$ is a sequence of real numbers
for $i \leftarrow 0, P-1; j \leftarrow 0, Q-1$ **do**
    $(C_1, \dots C_9)$ are the adjacent cells to $A(i,j)$ and itself.
    $B(i,j) \leftarrow LWC(C_1, \dots, C_9)$ with weight $w_i, i = 1 \dots 9$ at $A(i,j)$.
end for

The filtering process on $SPD(2)$ grids behaves roughly like in image processing: when the weights are real numbers in the interval $[0,1]$ that sum to 1, then a weighted mean is produced. It tends to smooth out the grid, making spatially close matrices more similar. On the opposite, when weights sum to 0, the equivalent of a high pass filter is produced, that emphases sharp variations. Please note that the size of the grids after filtering is unaltered.

The second processing phase is simplification to reduce grid size. The main idea is to replace a block of grid cells by a single one using a digest. An obvious approach is to replace a block by its mean, that can be obtained from LWC by using equal positive weights $1/n$ if n is the number of cells in the block. A major drawback is that the important information tends to be lost, with matrices going close to multiples of the identity in many cases. Another way of dealing with the problem is to introduce an order on $SPD(2)$ and to select the largest (resp. lowest) element in the block. This procedure has two benefits:

- The selected matrix is an element of the original grid.
- As in deep learning networks, it will select the most representative elements.

After some experiments on simulated matrix images, the order chosen is a lexicographic one, the first comparison being made on the determinant of the matrices and the second on the trace. After the selection phase, the size of the grid is reduced by the ratio of the number of elements considered in a block. In the current implementation, it is 3×3, thus shrinking the grid by a factor 3 in each dimension. The filtering/selection phases may be chained in order to get smaller grids. As for the distance computation, it is quite easy to implement the process on a GPU, all operations being independent.

IV. Conclusion and Future Work

The work presented here is still in early stage of development. Only theoretical concepts and computer implementation of the traffic processing, filtering and selection phases are completed or nearly completed. Testing on real data is yet to be done, and a complete complexity computation metric has to be built. The next steps are:

- Constitution of a traffic database from surveillance (Radar) and ADS-B data. This work has been launched, and data collection is in progress.
- Complexity index coding. Although most of the software bricks needed are available or close to release, it remains to implement the overall process. A weight adjustment procedure is lacking for the filtering phase: it is the topic of a more theoretical work and involves some Lie group techniques.
- Evaluation against existing indicators and expert advices.

Based on the experience gathered on the topic, it is expected that the new approach presented here will outperform the current state-of-the-art metrics. Furthermore, thanks to the ability to compute the distance between two grids of $SPD(2)$ elements, it offers the unique opportunity to derive an index for a traffic situation database that will be an invaluable tool for practitioners in the field of air traffic management.

REFERENCES

[1] M. Prandini, L. Piroddi, S. Puechmorel, and S. L. Brazdilova, "Toward air traffic complexity assessment in new generation air traffic management systems," *IEEE Transactions on Intelligent Transportation Systems*, vol. 12, no. 3, pp. 809–818, Sept 2011.

[2] A. Cook, H. A. Blom, F. Lillo, R. N. Mantegna, S. Miccich, D. Rivas, R. Vzquez, and M. Zanin, "Applying complexity science to air traffic management," *Journal of Air Transport Management*, vol. 42, pp. 149 – 158, 2015. [Online]. Available: http://www.sciencedirect.com/science/article/pii/S0969699714001331

[3] L. I. S. Shelden, R. Branstrom, and C. Brasil, "Dynamic density: An air traffic management metric," NASA, Tech. Rep. NASA/TM-1998-112226, 1998.

[4] K. Lee, Feron, and A. E.and Prichett, "Air traffic complexity : An input-output approach," in *Proceedings of the US Europe ATM Seminar*. Eurocontrol-FAA, 2007, pp. 2–9.

[5] D. Delahaye and S. Puechmorel., "Air traffic complexity based on dynamical systems," in *Proceedings of the 49th CDC conference*. IEEE, 2010.

[6] V. A. Epanechnikov, "Non-parametric estimation of a multivariate probability density," *Theory of Probability & Its Applications*, vol. 14, no. 1, pp. 153–158, 1969. [Online]. Available: https://doi.org/10.1137/1114019

[7] P. Hall, N. I. Fisher, and B. Hoffmann, "On the nonparametric estimation of covariance functions," *Ann. Statist.*, vol. 22, no. 4, pp. 2115–2134, 12 1994. [Online]. Available: https://doi.org/10.1214/aos/1176325774

[8] Y. Li, N. Wang, M. Hong, N. D. Turner, J. R. Lupton, and R. J. Carroll, "Nonparametric estimation of correlation functions in longitudinal and spatial data, with application to colon carcinogenesis experiments," *Ann. Statist.*, vol. 35, no. 4, pp. 1608–1643, 08 2007. [Online]. Available: https://doi.org/10.1214/009053607000000082

[9] J. Yin, Z. Geng, R. Li, and H. Wang, "Nonparametric covariance model," *Statistica Sinica*, vol. 20, no. 1, pp. 469–479, 2010. [Online]. Available: http://www.jstor.org/stable/24309002

[10] E. A. Nadaraya, "On estimating regression," *Theory of Probability & Its Applications*, vol. 9, no. 1, pp. 141–142, 1964. [Online]. Available: https://doi.org/10.1137/1109020

[11] F. Nielsen and R. Bhatia, *Matrix Information Geometry*. Springer Berlin Heidelberg, 2012. [Online]. Available: https://books.google.fr/books?id=MAhygTspBU8C

Monitoring of Coastal Environments Using Data Mining

Corneliu Octavian Dumitru, Gottfried Schwarz, and Mihai Datcu
Remote Sensing Technology Institute, German Aerospace Center (DLR),
82234 Wessling, Germany
email: corneliu.dumitru@dlr.de, gottfried.schwarz@dlr.de, mihai.datcu@dlr.de

Abstract—**Current satellite images provide us with detailed information about the state of our planet, as well as about our technical infrastructure and human activities. A range of already existing commercial and scientific applications try to analyze the physical content and meaning of satellite images by exploiting the data of individual, multiple or temporal sequences of images. However, what we still need today are advanced tools to automatically analyze the image data in order to extract and understand their full content. In this paper, we propose a highly automated approach for application-adapted image content exploration, targeting coastal environmental monitoring. For the selected coastal areas, different use cases can be considered such as: detection of wind turbines *vs.* boats, differences between beaches, tidal flats, and dams, and identification of fish cages/aquaculture. The average accuracy is ranging from 80% to 95% depending on the satellite images.**

Keywords- coastal monitring; data mining; Sentinel-1; Sentinel-2; TerraSAR-X.

I. Introduction

In Earth observation, a very popular satellite image analysis system is the one from Digital Globe, named Tomnod, or Google Earth together with its related tools, which are targeting general user topics. In the Earth observation (EO) domain, there are systems such as LandEX [1], which is a land cover analysis system, while GeoIRIS [2] is a system that allows the user to refine a given query by iteratively specifying a set of relevant, and a set of non-relevant images. A similar information retrieval system is IKONA [3], which is using relevance feedback in order to exploit very high resolution EO images. Further, the Knowledge-driven Information Mining (KIM) system [4] is an example of an active learning system providing semantic interpretation of image content. The KIM concept evolved into the TELEIOS prototype [5], complementing the scope of searching for EO images with additional geo-information and in-situ data integrated into an operational EO system [6] to interpret TerraSAR-X images. Similar concept with KIM concept is presented in [29] while in [30] a data mining approach for Big Data is described.

The proposed system is very fast compared with the existing systems and with only few examples can retrieve the desired category with higher accuracy. The diversity of applications that can be considered for such systems are rather broad and include, for instance, coastal environmental monitoring (sea level, tides and wave direction), land cover/use changes, disaster monitoring, forest management, ice monitoring, monitoring of active volcanoes, waste deposit site management, traffic monitoring, vegetation monitoring, urban sprawl, soil moisture dynamics, etc.

The paper is organized as follows. Section II describes the selected test areas. Section III presents our datasets. Section IV details the data mining methodology applied in this paper. Section V shows the results and we conclude the paper in Section VI. The acknowledgements close the paper.

II. Selection of Test Areas, Use Cases, and Applications

We emphasize here three use cases for monitoring coastal environments. For these use cases, we selected for our investigation the Wadden Sea with the Dutch Delta (in the Netherlands), the Danube Delta (in Romania), and the Curonian Lagoon (in Lithuania and Russia) which are internationally recognized protected areas as UNESCO (United Nations Educational, Scientific and Cultural Organization) Natural Heritage sites.

A. *The Wadden Sea, Netherlands*

Site description: The Wadden Sea (Dutch: Waddenzee, German: Wattenmeer, Danish: Vadehavet) is an intertidal zone in the south-eastern part of the North Sea. It lies between the coast of N-W continental Europe and the range of Frisian Islands, forming a shallow body of water with tidal flats and wetlands [7], protected by a 450 km long chain of barrier islands, the Wadden Islands. The Wadden Sea region measures about 22,000 km^2, divided between land and sea. About 63% of the region lies in Germany, with about 30% in the Netherlands, and 7% in Denmark [8]. In 2009, the Dutch-German Wadden Sea was inscribed on the UNESCO World Heritage List and the Danish part was added later in 2014.

The landforms in the Wadden Sea region have essentially been created from a marine or tidal environment [9].

Typical for the Wadden Sea are large tidal flats, which are characterized by very high benthic biomass and productivity, dominated by molluscs and polychaetes.

State-of-the-art publications: In the research literature there are several studies treating the Wadden Sea area along the years. In order to understand the Wadden Sea dynamics, a number of recent publications [10]-[13] already used remote sensing images and addressed the issue of Synthetic Aperture Radar (SAR) satellite image classification and interpretation in these areas. At present, the option of data fusion from different sensor has not yet been fully exploited.

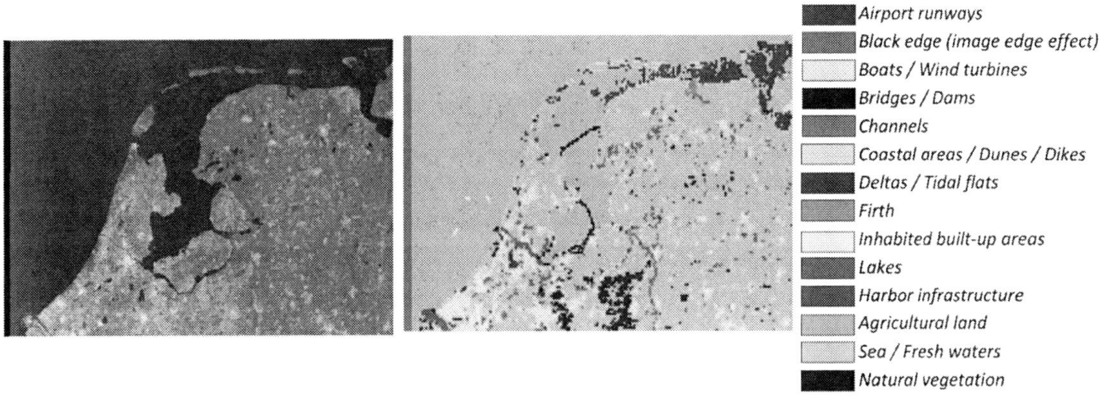

Figure 1. Sentinel-1A quick-look view (left) and classification map (right) for an image of the Wadden Sea, Lake IJssel, and Marker Lake, and the surrounding areas.

Image interpretation goal: The Wadden Sea area faces a strong economic impact due to recreation, fisheries and maritime traffic. The last impact is due to, e.g. the ports of Bremerhaven, Hamburg, and Rotterdam whereby the traffic runs through or nearby this area, which makes that monitoring of sand banks and any decrease of the water depth and the tide levels in this area is a critical topic for maritime security. A second important topic is the monitoring of biodiversity as described by [14].

Typical examples: The diversity of categories identified from a single image and a typical classification map of the Wadden Sea and its surrounding areas are shown in Figures 1 and 2.

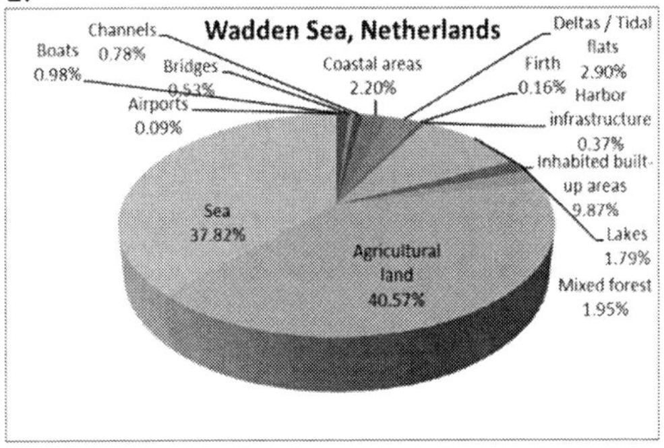

Figure 2. Diversity of categories identified from a single image of the Wadden Sea, the Netherlands.

B. The Danube Delta, Romania

Site description: The Danube Delta is the second largest river delta in Europe and is the best preserved one on the continent [15].

Formed over a period of more than 10,000 years, the Danube Delta continues to grow due to the 67 million tons of alluvia deposited every year by the Danube River [16]. The delta is an ideal test and validation area for vegetation monitoring as it is characterized by high biodiversity and various crops.

The Delta is formed around the three main channels of the Danube, named after their respective ports Chilia (in the north), Sulina (in the middle), and Sfantu Gheorghe (in the south).

The greater part of the Danube Delta lies in Romania (Tulcea County), while its northern part, on the left bank of the Chilia arm, is situated in Ukraine (Odessa Oblast). Its total surface is 4,152 km^2 of which 3,446 km^2 are in Romania. The waters of the Danube, which flow into the Black Sea, form the largest and best preserved delta in Europe. In 1991, the Danube Delta was inscribed on the UNESCO World Heritage List due do its biological uniqueness.

State-of-the-art publications: In the image processing literature there are not many studies treating the Danube Delta especially for SAR data [17]-[19]. However, the monitoring of biodiversity from in-situ measurements has attracted more interest [20].

Image interpretation goal: At the mouth of the Danube, the alluvial discharge decreases every year from 81 million tons in 1894, to 70 million tons in 7939, 58 million tons in 1982, and about 22 million tons in 2015. This makes it interesting to monitor the evolution of the alluvial discharge and to investigate its impact on the Danube Delta and the three channels together with their ports (Chilia, Sulina, and Sfantu Gheorghe) through the years.

The data can be combined with other types of information, such as the volume of water of each channel in order to prepare risk flood maps needed for the safety of the

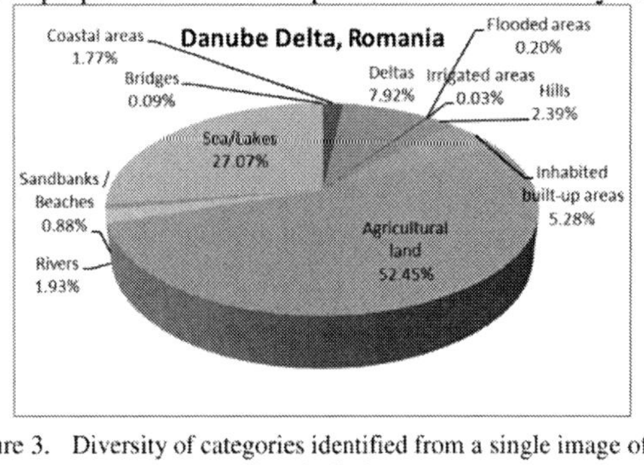

Figure 3. Diversity of categories identified from a single image of the Danube Delta.

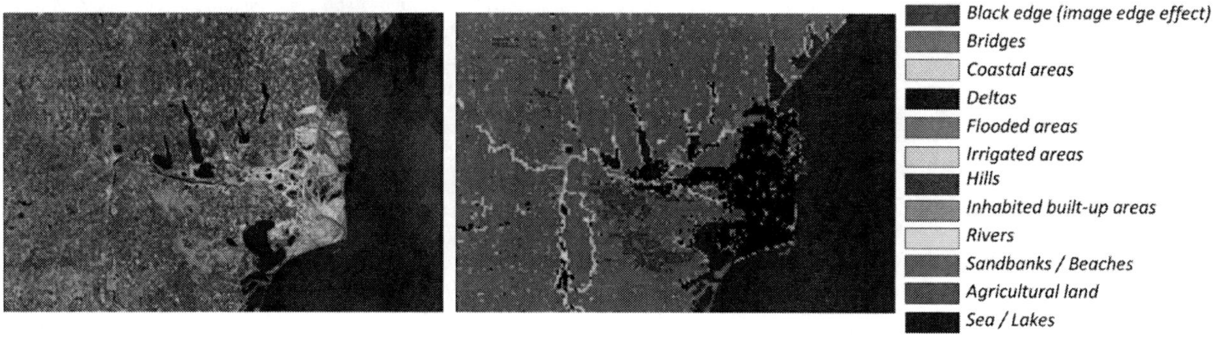

Figure 4. Sentinel-1A quick-look view (left) and classification map (right) for an image of the Danube Delta and the surrounding areas.

shipping traffic and also for the local authorities to protect the human settlements. Another image interpretation goal is vegetation monitoring, in particular, biodiversity issues and crop type analyses.

Typical examples: The diversity of categories identified from a single image and a typical classification map of the Danube Delta and its surrounding areas are shown in Figures 3 and 4.

C. The Curonian Lagoon, Lithuania and Russia

Site description: The Curonian Lagoon is the largest European lagoon. Situated in the southern part of the Baltic Sea with a total area of 1584 km^2, the lagoon receives water from the River Nemunas. The salinity of the water is higher and fluctuates between the northern and southern part of the lagoon [14]. The entire Lithuanian part of the Curonian Lagoon has been designated as a NATURA 2000 area and in 2000 the Curonian Spit cultural landscape was as well inscribed on the UNESCO World Heritage List.

State-of-the-art publications: In the remote sensing literature, there are not many studies treating the Curonian Lagoon especially for SAR data. However, the monitoring of biodiversity has attracted greater interest [21]-[23].

Image interpretation goal: We analyzed the effect of socio-economic activities of the area regarding: the ceasing commercial fisheries, the prohibition of the extraction of mineral resources, the agricultural sector, the hunting sector, the restriction of recreational use of the aquatic areas, and the oil drilling/pollution of the area.

Typical examples: The diversity of categories identified from a single image and a typical classification map of the Curonian Lagoon and its surrounding areas are shown in Figures 5 and 6.

III. DATASETS

An important aspect to be addressed is the creation of a reference dataset for test and validation of the different systems. We already possess an initial synthetic aperture radar dataset composed of 1000 TerraSAR-X images and 100 Sentinel-1 images covering target areas from around the world.

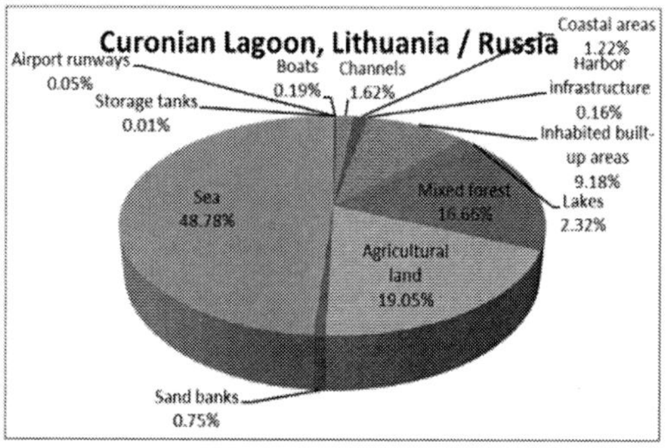

Figure 5. Diversity of categories identified from a single image of the Curonian Lagoon.

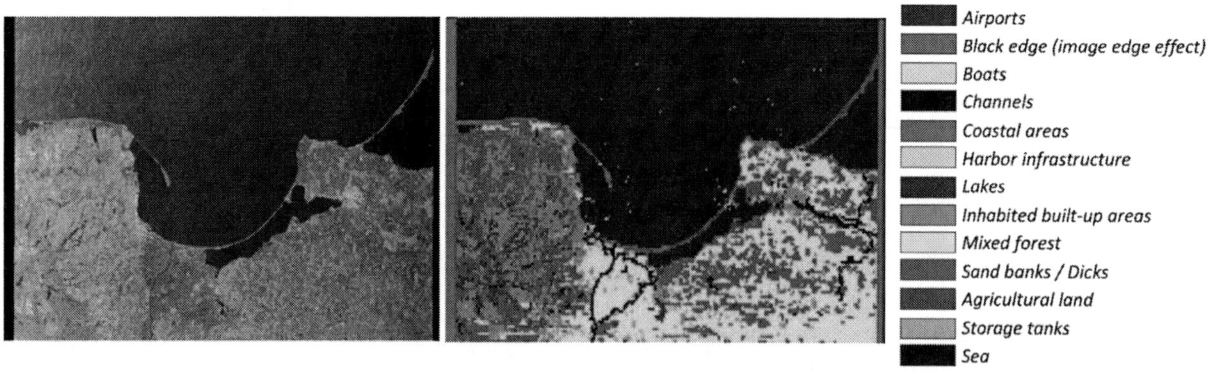

Figure 6. Sentinel-1A quick-look view (left) and classification map (right) for an image of the Curonian Lagoon and the surrounding areas.

From this database, about 295 TerraSAR-X and 25 Sentinel-1A images have already been annotated by a remote sensing expert using a semi-automatic semantic annotation system resulting in a semantic catalogue of hundreds of semantic labels grouped in a 3-level hierarchical scheme [24]. This annotated database mainly covers urban and industrial areas together with their infrastructure predominantly from Europe, and can be considered as our initial ground truth dataset [25].

Our latest dataset also contains optical satellite data with multi-spectral images (e.g., Sentinel-2A), and synthetic aperture radar images (e.g., TerraSAR-X and Sentinel-1A / 1B). These data cover 10 protected areas from Europe (national parks, mountains, arid and semi-arid areas, and coastal and marine ecosystems) [14].

IV. METHODOLOGY

The data mining system [6] (used in this paper) is composed of four main modules: Data Model Generation (DMG), Database Management System (DBMS), Knowledge Discovery in Databases (KDD), and Statistical Analytics (SA).

The DMG module transforms the original format of original Earth observation products into smaller and more compact product representations that include image descriptors, metadata, image patches, etc. The DBMS module is used for storing all the generated information and allows querying and retrieval of the available image data. The KDD module is in charge of finding patterns of interest from the processed data and presenting them to the user. Moreover, the KDD module allows annotating the image content by using machine learning algorithms and human interaction resulting in physical categories. The SA module provides classification maps of each dataset and distribution results of the retrieved categories in an image. These four modules are operated automatically and interactively with and without user interaction.

We summarize our data mining methodology as a pseudo-code segment in Table 1.

TABLE 1: THE PROPOSED METHODOLOGY.

Step 1: EO Dataset
Select and download typical EO images.
Step 2: Data Model Generation (DMG)
for each EO_i image (i=1…N) **do**
<u>tile</u> EO_i into $p_{i,j}$ patches (j=1…M), where the size of the patches depends on the image resolution
<u>store</u> all $p_{i,j}$ into the DBMS
for each $p_{i,j}$ patch **do**
<u>extract</u> an $f_{i,j}$ primitive feature vector from optical / SAR algorithms
//e.g., Gabor filters with 5 scales and 6 orientations and compute the means and standard deviations of the coefficients //
<u>store</u> all $f_{i,j}$ vectors into the DBMS
end
end

Step 3: Knowledge Discovery in Databases (KDD)
if r_k (k=1…K) ∄ **do** //if the patch reference label has not yet been generated//
for all $f_{i,j}$ primitive feature vectors **do**
<u>group</u> the $f_{i,j}$ into g_k clusters and group them into c_k categories using an SVM (Support Vector Machine)
for each c_k category **do**
<u>select</u> an r_k semantic annotation label //visual support via Google Earth //
<u>store</u> reference r_k labels into the DBMS
end
end
else // routine processing after label generation//
for all $f_{i,j}$ primitive feature vectors **do**
<u>group</u> the $f_{i,j}$ into g_l clusters (l=1…L) and group them into c_l categories using an SVM
<u>store</u> all g_l into the DBMS
for each c_l category **do**
<u>select</u> an a_l semantic annotation //visual support via Google Earth//
<u>store</u> a_l labels into the DBMS
end
end
end

Step 4: Statistical Analytics (SA)
for selected EO_i and its a_l **do**
<u>generate</u> classification maps
<u>compare</u> obtained a_l annotations with r_k //reference annotations (generated previously)// and <u>generate</u> change maps
<u>compute</u> characteristic metrics //e.g., precision/recall by comparing the results with the r_k //
end

V. RESULTS AND DISCUSSIONS

For the selected areas of interest, different use cases can be considered such as: *detection of wind turbines vs. boats*; *differences between beaches, tidal flats,* and *dams; fish cages/aquaculture;* etc.

For example, we selected the Wadden Sea area and we show the results for the *detection of wind turbines vs. detection of boats*. The images were acquired in order to cover, as much as possible, the same area on the ground and/or the same acquisition date or a date closer between the acquisitions. The data set consists of different images acquired by three different satellites: a TerraSAR-X image acquired on May 13, 2015 with a resolution of 2.9 meters, a Sentinel-1A image acquired on May 15, 2015 with a resolution of 20 meters, and a Sentinel-2A single quadrant-image acquired on April 21, 2016 with a resolution of 10 meters (considering only the RGB bands). In Figure 7, we show the available data for the Wadden Sea protected area.

All these images were tiled into patches and from each patch a feature vector was extracted. We classified the images considering only two categories of interest, namely *Wind turbines* and *Boats* (see Figure 8). Based on the extracted features and the specific patterns of these categories we were able to separate them during classification. Figures 9, 10, and 11 illustrate the retrieved categories after the classification projected on the quick-look of each image product. For each image product the locations of *Wind turbines* and *Boats* are marked in green and blue, respectively.

The complete processing chain from ingestion to annotation was run on a desktop PC with software coded in Java 8 and Matlab R2105a. The PC used for our experiments had a processor clock rate of 2.40 GHz, and a RAM capacity of 8 GB. Typically, we obtain a CPU usage of less than 25% as we store all image files onto a disk and have to wait for the completion of all data transfers. The actual memory consumption of our PC configuration is less than 50 MByte per image. The classification and display of a new set of retrieved patches needs about 4 to 6 ms when we have a collection volume of 2 GByte of image data.

The accuracy of the results was computed for each sensor and for each retrieved category. For each image (EO_i) we compared the category al with its corresponding reference category r_k and we computed its classification accuracy. The attained average accuracy is 93%, ranging from 80% to 95% depending on the image type (e.g., TerraSAR-X, Sentinel-1A or Sentinel-2A). When we compare the different SAR sensors, we notice that the overall classification accuracy is higher for the high resolution instruments, for example for TerraSAR-X.

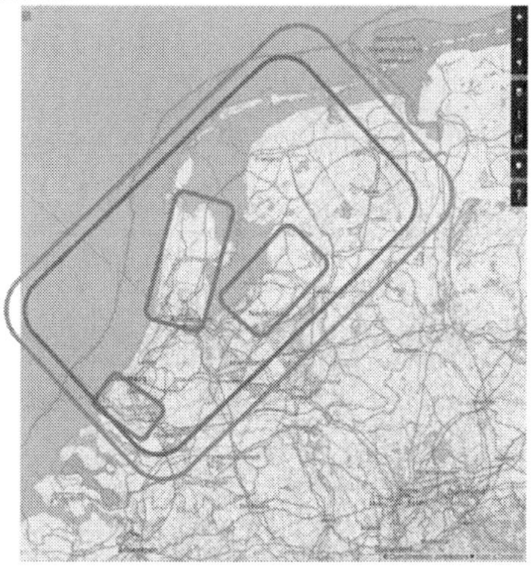

Figure 7. Locations of the Wadden Sea shown on OpenStreetMap; the TerraSAR-X footprints are in green, the Sentinel-1A footprint is in orange, and the Sentinel-2A footprint (all quadrants) is in blue.

Figure 8. In-situ data: wind turbines *vs.* boats.

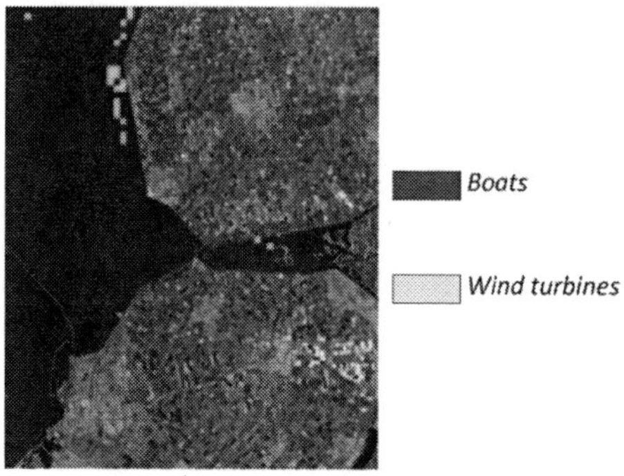

Figure 9. TerraSAR-X "patch-based" classification results projected on a SAR image of Flevoland, the Netherlands.

Figure 10. Sentinel-1A "patch-based" classification results projected on a SAR image of the Wadden Sea, Lake IJssel, and Marker Lake, and the surrounding areas in the Netherlands.

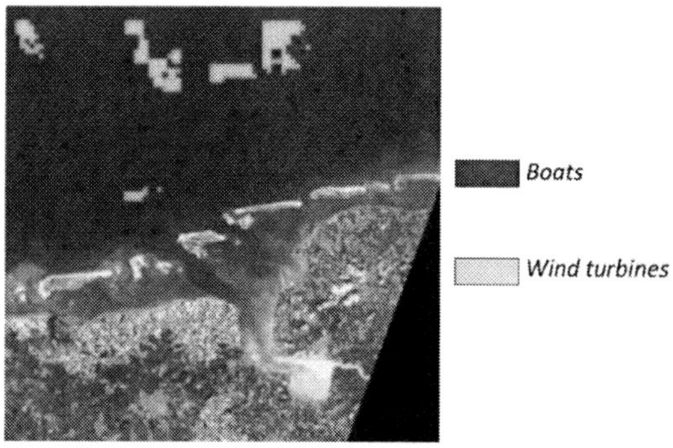

Figure 11. Sentinel-2A "patch-based" classification results projected on a (gray level) image of the German and Dutch Wadden Sea.

VI. Conclusions and Future Work

In this paper, we analyzed several protected areas all over Europe by a high- and a medium-resolution space-borne instrument (SAR and multi-spectral images).

By exploiting the specific imaging details and the retrievable semantic categories of these three image types (TerraSAR-X, Sentinel-1, and Sentinel-2), we can semantically fuse the image classification maps. In order to verify the classification results, we need to compare them with in-situ data.

Another example would be the *difference within beaches, tidal flats, and dams* that we can find from the images available in our dataset (e.g., the Danube Delta, the Curonian Lagoon, or the Wadden Sea). In this case, we obtained similar accuracy results with the case described in Section V.

For future evaluation, we plan to compare the classification accuracy of the wind turbines considering more parameters such as: the size of the pylon, the blade angles of the wind turbines, the rotation rate of the propeller, and the viewing direction and the resolution of the satellite image.

At this moment, there exist some studies about wind turbines [26]-[28] using SAR images but none of the existing papers analyzes all these parameters simultaneously. We will also compare the results from the point of view of accuracy between high-resolution *vs.* medium-resolution and between SAR sensors *vs.* multi-spectral sensors.

ACKNOWLEDGEMENTS

This work was supported by the H2020 ECOPOTENTIAL project. We thank the TerraSAR-X Science Service System for the provision of images (Proposals MTH-1118 and LAN-3156).

REFERENCES

[1] T. Stepinski, P. Netzel, and J. Jasiewicz, "LandEx-A GeoWeb Tool for Query and Retrieval of Spatial Patterns in Land Cover Datasets", IEEE JSTARS, 7(1), pp. 257-266, 2014.

[2] C.R. Shyu, M. Klaric, G. Scott, A. Barb, C. Davis, and K. Palaniappan, "GeoIRIS: Geospatial Information Retrieval and Indexing System – Content Mining, Semantics Modelling, and Complex Queries", IEEE TGRS, 45(4), pp. 839-852, 2007.

[3] N. Boujemaa, "Ikona: Interactive Specific and Generic Image Retrieval", in Proc. of MMCBIR, Glasgow, UK, pp. 1-4, 2001.

[4] M. Datcu et al., "Information Mining in Remote Sensing Image Archives: System Concepts", IEEE TGRS, 41(12), pp. 2923-2936, 2003.

[5] TELEIOS project [accessed March 2018]. Available: http://www.earthobservatory.eu/.

[6] EOLib project, [accessed March 2018]. Available: http://wiki.services.eoportal.org/tiki-index.php?page=EOLib.

[7] ECOSTRESS (Ecological Coastal Strategies and Tools for Resilient European Societies) project, [accessed March 2018]. Available: http://ecostress.eu/pilot-areas/dutch-german-wadden-sea/.

[8] Wadden Sea World Heritage, 2017. Available: http://www.waddensea-worldheritage.org/.

[9] K.S. Dijkema, J.H. Bossinade, P. Bouwsema, and R.J. de Glopper, "Salt Marshes in the Netherlands Wadden Sea: Rising High-Tide Levels and Accretion Enhancement", in "Expected Effects of Climatic Change on Marine Coastal Ecosystems", Kluwer Publishers, Dordrecht; pp 173-188, 1990.

[10] S. Brusch and S. Lehner, "Monitoring River Estuaries and Coastal Areas using TerraSAR-X", in Proc. of OCEANS, Bremen, Germany, pp. 1-4, 2009.

[11] S. Wiehle and S. Lehner, "Automated Waterline Detection in the Wadden Sea Using High-Resolution TerraSAR-X Images", Hindawi Journal of Sensors, pp. 1-6, 2015.

[12] G. Heygster, J. Dannenberg, and J. Notholt, "Topographic Mapping of the German Tidal Flats Analyzing SAR Images with the Waterline Method", IEEE TGRS, 48(3), pp. 1019-1030, 2010.

[13] M. Gade and S. Mechionna, "The Use of High-Resolution RADARSAT-2 and TerraSAR-X Imagery to Monitor Dry-Fallen Intertidal Flats", in Proc. of IGARSS, Quebec, Canada, pp. 1218-1221, 2014.

[14] ECOPOTENTIAL project, 2017. Available: http://www.ecopotential-project.eu/.

[15] Danube Delta, 2016. Available: http://romaniatourism.com/danube-delta.html.

[16] Danube Delta World Heritage, 2017. Available: http://whc.unesco.org/en/list/588.

[17] S. Niculescu, C. Lardeux, I. Grigoras, J. Hanganu, and L. David, "Synergy between LiDAR, RADARSAT-2, and Spot-5 Images for the Detection and Mapping of Wetland Vegetation in the Danube Delta", IEEE JSTARS, 9(8), pp. 3651-3666, 2016.

[18] M. Mierla, G. Romanescu, I. Nichersu, and I. Grigoras, "Hydrological Risk Map for the Danube Delta – A Case Study of Floods Within the Fluvial Delta", IEEE JSTARS, 8(1), pp.98-104, 2015.

[19] R. Tanase, A. Radoi, M. Datcu, and D. Raducanu, "Polarimetric SAR Data Feature Selection using Measures of Mutual Information," in Proc. of IGARSS, Milan, Italy, pp. 1140-1143, 2015.

[20] P. Gastescu, "The Danube Delta Biosphere Reserve. Geography, Biodiversity, Protection, Management", Romanian Journal of Geography, 53(2), pp. 139-152, 2009.

[21] D. Vaičiūtė, I. Olenina, R. Kavolytė, I. Dailidienė, and R. Pilkaitytė, "Validation of MERIS chlorophyll a products in the Lithuanian Baltic Sea case 2 coastal waters", in Proc. of IEEE/OES Baltic International Symposium (BALTIC), Riga, Latvia, pp.1-2 , 2010.

[22] G. Garnaga and Z. Stukova, "Contamination of the south-eastern Baltic Sea and the Curonian Lagoon with oil products," in Proc. of IEEE/OES US/EU-Baltic International Symposium, Tallinn, Estonia, pp. 1-8, 2008.

[23] S. Gulbinskas, E. Trimonis, and I. Mineviciute, "Sedimentary fluxes in the marine-lagoon (Baltic sea – Curonian Lagoon) connection," in Proc. of IEEE/OES Baltic International Symposium (BALTIC), Riga, Latvia, pp. 1-6, 2010.

[24] C.O. Dumitru, G. Schwarz, and M. Datcu, "Land Cover Semantic Annotation Derived from High Resolution SAR Images", IEEE JSTARS, 9(6), pp. 2215-2232, 2016.

[25] C. Dumitru, G. Schwarz, and M. Datcu, "SAR Image Land Cover Datasets for Classification Benchmarking of Temporal Changes", IEEE JSTARS, 11(5), pp.1-21, 2018.

[26] C. Clemente and J.J. Soraghan, "Analysis of the effect of wind turbines in SAR images," in Proc. of IET International Conference on Radar Systems (Radar 2012), Glasgow, UK, pp. 1-4, 2012.

[27] T. Cuong, "Radar cross section (RCS) simulation for wind turbines", Master Thesis, Naval Postgraduate School, California, 94 pages, 2013.

[28] M.B. Christiansen and Ch.B. Hasager, "Wake effects of large offshore wind farms identified from satellite SAR", Remote Sensing of Environment, 98(2-3), pp. 251-268, 2005.

[29] J. Zhang, W. Hsu, and M.L. Lee, "Image Mining: Trends and Developments", 2002. Available: http://www.comp.nus.edu.sg/~whsu/publication/2002/JIIS.pdf.

[30] X. Wu, X. Zhu, G.-Q. Wu, and W. Ding, "Data Mining with Big Data", IEEE TKDE, 26(1), pp. 97-107, 2014.

Descriptive Sentence Extraction for Text to 3D scene Generation

Valentina Bova
Department of Informatics, Modeling, Electronics and System Engineering
University of Calabria
Rende, Italy
e-mail: valentina.bova@dimes.unical.it

Elena Cardillo
Institute of Informatics and Telematics
National Research Council
Rende, Italy
e-mail: elena.cardillo@iit.cnr.it

Abstract—**Three-dimensional objects (3D) allow extensive and heterogeneous information to be stored in single models which can be exploited by users to satisfy various research and study needs. Moreover, the 3D visualization would be even more interesting if it were the result of the "materialization" of descriptive sentences extrapolated from texts related to the subject matter. In other words, a direct connection between 3D models and the associated texts or drawings could provide a useful and stimulating explication of the case of study. The extrapolation of specific information from texts, however, is time-consuming and it requires the user to have in-depth knowledge of the referring domain. An innovative solution to the problem, then, would be to develop a system that can analyse and "comprehend" the documents in order to automatically provide, as output, portions of text containing geometric and spatial information useful for the 3D scenes generation. In this paper, the analysis of the framework of the above-mentioned system is presented and its implementation on a specific corpus concerning the "World City" project, is evaluated.**

Keywords-Sentence Extraction; 3D Models; World City project; Text-to-Scene Conversion.

I. Introduction

Three-dimensional (3D) reconstruction is an emerging methodology used in several areas, such as art, education, robotics and, nowadays, it is also developing in the Cultural Heritage field. According to the principles for the Conservation and Restauration of Built Heritage "In the protection and public preservation of archaeological sites, the use of modern technologies, databanks, information system and virtual presentation techniques should be promoted" [1]. But that is not all, because the relationship between Cultural Heritage and Information and Communication Technologies (ICTs) could be exploited not only to represent sites and artworks of the past, still existing or no longer existing, but also to spread the knowledge of projects never realised. Thanks to virtual models, in fact, researchers have the possibility to study and formulate conclusions about sites and object placements, characteristics and configurations, while, more general users may discover and understand their beauty and importance.

The aim of this work is to spread knowledge of a worldwide known project developed by the French bibliographer Paul Otlet in collaboration with international architects such as Andersen, Hébrard, Le Corbusier and Heymans [2]: the "World City" [3]. The complex project has been described in several drawings and textual documents which contain, in a dispersed and fragmented way, information of heterogeneous nature. Conversely, a 3D representation could include, in a single composite model, all the data that could be immediately transferred to the users. In fact, the 3D model has a strong communicative power in addition to the great advantage of being a "universal datum". This means that the transfer of information does not depend on the used written language, weakness of the texts, or on the users' domain knowledge and imagination, which often cause erroneous or different interpretations of the information. On these bases, this work aims to exploit a virtual 3D of the *World City* in order to describe the project in an innovative way: the creation of 3D scenes starting from spatial descriptions contained and extracted from a referent corpus of texts. The project, in fact, was the result of numerous years of study and research attested by primary and secondary sources.

The paper is divided into sections as follow: Section II provides an overview of similar systems. Section III summarizes the 5 different phases of the methodology and describes the first two in detail (Domain Analysis and Corpus Compilation, Information Extraction). Section IV shows the results of the sentence extraction system. In section V, concluding remarks are presented.

II. Background

The work proposes to achieve its aim by a methodology that, through a set of rules, will lead to the reconstruction of virtual scenes regarding the World City project. The idea is to generate associations between terms and 3D elements writing some scripts able to analyse the texts, extract the relevant information from them and handle the location of the three-dimensional objects in the virtual environment.

A. *Related works*

Several systems that can interpret natural descriptions to create a visual representation have already been developed in the past. A text-to-scene conversion system, frequently cited as the first in this field, is the tool SHRDLU [4], which allows users to insert, as input, commands written in natural language with the purpose of using them to move virtual objects around in a small "blocks world". Likewise, Natural Language Image Generation (NALIG) [5] is able to generate scenes by tacking sequences of descriptions which concern the spatial relations between objects. The pioneering WordsEye [6] is one of the main works that focused on this theme, in fact, it creates three-dimensional scenes from input descriptions by converting a parse tree to a dependency representation that, in turn, is transformed into a semantic one. Other similar systems are [7] [8], which use manual links between language and objects in order to create three-dimensional scenes in a virtual space.

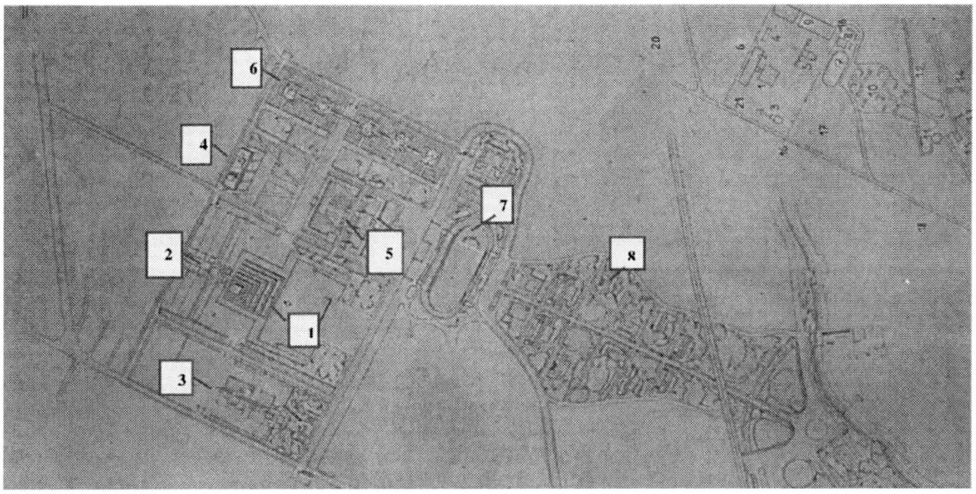

Figure 1. Perspective of the project, Archives of the "Fondation Le Corbusier"; Paris; (24525).

Chang et al. [9] present an advanced 3D generation approach able to learn from data; indeed, the system is capable of mapping, in an automatic way, textual terms to objects and of creating a 3D representation. Furthermore, other works like those described in [10] [11] addressed the development of systems able to infer the presence of implicit objects, or constraints on the objects, in a described scene and to generate a final 3D representation. Sproat [12], instead, focuses on the possibility of inferring the environment of the textual descriptions; for example, taken into account the sentence "Carl is having a shower" the system tries to infer that the scene is set in a bathroom and not in a bedroom or in a kitchen. Big efforts have also been spent, in the literature, to propose solutions for the automatic or semi-automatic extraction or annotation of spatial relations and spatial objects from texts in order to generate 3D scenes. The SpatialML annotation scheme, for example, aims to mark places, including buildings, mentioned in a text (indicated with PLACE tags) and map them to data from gazetteers and other databases. Semantic attributes, such as country abbreviations, subdivision and dependent area abbreviations, and geo-coordinates are used to help establish such a mapping. Rules are language-dependent for marking up SpatialML tags, while are language-independent for marking up semantic attributes of tags [13]. Also, Klien and Lutz [14] proposed a method based on spatial relations for automatizing the semantic annotation process. In particular, they showed how the use of spatial relations at the data level, thus expressed through spatial processing methods (e.g., the calculation of the topology, direction or distance between two spatial entities) can be exploited for the semi-automatic semantic annotation of geodata. Concept definitions and spatial relations here can be extracted from geographic domain ontologies. Other works are focused on the use of a markup language, based on the Text Encoding Initiative (TEI) Guidelines, for semantically annotating raw texts and, in particular, for the task of Named Entities Recognition and Spatial Role Labeling [15]. Regarding the use of ontologies, in [16] they are proposed to bridge between cognitive–linguistic spatial concepts in natural language and multiple qualitative spatial representation and reasoning models. To make this mapping, authors developed a novel global machine learning framework for ontology population.

Finally, a more recent initiative, using also ontologies and semantic web technologies is the Digital 3D Reconstruction in Virtual Research Environment project [17], which aims to define standards for the web-based delivery, e-documentation and presentation of 3D data sets of destroyed architectural landmarks and artworks. The results are concerned with indexing of sources, documentation, semantic modelling, and visualization of 3D data sets using WebGL-technology. Here the main contribution is the development of the Cultural Heritage Markup Language (CHML), a human and machine-readable XML Schema for semantic annotation and for the digital 3D reconstruction of the lost and/or never existing Cultural Heritage 3D objects. The advantages of this new data model is that it is mapped to CIDOC CRM, which is the referent ontology in the Cultural Heritage domain, and is ready to use for annotating and indexing cultural objects within a Virtual Research Environment [18].

B. *The World City*

The concept of the World City was born in the period that goes from 1910 to 1941.This city should have been a spatial non-space, i.e., a "home for men" after war and a world centre for the accumulation, organization, and dissemination of knowledge. The idea was to create a place where people could live in harmony and in universal cooperation and a site whose urban organization responds to precise philosophical, scientific and rational criteria. The City should have included numerous buildings which are the World Museum (1) [19], the Hall of Modern Times (2), the International Association (3), the Library (4), the University (5), the Stadium (6), the Pavilions (7) and the cité hôtelière (8). In Figure 1, a plan realised by the architect Le Corbusier is shown to facilitate the understanding of the composition.

III. Materials and Methods

In the few above-mentioned works (see Section II-A), as well as in others, the 3D scenes are generated starting from sentences written by the users or manually selected from a text. On the contrary, nothing has been done with regard to the automatic extraction of descriptive sentences from a large corpus containing various information. Therefore, the challenge of the present work is to develop a system capable of selecting, without human help, specific sentences from texts concerning the "World City" with the final purpose of spreading the knowledge of the project thanks to the generation of 3D virtual scenes.

The approach can be subdivided in 5 different steps, which are listed below:

1) *Domain Analysis and Corpus compilation*: collection of the relevant sources related to the "World City";
2) *Information Extraction*: extraction of sentences which contain spatial description from the corpus;
3) *Semantic Annotation and Spatial Roles labelling*: sentences annotation and automatic detection of the spatial roles;
4) *3D Objects modeling*: creation of the models which compose the city through a graphical tool;
5) *3D Scenes generation.*

In this paper, we focused on points 1 and 2, namely, on the study of the domain and on the possibility of automatically extracting all the spatial information from the heterogeneous texts that compose the corpus. Further works will deal with the Semantic Annotation and the automatic 3D scenes generation.

C. Domain Analysis and Corpus Compilation

The domain analysis consists in the study of the architectural and historical sources present in the literature in order to discover the specific terms or the multi-words used in the architectural domain, with particular attention to the terminology used in the descriptions of the "World City". For this purpose, a corpus has been created focusing on two important aspects [20]:

- Definition of the characteristics of the reference population from which a significant sample was extracted;
- Definition of qualitative and quantitative criteria for determining the representativeness of the corpus.

The corpus, in fact, must fulfil the role of a representative sample, in the statistical sense of the term, because all the observations obtained from its analysis must be valid and extendable to all the individuals of the population. Specifically, the extracted terminology must be as representative as possible of the one used in the reference domain, but, on a smaller scale. One of the criteria that contributes to ensure the representativeness of the corpus is its size. However, there are not yet precise directives concerning the right dimension. Moreover, given the large amount of information and documents in all areas of knowledge, determining the number of all the available sources, for a precise domain, is a difficult and significant issue.

During the first phase, we collected sources of heterogeneous nature, which include images or technical drawings, videos and textual documents but, for our corpus composition, we only used the texts, because we are interested in the generation of 3D scenes starting from texts written in natural language. On these bases, aiming to respect the criterion of quality, we selected the texts which respect the following requirements [21]:

1. The texts should be representative of the period taken into consideration that goes from the beginning of the nineteenth century to the present day.
2. The texts should be written by different authors: firstly by Paul Otlet, but also domain experts both of the time and contemporary;
3. The texts should be original and not translations;
4. The texts should be complete and not fragments of the whole documents.

All these criteria should guarantee the maximum reliability of all the texts which form the corpus that is composed by primary sources (in the specific case, Paul Otlet's publications or the correspondence between him and the architects), and secondary sources (articles and books of other authors related to the referent domain).

At the end of the analysis, we collected 29 texts in total, for an amount of 411,401 tokens. These documents, originally of different formats (.doc, .pdf, .jpeg) have all been transformed into .txt files through the software ABBYY [22], able to provide optical character recognition and document capture. The whole corpus could be subdivided into four sub-corpora, one for each language handled. In particular, 17 documents are in English (201,747 tokens), 6 documents are in French (85,738 tokens), 4 documents are in Italian (105,930 tokens) and only two documents are in Spanish (17,986 tokens). Once the corpus was created, we carried out an analysis on the natural language constructions useful to talk about spatial configurations. The study was carried out on the four above-mentioned languages because we wanted to work on original texts and not on translations to ensure that the terminology is original and appropriate with reference to the specific domain.

D. Spatial Information Extraction

One of the most important functions of natural language is to describe spatial relationships between objects through linguistic constructs containing spatial information. The latter are easily understandable by the human mind, but machines, on the contrary, have not the same cognitive capabilities and they cannot distinguish spatial and non-spatial data from . This means that it is difficult for computers to identify and extract from texts only the information useful for 3D scenes construction, which is our final task. Therefore, we developed a sentence extractor capable of parsing large data to automatically extract specific sentences from the aforementioned corpus [23]. The aim is to provide a great help to people that, instead of reading the whole texts to select precise information, may automatically obtain the required data.

A way to guide the computer to a correct extraction is to identify how the spatial information is expressed in natural language. We ascertained that is is generally provided by the use of prepositions that establish a relationship between two or more objects However, it is not sufficient, because the same preposition could also be used to talk about events or situations which do not involve spatial descriptions. For example, the preposition *on* could be used to describe spatial configurations like "the picture is *on* the wall" or "the bottle is *on* the table" but, the same preposition is also used in different contexts such as in the sentences "They need to concentrate *on* their studies" or "The discussion will be *on* a topic you have studied recently".

The first two sentences express spatial concepts, concepts of verticality or objects overlapping, while the last two sentences do not have any kind of reference to entities locations. This means that the usage of prepositions depends on several aspects like the entities involved in the scene or the general situation of speech. In other words, prepositions are often used in front of nouns or pronouns to show the relationship between them and other words in the sentence, but they can also be used to describe the time when something happens (*They arrived* **on** *Sunday*), the way in which something is done (*We went* **by** *train*) and even more. On this basis, the identification and the extraction of particular sentences from a large number of texts, characterised by heterogeneous information, is a big and interesting challenge. Therefore, in this work, a Python script able to read and analyse a text has been created with the purpose of extracting all the sentences containing spatial descriptions. The latter are composed by three central concepts belonging to the Holistic Spatial Semantic Theory [24] in which the three main spatial roles are defined. They are trajector(s), landmark(s) and spatial indicator(s) that, linked together, generate a spatial triplet. In particular:

- the *trajector (TR)* is a spatial role label assigned to a word that denotes a central object of a spatial scene;
- the *landmark (LM)* is a spatial role label given to a word that indicates a secondary object of a spatial scene (to which a possible spatial relation between two objects can be established);
- the *spatial indicator (SI)* is a spatial role label assigned to a word that indicates a spatial relation between objects (TR and LM) of a spatial scene.

To better understand, in the sentence "*The* [*car*]$_{TR}$ *is* [*under*]$_{SI}$ *the* [*tree*]$_{LM}$" the "car" is a trajector, the "tree" is a landmark and "under" is a spatial indicator. A key element of the system is a set of text extraction rules that identify relevant information to be extracted from the input text. In particular, the adopted extraction process is based on some word lists belonging to a "spatial domain" and on specific rules which guide the system to identify only the sought information.

The system is subdivided in four sections which, by successive and interconnected steps, gradually lead to a more accurate result. The general idea is to start from an entire document, written in one of the four languages mentioned above, and to parse it in order to identify the possible spatial indicators and labels (TR and LM) existing and interrelated. Although in this step, a difference between roles is not carried out, they are considered regardless of whether they are a trajector or a landmark. The assignment of the correct roles, in fact, will be done subsequently (see step 3 of the methodology described in section III), by using a probabilistic programming language called Saul [25]. For this purpose, two main operations are executed by the system: i) the division of the whole text into single sentences and, ii) their analysis to discard, step by step, those that are not useful for the final goal. The four scripts of the system are the following:

1- Sentence_Split.py = the system opens a document, in a .txt format, and separates strings using two specific delimiters, a dot ('.') or a long sequence of blank spaces. Then, it creates a .txt file (*Sentences.txt*) that collects all the sentences of the document.

2- Search.py = the system reads, as input, a .txt file containing all the possible prepositions or expressions that may be spatial indicators (e.g., *on, in the centre of, to the right*, etc.). Then, it opens the *Sentences.txt* file and it analyses if each sentence contains or does not contain one or more spatial indicator(s). Finally, it creates, as output, a .txt file (*outfile.txt*) including only the phrases with spatial indicator(s) inside.

3- CountOccurrences.py = the system reads two .txt files, the previous *outfile.txt* and *domainNouns.txt*, which is a list containing terms or multi-words that may be TR(s) or LM(s) of the sentences. The latter are all written with lowercase letters so, the next step of the system is to replace all the capital letters, present in *outfile.txt* file, with lowercase letters in order to be case-insensitive. In the end, the system counts the number of labels occurrences (number of time that TR(s) and/or LM(s) appear in each sentence) and, if it is greater than two, it extrapolates the sentences from the *outfile.txt* file and writes them into another .txt file (*labelSentences.txt*). In this way, it is hoped that, at least, one label is the TR of the sentence and another one is its LM and that they are connected through a spatial indicator detected in the previous step.

4- Last.py = in this phase the system improves the results establishing which are the positions that can be occupied by the labels in order to be possible TR(s) and LM(s). The locations are set up with reference to the positions of the spatial indicators taking into account some sentence structure rules. In Table I, the main rules adopted to identify a possible landmark in a sentence are illustrated. More specifically, by making reference to the location of the spatial indicator (signed as s_i) the LM may be located in the next position (s_i + 1), in (s_i + 2) or in (s_i + 3) position. Sample sentences are:

a) A [*zoo*]$_{TR}$ designed for children is located [*in the south of*]$_{SI}$ [*London*]$_{LM}$;

b) The [*fork*]$_{TR}$ is [*to the left of*]$_{SI}$ [*the*]$_{article}$ [*plate*]$_{LM}$;

c) Put the [*box*]$_{TR}$ [*on*]$_{SI}$ [*the*]$_{article}$ [*wooden*]$_{adjective}$ [*table*]$_{LM}$!

TABLE I. LANDMARK POSSIBLE POSITION

a	***SI***	LM		
b	***SI***	article	LM	
c	***SI***	article	adjective	LM
	SI Position: s_i	***LM position: s_i + 1***	***LM position: s_i + 2***	***LM position: s_i + 3***

A further case regards the lack of the landmark in the sentence. This happens when the description is characterized by the presence of an implicit LM like in the sentence: The [balloon] TR flown [up]SI where the LM is NIL (void). Once these rules have been taken into account, the system makes a screening selection of the input file (*labelSentences.txt*) and generates a final file (Last.txt),as output, which shall collect all the sentences containing spatial descriptions and spatial relationships. Table 2 summarizes the four abovementioned steps:

TABLE II SUMMARIZATION OF THE FOUR SCRIPT STEPS

Script	Action	Input	Output
1	**Subdivision** of the whole document into **single sentences.**	*Original document (File.txt)*	*Sentences.txt*
2	**Selection** of the sentences which **contain** one or more **spatial indicators.**	*Spatial_ indicator.txt* *Sentences.txt*	*Outfile.txt*
3	**Count** of the number of times that **words** representing TR or LM appear in each sentence. If num>2 the sentence is extracted.	*Domain Nouns.txt* *Outfile.txt*	*Label Sentences.txt*
4	**Application of rules**: assignment of the **positions** that can be occupied by the labels in order to be possible TR(s) and LM(s).	*Label Sentences.txt*	*Last.txt*

Since at step 3 of the methodology, the automatic assignment of roles (trajector, landmark) and spatial indicator in the sentences will be carried out using Saul, which works only for English, it has been necessary to translate of all the sentences extrapolated from the Italian, French and Spanish documents into English. More precisely, 146 sentences have been manually translated from French, 241 from Italian, and 48 from Spanish.

IV. RESULTS

In total, the system extrapolated 705 different sentences, originally in English (270 sentences) or translated into English (435 sentences), that may be classified into two different categories: "useful extractions" and "unuseful extractions". In particular, the sentences belonging to the first category are those that have been extracted by the system and that really contain spatial information, while, the ones belonging to the second category, are the sentences extracted even if they do not contain spatial data. The number of "useful extraction" sentences is 578, while, the amount of "unuseful extraction" sentences is equal to127 units. In addition, there is a third category that includes all the sentences not detected by the system but which contains spatial information; in other words, the missing data. They are, in total, only 75, as depicted in Figure 2.

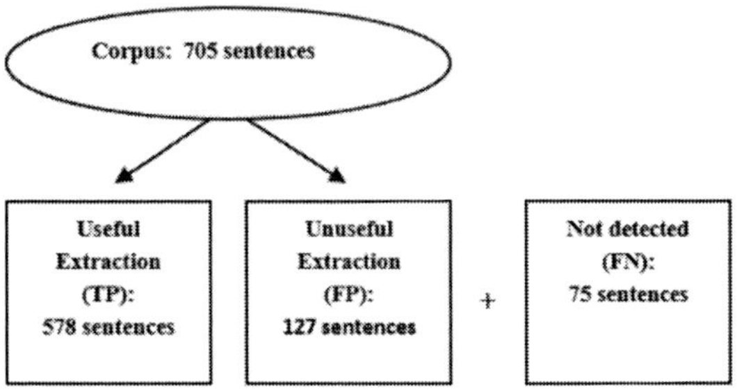

Figure 2. Schematization of the results.

The results have been estimated by the evaluation metrics of precision and recall defined as:

$$precision = \frac{TP}{TP+FP} \qquad recall = \frac{TP}{TP+FN}$$

where:
TP = is the number of system-extracted sentences that contain spatial information;
FP = is the number of system-extracted sentences that do not contain spatial information;
FN = is the number of sentences containing spatial information that the system does not extract from the texts.

The count of the exact number of sentences containing spatial information has been manually performed. They have been detected from the four *Sentences.txt* files (one for each language handled) and compared to the files automatically generated by the system: *Label Sentences.txt* and *Last.txt*. On this basis, the parameters of precision and recall have been estimated. Table 3 shows the results of the system run:

TABLE III. EVALUATION METRICS OF PRECISION AND RECALL

PRECISION	**0.820**
RECALL	**0.885**

These results certify that the used system has an adequate level of reliability because it is capable of responding to the task with a limited margin of error.

V. DISCUSSION AND CONCLUSION

Three-dimensional virtual reconstructions are used in various fields, such as playful or didactic, but play a predominant role in the Cultural Heritage sector. The 3D elements, in fact, allow complete and exhaustive knowledge of the object under consideration because they can be viewed from all points of view, rotated, inspected within them and exploded in their various components. Despite the multitude of 3D models designed to spread the knowledge of our Cultural Heritage, the innovative nature of this work is the connection between three-dimensional data and one-dimensional data. In other words, the will to materialize 3D scenes from descriptive sentences contained in texts of historical, artistic and cultural value that regard the project of the World City. Such interrelationship between reference textual sources and three-dimensional models would enrich the original texts with information that are often implied or scattered in the texts and cannot be viewed together. Furthermore, thanks to the system created and described in this work, it is possible to overcome the problem associated with the manual extraction of spatial descriptions that is a time consuming operation, which becomes more and more complicated in the growth of the size of the examined corpus. On the contrary, the automatic extrapolation of sentences to materialize in virtual space is the key to the problem and the innovation of the proposed work. These sentences will then become the starting point for virtual reconstructions of more or less complex scenes containing spatially related entities. Given the simple task evaluated, a future test will be to train a machine learning document classifier to see if the evaluation is improved with respect to the use of our rule-based approach.

The proposed methodology will provide a three-dimensional view of the World City, just as Paul Otlet and Le Corbusier designed it, and it will allow a simpler and quicker understanding of the complex project that, although it has great historical, artistic and cultural value, was never realized. Finally, we hope that the abovementioned methodology will be exploited in other contexts where there is a need to extrapolate sentences, containing entities and relationships between them, from documents. Especially when the documents, due to their large-scale, cannot be manually read and analysed by the user. Further work will test the potentiality of semantic web technologies and ontologies to improve the results as experimented in [18].

REFERENCES

[1] K. Charter, "Principles for conservation and restoration of built heritage", Marsilio, Venice, 2000.

[2] G. Gresleri and D. Matteoni, "La città mondiale". Andersen, Hébrand, Otlet, Le Corbusier, first edition, Polis/Marsilio Editori, 1982.

[3] P.Otlet, Cité Mondiale. Geneva : World Civic Center : Mundaneum, Publication n. 133 de l'Union des Associations Internationales, Palais Mondial, Bruxelles, 1929.

[4] T. Winograd, "Procedures as a representation for data in a computer program for understanding natural language (No. MAC-TR-84)," Massachusetts Inst of Tech Cambridge Project Mac, 1971.

[5] G. Adorni, M. Di Manzo and F. Giunchiglia, "Natural language driven image generation," in Proceedings of the 10th International Conference on Computational Linguistics and 22nd annual meeting on Association for Computational Linguistics, pp. 495-500, 1984.

[6] B. Coyne and R. Sproat, "WordsEye: An Automatic Text-to-Scene Conversion System," in Proceedings of the 28th annual conference on Computer graphics and interactive techniques (SIGGRAPH '01), ACM, New York, pp. 487–496,2001.

[7] L. M. Seversky and L. Yin, "Real-time automatic 3D scene generation from natural language voice and text descriptions," in Proceedings of the 14th Annual ACM International Conference on Multimedia, 2006.

[8] M. Savva, A. X. Chang, G. Bernstein, C. D. Manning, and P. Hanrahan, "On being the right scale: Sizing large collections of 3D models," in SIGGRAPH Asia, Workshop on Indoor Scene Understanding: Where Graphics meets Vision, 2014.

[9] A. Chang, W. Monroe, M. Savva, C. Potts and C.D. Manning, "Text to 3d scene generation with rich lexical grounding," arXiv In section V concluding remarks are presented.preprint arXiv: 1505.06289, 2015.

[10] A. Chang, M. Savva and C. D. Manning, "Learning Spatial Knowledge for Text to 3D Scene Generation," in Empirical Methods in Natural Language Processing (EMNLP), pp. 2028–2038, 2014.

[11] A. Cropper, "Identifying and inferring objects from textual descriptions of scenes from books," in OASIcs- OpenAccess Series in Informatics (Vol. 43), Schloss Dagstuhl-Leibniz-Zentrum fuer Informatik, 2014.

[12] R. Sproat, "Inferring the environment in a text-to-scene conversion system," in Proceedings of the 1st international conference on Knowledge capture, ACM, pp. 147-154, 2001.

[13] I. Mani, J. Hitzeman, J. Richer, D. Harris, R. Quimby and Ben Wellner, "SpatialML: Annotation Scheme, Corpora, and Tools", in Proceedings of the Sixth International Conference on Language Resources and Evaluation (LREC'08), Marrakech, Morocco, May 28-30, 2008.

[14] E. Klien and M. Lutz, "The Role of Spatial Relations in Automating the Semantic Annotation of Geodata, in Cohn, Anthony G. and Mark, David M. (eds.)", in Proceedings of the International Conference on Spatial Information Theory 2005, Springer Berlin Heidelberg, pp. 133—148, 2005.

[15] L. Moncla and M. Gaio, "A multi-layer markup language for geospatial semantic annotations", in Proceedings of the 9th Workshop on Geographic Information Retrieval, Paris, France, November 26-27, 2015, Article n. 5, ACM New York (USA), 2015.

[16] P. Kordjamshidi and M.F. Moens, "Global machine learning for spatial ontology population", Web Semantics: Science, Services and Agents on the World Wide Web, Vol. 30, January 2015, pp. 3-21, 2015.

[17] Digital 3D Reconstructions in Virtual Research Environments. Leibniz Association 2013-2016. [Online]. Available from: http://www.patrimonium.net. [retrieved: March, 2018]

[18] P. Kuroczynski, O. Hauck and D. Dworak, "3D Models on Triples Paths – new Pathways for documenting and Visualizing Virtual Reconstruction", in 3D Research Challenges in Cultural Heritage II: How to Manage Data and Knowledge Related to Interpretative Digital 3D Reconstructions of Cultural Heritage, LNCS, Spriger Verlag, pp. 149-172, 2016.

[19] W. Van Acker, "Opening the Shrine of the Mundaneum: The Positivist Spirit" in the Architecture of Le Corbusier and his Belgian 'Idolators', in A. Brown & A. Leach (Eds.), Proceedings of the Society of Architectural Historians, Australia and New Zealand: 30, Open: Gold Coast: SAHANZ, Vol. 2, pp. 791-805, 2013.

[20] A. Caruso and A. Folino, "Corpus-based knowledge representation in specialized domains," in Corpus-based studies on language verieties, Peter Lang, pp. 11-35, 2016.

[21] J. Pearson, "Terms in Context," Amsterdam-Philadelphia: John Benjamins Publishing Company, pp. 58-62, 1998.

[22] ABBYY FineReader, URL: < https://www.abbyy.com/it-it/> [retrieved: March, 2018]

[23] F. Bonin et all, "A Contrastive Approach to Multi-word Extraction from Domain-specific Corpora," in Proceedings of LREC'10, Valletta, Malta, 17-23, pp. 3222–3229, 2010.

[24] J. Zlatev, "Holistic spatial semantics of Thai, Cognitive Linguistics and Non-Indo-European Languages", pp. 305–336, 2003.

[25] P. Kordjamshidi, R. Dan, and W. Hao "Saul: Towards Declarative Learning Based Programming." *IJCAI*, 2015.

Application of Event Sourcing in Research Data Management

Jedrzej Rybicki
Juelich Supercomputing Center (JSC)
Juelich, Germany
Email: j.rybicki@fz-juelich.de

***Abstract*—Event sourcing is an architecture pattern successfully applied in modern microservice-oriented web applications. It enables better scalability, integration, and traceability by changing the way in which data are handled in those distributed systems. There are many differences, however, between data used by commercial applications and research data. In this paper, we examine if and how event sourcing can be applied in the field of research data management and what ramifications and benefits can it bring. One of the most important rules of the pattern is to record and publish all the changes ever done to a data item. Therefore, not only the current version of the item exists, but also older versions and all modifications can be traced back in time. As we will show, it opens new avenues to work with research data. The publication of the changes makes it easy to replicate the data, and collaborate on them without a central authority. All these are features often required in the modern data-driven science. The concept, its suitability, ramifications, and initial performance evaluations are presented in two real world usage scenarios. The preliminary results corroborate the assertion of suitability of event sourcing in this particular field.**

Keywords–Data Management; Event sourcing; Replication; Performance evaluation.

I. INTRODUCTION

The research data come in all kinds and flavors. Spanning from small items like single measurement of a parameter value, through all kinds of documents, or recordings, up to large size genome sequences or results of astrophysical observations. Data can be raw and unprocessed or curated to form highly processed secondary data. Also, there is a high veracity with regard to the intended use of the data: some of them are expected to be just safely stored (archived), some are shared (downloaded) or collaboratively edited by researchers spread all over the world. Finally, there is an option for processing the data with High-Throughput Computing (HTC) or High-Performance Computing (HPC) facilities. The variety along all the dimension, suggest that there is not a single optimal storage solution, but rather one has to decide on case-by-case basis which solution best suits the particular data and envisioned usages.

One common feature of research data is the time dimension. It can either be explicit like in case of subsequent measurements, but also implicit like different versions of curated document. Closely related to this subject is the question if the research data change at all. Does a new, modified version of the data really substitute the old one, or should the old one be kept? One could argue that for the sake of data understandability and research transparency both versions should exist with a link (or other indicator) between them in the logical data access layer. In that sense, the research data are immutable, i.e., they never change but rather new versions emerge along the old ones. Each new version or each new measurement is yet another *event* on the time axis, that should be recorded and stored to enable better understanding of the current versions.

If the data are used as input for scientific processing, researcher often requires means to define exactly the set of inputs. A *snapshot* composed of many data objects could be a useful abstraction for that. In many cases, it might also be relevant how the output of the processing changes depending on the selected data. In that case, the snapshots must be parameterized, e.g., to include only measurements from given region or time interval. If the processing supports the notion of snapshots for inputs it is also possible to create "alternative past models", for instance to examine what results alternative measurements would led to.

A common problem with research data is the distribution. The data often need to be replicated to make distributed processing more efficient. In some of the cases, *sharding* makes more sense than full replication: on a given location only a partition of data is stored. A reason could be that a local facility is only interested in parts of the data. The problem of data distribution can also be understood as a generalization of snapshotting mentioned above. Local replica is then a snapshot and replication is creation of parametrized snapshots with final location of the data as one parameter. Replication and sharding are hard engineering problems and become even more challenging when data are modified in a distributed fashion. Some coordination is required to keep track of such changes and potentially propagate them to all interested parties. Preferably this should happen with as little overhead as possible, in particular global "locks" as in case of well-known two-phase commit distributed transactions might not be acceptable. Yet there are high expectations in regard to data consistency. As we show latter, the distributed modification of data can be better understood and solved with the notion of events mentioned above.

In this paper, we propose how modern software architecture principles subsumed under the term of event sourcing can be applied to research data. In particular, this approach seems to suit well the distributed, collaborative storing and processing of data. The paper is a work-in-progress report on our experiences with application of event sourcing paradigm in research data management. We will present two distinct use cases of storing research data with the proposed architecture and shed some light on the technical details of our approach. The paper also includes preliminary performance assessments of applications employing the concept.

The rest of the paper is structured as follows. In Section II, we shortly summarize some of the previous work on event sourcing and its application in research. Then, follows a section describing the different flavors of event-driven architectures to finally formulate event sourcing pattern and give some insights on how it can be implemented with help of Apache Kafka. The main part of this paper is the evaluation of event sourcing for managing research data, this is done based on two real-world inspired use cases which we describe in Section V. The results obtained in our preliminary evaluations are discussed before the papers ends with a conclusion and outlook on future work.

II. Related Work

Event sourcing was and is successfully applied in the domain of commercial applications [1]–[3], because of the performance, distribution, and ease of integration (especially in microservice-oriented systems) it offers. There are many evaluations of using event sourcing with particular languages or frameworks [4] [1] [5]. There is not much work, however, on how this kind of architecture approach can be applied in research data management. Of course, emerging research infrastructures should follow best development and architectural practices obtained in the commercial setting. On the other hand, there are some unique aspects of managing research data that need to be addressed. The most prominent difference seems to be caused by the Open Data Movement [6]. Research data are expected to become open, and accessible, at least in in the long term. Also, the transparent provenance standards resulting from the need of reproducibility are probably higher in the academic context. In this paper we show how event sourcing can help in achieving these features.

Müller [7] showed how event sourcing can enable retroactive computing, i.e., to examine how alternative chains of events could lead to a different final state of the system. This interesting use case can be realized if the research data are stored in an event-driven fashion and is therefore orthogonal to our work. Another application of event sourcing in broad context of research data comes from Erb and Kargl [8]. They analyzed how event sourcing architecture can be incorporated into discrete event simulations to make them better to understand, debug, and evaluate. The work is less focused on managing research data (although it is relevant in this context) but provides important insights and use cases for the event sourcing architecture.

One of the use cases discussed in this paper is replication of research data repository. State-of-the art research data management solutions like iRODS [9] or Fedora Commons [10] store data on the backend file system and metadata in a relational database. iRODS provides its own means to facilitate replication. Upon ingest of new data they can be copied to remote repository with proprietary transport protocol. To replicate an existing repository, its backend filesystem and metadata database has to be copied to a remote location by other means. To create such a consistent snapshot, original repository has to be either stopped or set into read-only mode. In this paper we will show that event store has some clear advantages over the mixture of database and file system in this scenario. In particular, it enables replication during normal operation of the original repository. By playing back all the past operations on the original repository it can be guaranteed that the replica is in a consistent (even if not most up-to-date state) state. The messaging features of event stores, guarantee that the future updates will be propagated to existing replicas. Lastly, the event stores allow for replication in the time which are convenient to the receiver, e.g., during the night hours.

The popularity and usability of event-oriented approaches in the modern microservice architectures led to availability of at least few products that can be used to built event sourcing solutions. Apache Kafka [11] is one of the most popular and we used it as a backbone of our solution. Furthermore, we already have used Kafka in context of research infrastructure, namely to extend Swift [12] with flexible namespaces [13]. Thus, some initial experiences with this product that we could build upon were available. The basic workings and most prominent features of Apache Kafka will be explained later in this paper.

For our experiments we selected Kafka as an event store. The idea of event sourcing is to store all the changes done to entities as events. Thus, to obtain a valid state of an entity, it is required to replay all the events that happened to it. We did this by retrieving the events from event store, an alternative approach would be to use one of the streaming platforms like Samza [14] or Spark [15] or streaming features of Kafka. These platforms can read data from Kafka and direct process the data, e.g., to obtain an aggregate or entity state. Such a processing is usually done in close to real-time manner. This was not required in our scenarios. In opposite we were interested in the past versions of entities. Thus, streaming platforms may combine well with our approach but their application is depending on the user requirements.

III. Event-driven architectures

Before we explain what kinds of event-driven architectures are common in distributed systems, we shall first define some basic terminology. In the remainder of this paper, we will use terms entity, aggregate, and event as defined by domain-driven design [16]. In short, *entity* is characterized by the possession of identity, a group of entities can form an *aggregate*, and changes in state of entities or aggregates are called *events*. Especially the last definition is not so common in the event-driven approaches as we will see later in this section.

Fowler presented an excellent discussion of the different kinds of event-driven architectures [3], we include only a short summary of his arguments. One of the first examples of an event-oriented approach were systems using notifications distributed through a common Enterprise Service Bus (ESB) [17]. This solution was used for enterprise-wide integration of services. In particular, upon a change within the system, a notification was sent to the bus, and then distributed to all interested parties. This was achieved in publish/subscribe fashion. The messages were usually simple in form and to actually get information about what changed, the interested party had to contact the message originator. Soon, this subsequent communication was identified as a bottleneck and new architectures emerged where messages included sufficient description of the actual change to eliminate the need for additional communication. Usually, it would include an identifier of the entity or aggregate and new values of its attributes. Such approaches were subsumed under the term event-carried state transfers, they were still relying on publish-subscribe message buses and were oriented on costly immediate information delivery.

The final evolution of message-driven architectures, and the one that is relevant for the rest of the paper is called event sourcing. Here again each change in the entity or aggregate state is recorded as an event and published. But unlike the previous approaches the publication is done with help of an event store. This component stores the events for longer period of time and beside supporting publish-subscribe interface for immediate event distribution, it also provides access to stored events from the past. Thus, the subscribers can not only just express their interest for the future events (like in approaches described above), but also request the past events. Events follow time order, and each consumer can request all the messages starting from a given time offset. At the first glance, the change might not seem to be very substantial but it has a lot of implications. In particular, each service in the system can maintain its own state replica, and thanks to the notifications the state can be kept up-to-date. Importantly, changes of the state can be done in a consistent manner even without costly distributed transactions or central coordination in form of global locking. Further, the local state can be erased and rebuild from the past events. As all the changes in the system are stored as events, it is only required to play all the events in timely order to recreate the final state.

We believe that event sourcing can be successfully applied to manage research data. Since modification of an entity is done by publishing a "modification" event, no information is lost and old versions of the entities can always be retrieved. It is much more meaningful, for instance, to see that a value was added and then removed from a stream of measurements, rather than have just the final version without the given value. Furthermore, the event sourcing removes the need for central coordination when working with research data. Each researcher can pick and choose the events she is interested in, publish her modifications, or withheld modifications from others in her local version. This is not only a technical argument but also a social one as it plays well with the open nature of modern data-driven research.

It should be stressed that event sourcing is not a plug-and-play solution that can be easily included in the existing systems. It is an architecture decision that strongly influence the design of the system especially in data access layer.

IV. Implementation of Event Sourcing

In this paper, we aim at evaluating the general suitability of event sourcing architectures to manage research data. We are more focused on general insights rather than rigorous performance evaluations (which might follow up this paper).

A. Apache Kafka

Kafka is a "distributed streaming platform" [18], its functionality boils down to three main aspects:

1) publish/subscribe system,
2) fault-tolerant distributed storage,
3) processing of streams.

From our perspective the first two are the most important. Kafka uses notion of *records*, that are roughly equivalent to events from our previous definition. The records are very flexible structures comprising of a key, value, and timestamp. Both key and value are basically streams of bytes handled over to Kafka. Records belong to *topics*, i.e., categories of events. For efficiency Kafka divides them into *partitions*. Partition is an immutable sequence of records with strict time-based ordering. Upon publication of a new record *Publisher* assigns it to a partition. This can be done in a programmatic way (e.g.,

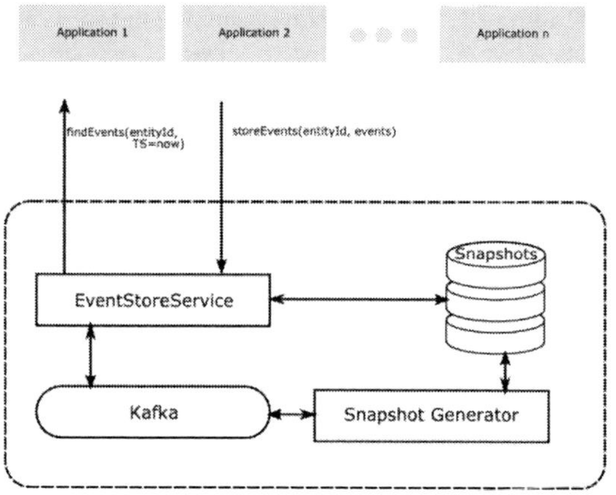

Figure 1. Architecture overview of our solution

based on hash of the message or any other information about the structure of records). *Consumers* can subscribe to given topic and will receive records in the same order as they were published. Each consumer can, also, select its offset in the topic, i.e., the position of the next message she would like to receive. It could be the newest one, but also the oldest one in case of rebuilding of an entity. The producer, on the other hand, only appends to new records to the partition log (which does not require random access to the storage and is very beneficial for the overall performance). If required, consumers can form groups per topic. In such case each record will be delivered to exactly one consumer from a group in a round robin fashion.

As already mentioned, Kafka is more than yet another publish/subscribe system. Its strength is the fact that the records are written to disk for defined periods of time in a fault-tolerant way. In particular partitions of a topic can be replicated and have their own retention policies. To increase data safety, consumer upon publication of a record, can wait for a defined number of acknowledgments from all replica managers.

A good intuition of what Kafka is and how it differs from other messaging and storage systems is to see it as a system that allows access to both past and future data [18]. Storage repositories, like filesystems or databases, are providing the data stored in the past. Whilst messaging systems allow to subscribe for the future data, i.e., data that will become available in the future will be distributed to all clients that subscribed.

B. Kafka deployment

There are many ways in which Kafka can be deployed. In general, Kafka servers can form a cluster and coordinate through Apache Zookeeper [19] (which can also be deployed as cluster). For our experiments we used, however, one host deployment, with one instance of Kafka and one instance of Zookeeper residing on the same host. The basis for our deployment were Docker images provided by Confluent Platform [20]. Docker enables rapid provisioning of software, thus this setup can be further extended towards cluster setting. With one exception that will be described later we used the pre-configured defaults of Kafka and Zookeeper as defined in the images.

Both Kafka and Zookeeper were deployed on a host with 1 VCPU, 2 GB RAM and 100 GB storage using Ubuntu 16.04

LTS and Docker in version 1.13.1. We used Confluent platform version 3.3.1 which included Kafka 0.11.0.1 and Zookeeper 3.4.10. To communicate with Kafka we used Python library `kafka-python` version 1.3.4.

C. *Programming interface*

As mentioned above, event sourcing is not a plug-and-play extension that can be added to an existing systems. It requires some changes in the persistent layer. Rather than performing fetches from a "source of truth" central database system to obtain current state of an entity, each service has to work with streams of events rather to build their states.

For a better understanding of the mental model required to work with events as persistence layer, let us discuss following code example.

```
# get current version
pastEvents = findEvents(entityId)
entity = new()
applyEvents(entity, pastEvents)

# do something with it
newEvents = processCommand(entity,...)
applyEvents(entity, newEvents)

# publish changes
storeEvents(entityId, newEvents)
```

In the first lines, a substitute for fetch command from traditional database-based approaches is presented. Crucial is the function `applyEvents` which applies all the events (stream of modifications) to a newly created, pristine entity. The modification to an existing entity is done with `commands`, which rather than modifying it directly, produce a list of events that need to be applied to the existing entity. Lastly, to make the changes induced by a command persistent, it is required to store the list of events.

To improve performance of such workflows it is possible to use snapshots. Snapshots would be entities which are rendered with `applyEvents` function and persisted together with a timestamp. The same function (without modifications) can be used to update snapshot or produce an entity for a timestamp of higher value than the timestamp of the snapshot.

A rudimentary overview of our architecture is depicted in Figure 1. Kafka is abstracted by an event source service which can also use snapshots if required. On the top level applications constituting user interfaces reside. In our case there are two web applications created. One is a simple research data repository and the other is a measurement display. These emulate a means in which data from event store would be served to end users.

V. USE CASES

We defined two use cases inspired by real-world usage of research infrastructures. The use cases are implemented with the application of event sourcing. In this section we will describe the use cases and how we implemented them.

A. *Measurements storage backend*

The inspiration to this use case was a common practice of collecting research data from a distributed network of sensors.

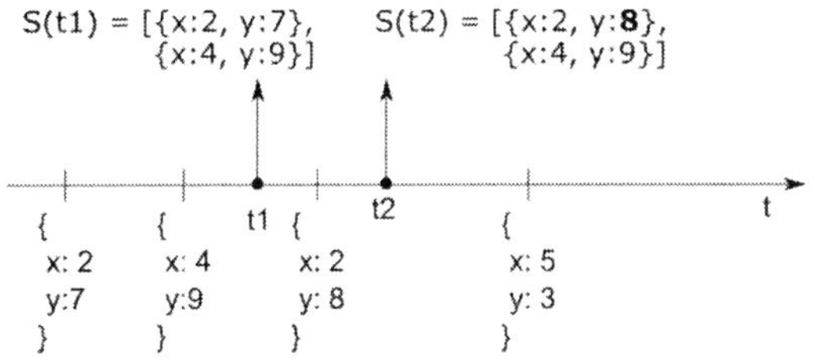

Figure 2. Modeling measurement stream as series of events. Aggregated states at $t1$ and $t2$.

We assumed that each station in the network periodically measure some values and uploads those to the central sink for further processing. We, also, wanted to account for a possibility to upload corrections of the previous measurements (e.g., upon detection of sensor malfunction). A simple domain analysis suggest a model in which each station in the network is an entity and each measurement would be an event. Hence, the state of the entity at given time would be a stream of measurements (and corrections) collected up to this moment. In fact, we are somehow close between discussing aggregates and entities but in general, this is not relevant here.

We implemented this use case in such a way that a process produces measurements of two values (x, y) which are then uploaded with a timestamp and station identifier to the central repository (i.e., Kafka server). The state of the entity is given by a $f(x) = y$. Therefore, if a measurement arrives with a value of x which is already present it would be treated as a correction. This approach is depicted in Figure 2. State of the entity requested at $t = t1$ would include values $x : 2, y : 7$ and $x : 4, y : 9$. Later, a correction of the first measurement arrives, thus the entity returned at $t = t2$ is built of values $x : 2, y : 8$ and $x : 4, y : 9$. It is worth noticing that the corrected measurement is still present in the event store and thus it is always possible to request state at $t1$.

Because the timestamps are also recorded it is possible to generate previous views of the entity state (e.g., before a correction). We implemented this functionality in form of a web application that connects to Kafka, pull all the relevant measurements and presents them in form of a x, y plot. Since building of the final state of a given entity boils down to replaying all the events (measurements), an obvious optimization would be to store previous states as snapshots and only apply events that happened between the snapshot time and the requested time. Many different strategies for generating snapshot are conceivable. A simple strategy is to store a snapshot depending on the number of events that needs to be read from Kafka to rebuild the requested entity state. If the number is higher than some pre-defined threshold a snapshot will be stored. This strategy aims at optimizing the overhead of communicating with the event store. An alternative like time-based snapshotting is less effective in this, especially when events are not evenly distributed in time. Two states of an entity, which are distant in time, might not differ very much in number of events that happened to them. All the code we developed can be found in the GitHub repository [21] for further analysis.

A system built in this manner would have to provide good performance on at least two fields. Firstly, a high throughput

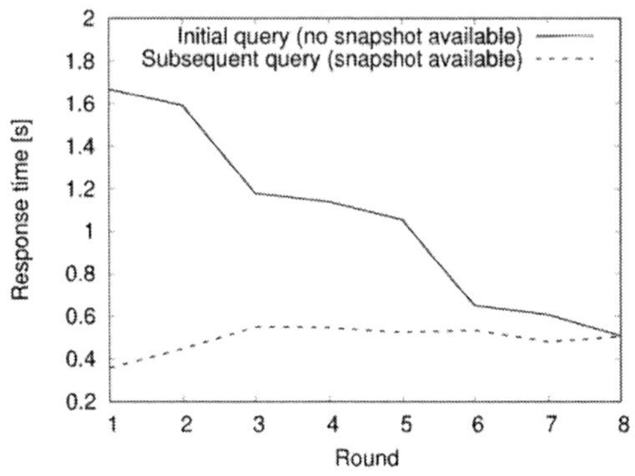

Figure 3. Querying measurements storage: In each round aggregated entity for decreasing timestamp is requested twice.

with regard to the uploading measurements must be granted. Secondly, the entity states delivered by aggregating the measurements should be produced quickly. The throughput was measured by uploading repeatedly large batches of measurements directly to Kafka. We tested batch sizes of 5 000, 10 000, and 50 000. The experiments were divided into 10 rounds, in each round a defined number of measurements were uploaded and time measurement was conducted. We summarize the obtained results in Table I. Our very rudimentary experiments suggest that it is possible to arrive at the throughput of almost 6 000 messages per second. Given, rather simple single-node deployment, we consider this performance sufficient.

TABLE I. MEASUREMENTS UPLOAD THROUGHPUT.

Batch size	Throughput (measurements/s)
5 000	5819.39
10 000	5938.39
50 000	5500.44

Our second heuristic was the performance of delivering the aggregated states of entities. For that we have conducted a two-phased experiment. Firstly, about 50 000 evenly distributed measurements were uploaded to Kafka. Subsequently, entity states for decreasing timestamps (i.e., from the most current downwards) were requested and response times were recorded. For each timestamp we performed two requests, thus the first response was produced solely based on measurements from Kafka and resulted in storing a new snapshot. It was in turn used to answer the subsequent query. The results are show in Figure 3. Solid line depicts the initial queries where no snapshot was available, subsequent query in each round benefited from the just-created snapshot and, thus, were answered quicker (dashed line). It can be seen that snapshots indeed improve the response times and are crucial especially for more complex entities aggregating large number of measurements (left side of the plot). This experiment was intended to show the best possible gains obtained by creating snapshots. The initial query always required full list of events for the requested entity. It is worth mentioning that we stored the snapshots in a simple in-memory store, so the difference in response times is mainly caused by retrieval of events from Kafka and process of rebuilding of the requested entity.

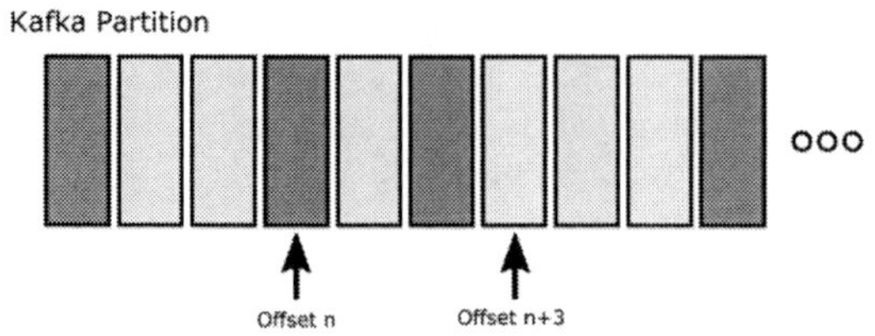

Figure 4. Storing data objects (dark gray) and files (light gray) in Kafka.

B. Replication of research data repository

Research data often need to be replicated. The reasons for that might be the data-preservation policies that require multiple copies, or efficiency considerations. To this end, we want to examine how event sourcing can be used to implement such replication.

For our tests we used data from a real-world research data repository EUDAT B2SHARE [22]. It is part of the EUDAT research data infrastructure built to serve researchers from all across Europe [23]. The data model used by B2SHARE defines data objects as a set of metadata, persistent identifier (PID), and a list of files. Current model does not support versioning of the objects and files. B2SHARE is based on open-source Invenio system [24] which offers an API that we used to download all the data from the repository. We obtained 538 objects and total size of data amounted to about 40 GB. Subsequently, we uploaded the data objects and files to our Kafka instance. Data objects were just JSON documents as downloaded from B2SHARE, they included basic metadata and names of files attached to the object, we used their PIDs as keys in Kafka. Files were uploaded with filenames as keys, and binary content as values. Larger files needed to be split into chunks of 40 MB. Such large records required a change in the default configuration of Kafka. All the data were put into one partition in Kafka and objects were put before files they referred to. We used creation time to sort the data objects, i.e., newer data objects have higher offsets in the partition. The code we developed for both scrapping the original data, as well as replicating it can be found in GitHub repository [25].

It might not be immediately clear from the above description what are the entities and events in this scenario. The entities in the system are the data objects, and events are modifications (or creations) of metadata descriptions which are stored in Kafka and uploads (or modifications) of files belonging to the data objects. The approach is shown in Figure 4. The dark gray rectangles depict events of uploading metadata descriptions of objects, and light gray rectangles are the upload of files corresponding to the objects. For example at offset n in partition there is a metadata object, at offset $n+3$ starts a list of three files belonging to an object at $n+2$ (it could also be three chunks of a larger file).

The evaluation of this use case comprised of two phases. First, the time required to upload the content of the B2SHARE repository to Kafka was measured. Afterwards, the repository was restored at the target site. These two phases simulate full replication of the research data. In total, 4267 events were generated to upload the content. The results are summarized in Table II.

There is apparently not much difference in performance of uploading and downloading. For comparison we copied

TABLE II. REPLICATION TIMES.

Phase	Time (s)
Upload	2170
Download	2282

the same data between the same hosts using Secure Copy Protocol (SCP) which completed the task in about 17 minutes. It should be stressed that the upload and download to Kafka can be done at the same time so that complete replication of B2SHARE data would needed about 30 minutes.

VI. DISCUSSION

To evaluate the applicability of event sourcing in research data management we implemented two use cases. In the first one we emulated gathering and evaluating of measurements from a distributed sensor network. We have identified two critical aspects for performance of event sourcing here. Firstly, the throughput for collecting the measurements. The values obtained in our experiments are pretty high. This comes at no surprise as event sourcing allows for efficient resources usage, there is no need for random access or costly data removal, it only has to support addition of data to the log. The other performance aspect were the response times of the interface serving aggregated entities. Here we have noticed that even a simple snapshotting strategy can substantially improve response times. When discussing this use case it is important to ask a question how hard would it be to change an existing application to support event sourcing. It would clearly require a change in the user-facing application, it must support Kafka as the source of information and being able to reconstruct the state of entity (as a stream of measurements in our case) from recorded events. By offering retrospective views on data it gives direct advantages to the researchers. One further advantage would be the ease of integration with other services and easy way towards replication of the data.

The replication of data constituted the central point of our second use case. We used data from existing repository to make the evaluation results more meaningful. The main challenge here was coping with the large files, they need to be split into chunks before uploading. We measured time for complete replication of the repository. There are many more possible aspects of this use case that might be relevant in the future. First one, is the need of keeping replicas up-to-date this would require changes in the existing repository software so that it would emit information about user actions (upload/modification of objects) and thus inform replicating sites about availability of new data. There could also be possibility of creating shards (i.e., partial replicas of the data), for that a way of defining sharding strategy needs to be put in place. This questions are pretty specific to particular use case, a research infrastructure is addressing and thus were not included into the evaluation. Since we are replaying the events from the oldest one, the target repository remains in a valid (i.e., consistent) if not most up-to-date state during the on-going replication.

There are some common aspects for both use cases. On very high level event sourcing requires a different mindset when dealing with data. In particular, deleting data is almost impossible. It is possible to create a correction (as we discussed), but the original event will remain in the event log. Developers should always be aware of this, especially when dealing with sensitive data like personal health data. Somehow related is the problem of event modeling. In this paper we used very simple modeling that might not be optimal. A solution is always specific to the problem that is to be solved. Another question is the evolution and extension of the event models. It is possible to do this, but it requires changes in the `applyEvent` function.

Event sourcing is not just new approach to data management but also an integration pattern. It might require some changes in the existing applications but as soon as they begin to use event store as persistence layer, it is very easy to add new services that can use the data. The application can run in parallel, use the same data, there is no need for coordination or global locking. The applications can be stateless and thus it is also possible to create multiple instances of the same application for instance to improve response times. In our cases, it would be easy to create one more replica of the repository or spin off one more user interface to present aggregated measurements.

VII. CONCLUSION AND FUTURE WORK

In this paper, we evaluated the application of event sourcing for managing research data. We defined two use cases and examined how they can be implemented in this architecture style and what performance they display. We also showed the functional benefits of this approach: how old versions of the data can be retrieved and how data can be seamlessly replicated. Although, these are preliminary experiences we believe that they can be valuable for both developers and researchers. The results obtained in the performance evaluation indicate the applicability of the approach and particular technology (Apache Kafka) in the real world scenarios. Also, the high-level ramifications of the proposed approach, in particular the concept of making the research data *de facto* immutable is a profound change in way we think about data.

In our future work, we plan to put the gained experiences into practice by implementing event sourcing in the context of research data infrastructures.

REFERENCES

[1] D. Betts, J. Dominguez, G. Melnik, F. Simonazzi, and M. Subramanian, Exploring CQRS and Event Sourcing: A journey into high scalability, availability, and maintainability with Windows Azure. Microsoft patterns & practices, 2013, ISBN: 978-1-62-114016-0.

[2] G. Young, Event Centric: Finding Simplicity in Complex Systems. Addison-Wesley, 2012, ISBN: 978-0-32-176822-3.

[3] What do you mean by "Event Driven"? [Online]. Available: https://martinfowler.com/articles/201701-event-driven.html [retrieved: Mar., 2018]

[4] B. Nobakht and F. S. de Boer, Programming with Actors in Java 8. Springer Berlin Heidelberg, 2014, pp. 37–53, ISBN: 978-3-66-245231-8.

[5] K. Lee, Event-Driven Programming. Springer London, 2011, pp. 149–165.

[6] M. B. Gurstein, "Open data: Empowering the empowered or effective data use for everyone?" First Monday, vol. 16, no. 2, 2011, ISSN: 13960466.

[7] M. Müller, "Enabling retroactive computing through event sourcing," Master's thesis, University of Ulm, 2016.

[8] B. Erb and F. Kargl, "Combining discrete event simulations and event sourcing," in Proceedings of the 7th International ICST Conference on Simulation Tools and Techniques SIMUTools '14, 2014, pp. 51–55, ISBN: 978-1-63-190007-5.

[9] A. Rajasekar, R. Moore, C.-Y. Hou, C. A. Lee, R. Marciano, A. de Torcy, M. Wan, W. Schroeder, S.-Y. Chen, L. Gilbert, P. Tooby, and B. Zhu, iRODS Primer: Integrated Rule-Oriented Data System, ser. Synthesis Lectures on Information Concepts, Retrieval, and Services. Morgan & Claypool Publishers, 2010, ISBN: 978-1-62-705972-5.

[10] D. Wilcox. Stewarding research data with Fedora. [Online]. Available: http://library.ifla.org/id/eprint/1796 [retrieved: Mar., 2018]

[11] J. Kreps, N. Narkhede, and J. Rao, "Kafka: A distributed messaging system for log processing," in Proceeding of 6th International Workshop on Networking meets Database (NetDB '11), Jun. 2011, pp. 1–7.

[12] J. Arnold, OpenStack Swift: Using, Administering, and Developing for Swift Object Storage. O'Reilly Media, 2014, ISBN: 978-1-49-190082-6.

[13] B. von St. Vieth, J. Rybicki, and M. Brzeźniak, "Towards flexible open data management solutions," in Proceedings of the 40th IEEE International Convention on Information and Communication Technology, Electronics and Microelectronics (MIPRO '17), May 2017, pp. 233–237, ISBN: 978-9-53-233090-8.

[14] S. A. Noghabi, K. Paramasivam, Y. Pan, N. Ramesh, J. Bringhurst, I. Gupta, and R. H. Campbell, "Samza: Stateful scalable stream processing at LinkedIn," Proc. VLDB Endow., vol. 10, no. 12, Aug. 2017, pp. 1634–1645, ISSN: 2150-8097.

[15] M. Zaharia, R. S. Xin, P. Wendell, T. Das, M. Armbrust, A. Dave, X. Meng, J. Rosen, S. Venkataraman, M. J. Franklin, A. Ghodsi, J. Gonzalez, S. Shenker, and I. Stoica, "Apache spark: A unified engine for big data processing," Communications of the ACM, vol. 59, no. 11, Oct. 2016, pp. 56–65, ISSN: 0001-0782.

[16] E. Evans, Domain-Driven Design. Addison-Wesley, 2004, ISBN: 978-0-32-112521-7.

[17] D. Chappell, Enterprise Service Bus. O'Reilly Media, 2009, ISBN: 978-0-59-600675-4.

[18] Apache Kafka. [Online]. Available: https://kafka.apache.org/ [retrieved: Mar., 2018]

[19] F. Junqueira and B. Reed, ZooKeeper: distributed process coordination. O'Reilly Media, 2013, ISBN: 978-1-44-936130-3.

[20] Confluent Platform Docker Images. [Online]. Available: https://github.com/confluentinc/cp-docker-images [retrieved: Mar., 2018]

[21] J. Rybicki. GitHub repository with the source code for measurements use case. [Online]. Available: https://github.com/httpPrincess/measurements2kafka [retrieved: Mar., 2018]

[22] EUDAT B2SHARE. [Online]. Available: https://b2share.eudat.eu/ [retrieved: Mar., 2018]

[23] W. Gentzsch, D. Lecarpentier, and P. Wittenburg, "Big data in science and the EUDAT project," in Proceedings of the Service Research and Innovation Institute Global Conference, Apr. 2014, pp. 191–194, ISBN: 978-1-47-995193-2, ISSN: 2166-0786.

[24] Invenio. [Online]. Available: http://invenio-software.org/ [retrieved: Mar., 2018]

[25] J. Rybicki. GitHub repository with the source code for replication use case. [Online]. Available: https://github.com/httpPrincess/b2kafka [retrieved: Mar., 2018]

A Big Data Quality Preprocessing and Domain Analysis Provisioner Framework using Cloud Infrastructures

Dirk Hölscher*, Timo Bayer*, Philipp Ruf*, Christoph Reich* and Frank Gut†
*Institute for Cloud Computing and IT Security, Furtwangen University of Applied Science, 78120 Furtwangen, Germany
Email: {dirk.hoelscher, timo.bayer, philipp.ruf, christoph.reich}@hs-furtwangen.de
† Daimler AG, 70565 Vaihingen, Germany
Email: frank.gut@daimler.com

Abstract—**Big data is a new economic driver for many advanced technology domains, such as autonomous driving, reusable rockets or cancer research. Generating knowledge from large amounts of data in such domains, will become increasingly important. Management and processing is done in powerful big data infrastructures located in the cloud. Diversifying requirements for the different big data domains require new uniform and adaptable architectural patterns that can be implemented and changed without much effort. This paper introduces a generic domain independent cloud big data framework, focussing on simplifying data preprocessing tasks and the deployment of data analysis environments by using adaptable and easy to configure domain specific components.**

Keywords–Domain Analysis Provisioner; Big Data Frameworks; Reusable Architectural Patterns; Cloud Computing

I. INTRODUCTION

Requirements for big data infrastructures strongly differ depending on the domain and individual/statutory provisions. As rapidly as data volumes change, business objectives will change based on newly discovered knowledge. The fast-growing need for integrating new data to analyze an increasing amount of data in new analysis domains and for provisioning new analysis methods/approaches for big data analysis requires fast and simple adjustable big data infrastructures that easily cope with changing requirements.

Limiting the administrative effort by using reusable components based on common and interchangeable technologies would also enable small and middle-class businesses to do big data analysis. Due to the continuously increasing data volumes more and more resources are needed for fast and reliable analysis task execution. Relocating traditional big data infrastructures into the cloud using virtualized environments, benefiting from the cloud's essential characteristics (resource pooling or rapid elasticity) will help reduce costs, by providing less complex and reusable frameworks. Big Data infrastructures can be operated as a private cloud (self-hosted service) or in a multi-tenant public cloud environment, depending on company's preferences and guidelines. Encouraging businesses of all sizes to use and analyse their data, non-abstract and easy adaptable infrastructure patterns are needed.

The main contribution of this paper introduces a generic data analysis framework, which can be adapted to fulfil different domain and data analyst's requirements. The to be introduced infrastructure consists of two main components, the preprocessing framework and the domain analysis provisioner framework. The preprocessing framework is responsible for transferring, storing, persisting and processing data provided by various data sources, whereas the domain analysis provisioner framework provides Platform-as-a-Service(PaaS) environments providing necessary analytical tools.

The paper is organised as follows: In Section II, related work will be presented. Section III describes components and functionality of the preprocessing framework. In section IV, the domain analysis provisioner framework, providing machine-learning and analytic environments is described. The next section elaborates important characteristics of the proposed framework followed by section VI, which summarizes and concludes the paper.

II. RELATED WORK AND STATE OF THE ART

In the following subsections, we present related work about big data architectural patterns and broker-based systems.

A. Architecture Patterns

In the field of big data architectures, there are several best practice design patterns that can be used.

The goal of the *Lambda* architecture pattern (Marz and Warren [1]), is to redefine classic data computation using modern big data technologies, while focusing on high scalability, realtime and immutability data processing. While scalability and realtime capabilities are achieved by using modern big data technology, achieving immutability requires a particular design. They described an architecture, in which input data is computed twice using batch processing as well as stream processing while the corresponding results are stored separately. This approach enables to recompute the processing results in the case of possible malfunctions. The disadvantages of this design pattern are (i) the necessity to develop and maintain redundant program logic within the two processing models and (ii) the resulting storage overhead.

To address these problems another design pattern, called *Kappa* architecture, was introduced by Kreps in [2]. The *Kappa* architecture focuses on the capability to recompute the processing results in case of possible malfunctions but eliminates the necessity to manage redundant program logic. To achieve this, the *Kappa* architecture utilizes the messaging system *Apache Kafka* to integrate data streams into the processing engine. Due to the capability of *Apache Kafka* to persist messages for a given time period, it is possible to recompute the data streams in case malfunctions were detected. The infrastructure mentioned in this paper is strongly based on the principles of these two architectural patterns.

The National Institute of Standards and Technology (NIST) defined a general reference architecture for big data applications. As described in [3], the proposed architecture comprises the five functional components *System Orchestrator, Data Provider, Big Data Application Provider, Big Data Framework Provider* and *Data Consumer*, which describe common functionalities big data applications should have. Based on the NIST's big data Reference architecture, we built a generic framework utilizing the components defined by NIST.

Rahmen et al. describe in [4] a platform to process and analyze healthcare information. The platform mainly relays on predefined functionalities and hides technology-specific implementations. The work introduces centralized approaches to manage the platform and deploy customized applications. Our platform, considers several of the introduced approaches while trying to fill the gap of domain-independent platforms. The purpose of the Cask Data App Platform [5], is to speed up the development of data analysis tasks. Therefore, several layers of abstraction are provided, such as an easy to use API and container based runtime environments to run and deploy analysis tasks. They provide graphical interfaces to quickly create ad hoc analysis tasks. Due to the limitations, of their imperative approach, we introduce a declarative solution to achieve maximum flexibility for analysis tasks.

B. Broker Systems

There is a wide variety of cloud based broker systems supporting the intermediation and aggregation of services offered by heterogeneous Cloud Service Providers (CSP) containing potential complex mechanisms related to any subdomain. A cloud broker is the basis of our domain analysis provisioner framework.

Roy et. al. show a Quality of Service (QoS) enhanced virtual resource broker [6] that allow different CSPs to register their resources at the broker by declaring, e.g. non-functional properties of their services. A broker client may request a virtual resource with a certain amount of assured quality by utilising the systems inter-CSP manager. The work on hand delimits itself from the QoS brokerage and the dedicated cost- and billing system, but focusses on the request analyzer as well as on the resource allocation manager.

Another economic driven cloud service facilitator was presented by Kim et. al. in [7]. The Virtual Machine (VM) reservation based cloud service broker considers the executed applications inside the leased resources, which overlaps with the scope of the work on hand. As workload increases, the *VM reservation module* starts to conduct demand prediction and reservation planning for new resources.

In order to develop efficient scheduling strategies of jobs in federated cloud environments, Pacini et. al. suggested an Ant Colony Optimization (ACO)-based approach, implemented as a three-layered broker in [8]. An underlying layer of the broker calculates the most suitable datacenter for a particular job, depending on the results of a parameter sweep experiment (e.g., simulations with repeatedly changing input parameters).

III. A Reusable Big Data Infrastructure for Processing Massive Datasets

The interpretation of massive datasets called big data analysis offers a promising potential for various industries and research fields. Due to the characteristic properties of these datasets (see [9]) as their volume, variability, and velocity, the development of such an application poses a particular challenge. In order to reduce the emerging development costs for adapting the data analysis task caused by different analysis domains, it is important to identify general-purpose concepts. In the following section, we introduce a configurable, expandable and reusable big data infrastructure to address these problems.

A. Framework Requirements

The main objective of the described framework is to abstract universally valid concepts, such as collecting and provisioning input data and orchestrating them in an architectural pattern, which is easily adaptable for domain-specific use cases. To address these challenges, we defined modular layers, which can be easily applied individually or combined to build up larger data analysis tasks. As depicted in Figure 1 these layers consist of various parts that can be divided into infrastructural system and domain-specific components. The infrastructure components are designed and implemented according to common big data application functionalities (see [10]). To tackle the big variety of scenarios the approach is focusing on domain-specific components. The functionality of these components depends on the provided data structures, data sources, and required processing tasks. Therefore, the framework comprises generic implementations to abstract the usage of technologies, as well as providing easy to use and flexible interfaces including communication functionalities for the combined infrastructure. Besides the identification and concatenation of suitable technologies and universally valid functionalities, another aspect comprises the definition of consistent interfaces and the logical separation of application components from collecting raw data until their final usage. The following subsections describe the responsibilities of the defined layers and the involved components.

B. Information Layer

Selecting and integrating relevant data sources for data collection is the foundation of every big data application. Large amounts of data sources, such as smart devices, wearables or sensors in manufacturing facilities, result in the necessity to involve multiple data sources and correlate the gathered data. Therefore, the *Information Layer* can be considered as a logical representation of various data sources.

C. Messaging and Distribution Layer

The main goal of the *Messaging and Distribution Layer* (see Figure 1) is to integrate the data sources and provide generated data to the succeeding infrastructure components. A domain-specific *Connector* has to be extended with specific collection functionalities to integrate data sources. For example, this may be used to establish a connection to a remote data store, understand the dataset format and much more. Depending on the application the data sources can vary from static datasets to realtime data collected by sensors.

Integrating Static Datasets: While dealing with batch data the connector will initially store new data within the *FileCache*. The *FileCache* is realized as a distributed Network File System (NFS) using the Parallel NFS (pNFS) standard providing fast and scalable functionality to store data within the infrastructure for further distribution. After uploading the data into the *FileCache* the *StorageConnector* is informed about the occurrence of new data. The responsibility of this component comprises uploading data from *FileCache* to a distributed storage engine

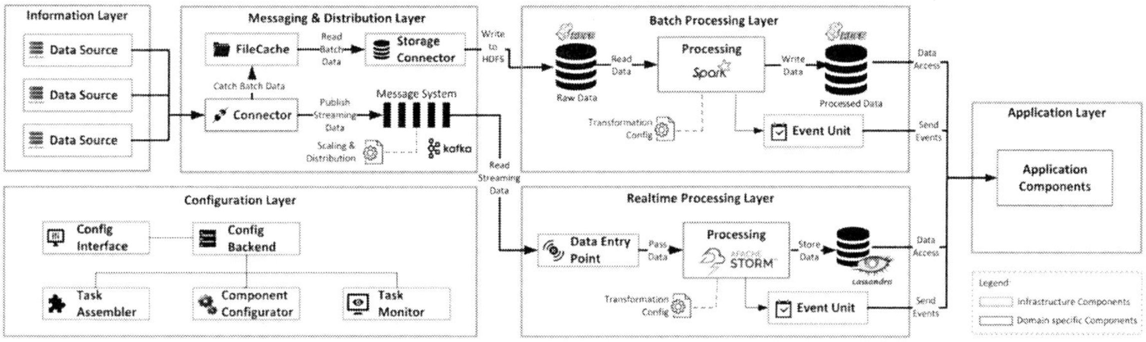

Figure 1. Architecture of the big data preprocessing framework

realized as a Hadoop Distributed File System (HDFS) cluster. Depending on the size of data, uploading to a HDFS cluster can be very time consuming, due to the necessity of splitting data into several blocks, which will be replicated and distributed in the storage cluster. In order to be able to manage massive datasets in a timely manner, this functionality can be highly parallelized using multiple instances of the *StorageConnector*. Using the *Messaging and Distribution Layer*, processing this kind of data only requires the definition of how to read data within the *Connector*. To speed up the development of such a component a base class was implemented providing functionalities for the *FileCache* and data persistence.

Integrating Realtime Data: Dealing with streaming data requires a different behaviour from the *Messaging and Distribution Layer*. In this case, the *Connector* has to continuously read small datasets and distribute it to the succeeding infrastructure components. The base class for implementing a *Connector* provides the functionality to distribute data within the infrastructure. To ensure a scalable and reliable data distribution the messaging system *Apache Kafka* has been chosen. Therefore, the base class acts as a *Producer* and provides the functionality to publish new data to multiple broker instances, which subsequently can be processed in the *Realtime Processing Layer*.

D. Batch Processing Layer

While the *Messaging and Distribution Layer* can be used independently, most big data scenarios require further data investigation (e.g, quality check, improvement, etc.) by a domain-specific *Apache Spark* job. Using *Apache Spark* for this kind of processing benefits from high scalability, fault tolerance and in-memory processing capabilities, which are required for processing large data sets efficiently. Implementing such a task strongly depends on the provided data structures and therefore, predefining general valid functionalities is impossible. Therefore, our approach focuses on integrating the preprocessing tasks within the infrastructure. Our approach provides base implementations for storage engine connections and for the integration of result postprocessing. The results of such a task can be divided into two categories: a) Generating new data (e.g., aggregations or enhanced data records). To store and provide the results for further usage, the base implementation allows to store new data into the HDFS cluster. b) Storing data tags that can be found looking for specific data patterns through data correlation. The *EventUnit* can be used within processing jobs to inform succeeding components about new results (data tags) or to directly exchange the achieved results. The *EventUnit* uses the messaging system *Apache Kafka* to enable a nearly linear scalability and can be configured as a *Producer* or a *Consumer*.

E. Realtime Processing Layer

The realtime layer enables the processing of streamed data individually or by combining it with layer described in previous sections to cover more complex processing scenarios (e.g., creating a *Lambda* architecture). The collected data for the *Realtime Processing Layer* is provided by the messaging system *Apache Kafka* and integrated by the *DataEntryPoint* component. This component acts as a *Apache Kafka Consumer* and can be configured for the given data structures. The processing task can be developed by implementing a domain specific *Apache Strom Topology* with nearly linear scalability, fault tolerance and realtime capabilities, representing important requirements in realtime scenarios. Furthermore, a general-purpose data quality module, validating input data against user configured thresholds for missing values, outliers or min/max values was implemented. Data composition is described using *XSD* schemes defining data structures and constraints for a given dataset. Processing realtime data mainly relies on the discovery of patterns within a given time frame, to generate more significant events for further operations. Furthermore, it is possible to use the previously described *EventUnit* to inform succeeding components about the occurrence of such events. If the processing task involves data manipulation it is possible to store the results within an *Apache Cassandra* cluster.

F. Application Layer

Depending on the given use case, there is a wide range of possible tasks to perform after processing the input data, like building models using machine learning technologies. To tackle the high variability of analysis tasks the *Application Layer* contains domain-specific components, which will access and utilize interfaces provided by the underlying layers. The *EventUnit* abstracts the direct data access to the corresponding storage engine.

G. Configuration Layer

The *Configuration Layer* contains all necessary components to provide centralized infrastructure management, enabling the implementation of different analysis tasks. One important responsibility of this layer includes a centralized and automated deployment of domain-specific components. To automate the distribution of components and their correct configuration, *DeploymentPackages* are introduced, containing the executables and specific configuration files representing the component's type (e.g., *Connector*, *Application* or *Processing* Component) and their expected parameters.

While the component type defines how the corresponding executables will be distributed and executed within the cluster, parameters can be used to execute multiple instances of the same processing task individually. Starting a processing task relies on an uploaded *DeploymentPackage* using a web interface (see Figure 2). After the *DeploymentPackage* is uploaded,

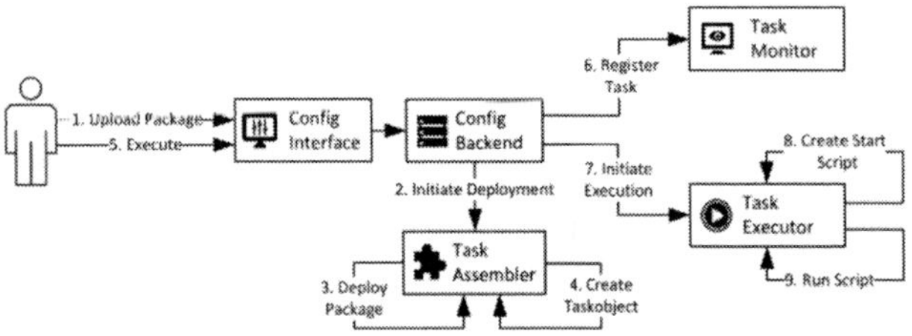

Figure 2. Process to Execute a Processing Task

the involved components are deployed to their assigned nodes by the *Task Assembler* component. Furthermore, this component creates a *Task object*, which is applied to orchestrate the domain-specific components and manage their execution. The *Task object* is also used to dynamically create a form within the user interface to execute a parameterized instance of the processing task. After a configured processing object was established, the *Task Executer* creates and executes a start script, connecting to the corresponding nodes and executing the involved components, while mapping the specified parameters. For the possibility to receive notifications and manage the running components, the *Task object* has to be registered by the *Task Monitor*. The *Configuration Layer* also provides functionalities to dynamically scale the cluster by adding exclusive nodes for each processing task.

IV. A GENERIC PROVISIONER ARCHITECTURE FOR SCHEDULING DATA ANALYSIS ENVIRONMENTS

Using Cloud Management System (CMS) or hypervisor technologies, predefined cloud images enable different isolated processing platforms to be used by a data analyst. Instantiating these non-universal VMs requires an initial configuration with the to be processed data source. These instances implement the proper data processing tasks, using adjusted software, system packages on top of an underlying operating system. A domain analysis provisioner framework using a web dashboard is proposed that accumulates different cloud images with their corresponding data sources and establishes a self-service for users to deploy a personalized data analysis environment.

The raw data of any data source always contains meta data, which has to be translated into meaningful attributes to enable the users to identify and select the desired dataset. Executing an action on these datasets results in a VM containing the required data source and a pre-configuration of analysis or processing tools. Once a validation of data accessibility from the instances point of view is confirmed, the processing tool is executed automatically. Additionally, this proposed configuration enhances usability as well as the convenience level.

A. Architecture Overview

As depicted in Figure 3, the domain analysis provisioner framework architecture consists of multiple dynamic modules, which are partially generated by model driven software development. To separate these structures, the provisioning engineer divides involved subsystems into different domain scopes. The domain analysis provisioner framework scope contains modules regarding the definition of tasks and must adjust itself to the referenced data source. A platform image is always linked to a data source and is responsible for executing the intentions of the domain analysis provisioner framework's scope. Resource provisioning is the central execution of processing platforms and rests upon CMS interaction. Each component may be implemented in a specialized way, maximizing domain specific requirements realization. A *User Interface* displays all data sources and possible actions on different scopes while taking care of accountability requirements. Main focus of the *Task Definition Module* is the connection to the incoming data source technology, using a representation of emerging meta data. A defined task can consist of multiple data sources, requiring a separate connector implementing a `connectToData`, as well as a `getData` function. Using these functions as alternative views of remote data sources supports the engineer of such a system in case metadata is altered frequently. The *Task Management Module* defines basic mechanisms for instantiating and configuring platform images with data sources. For example, *OpenStack* and Amazons Elastic Compute Cloud (EC2) both provides a *user_data* parameter for popular custom commands and system calls executed at instantiation time of an image [11] [12]. With the definition of startup templates, realizing individual and task specific platform preparation is programmatically extended by dynamic metadata of the to be analyzed content. A processing platform is defined by the *Platform Image Definition Module* and must be registered with a CMS. Depending on the deployed software ecosystem and its configuration capabilities, the proper dynamic initiation script provided by the *Platform Instantiation & Configuration* module containing values defined by the metadata representation structure is deployed. Assigning a data source is done by manipulating different configuration files inside the VM. Since the CMS is able to push commands directly to the instances, every other method of registering or gathering data for processing is conceivable. The image ID resulting from the registration process with a CMS is the provisioner's reference for creating platforms inside the virtualized infrastructure. Once a platform is instantiated, the VMs static metadata is persisted inside an internal data store for further usage by the dashboard to visualize processing jobs, as well as manipulations by the *Cloud Resource Management* module. For example, a program executed inside the cloud image produces a log file, whose content may be interpreted by a status server, which returns feedback to the dashboard via REpresentational State Transfer (REST) paths. Thereby, the VMs assigned IP address is consulted from the provisioner's internal data store, requesting its current state at a predefined port and path to display it inside the user interface.

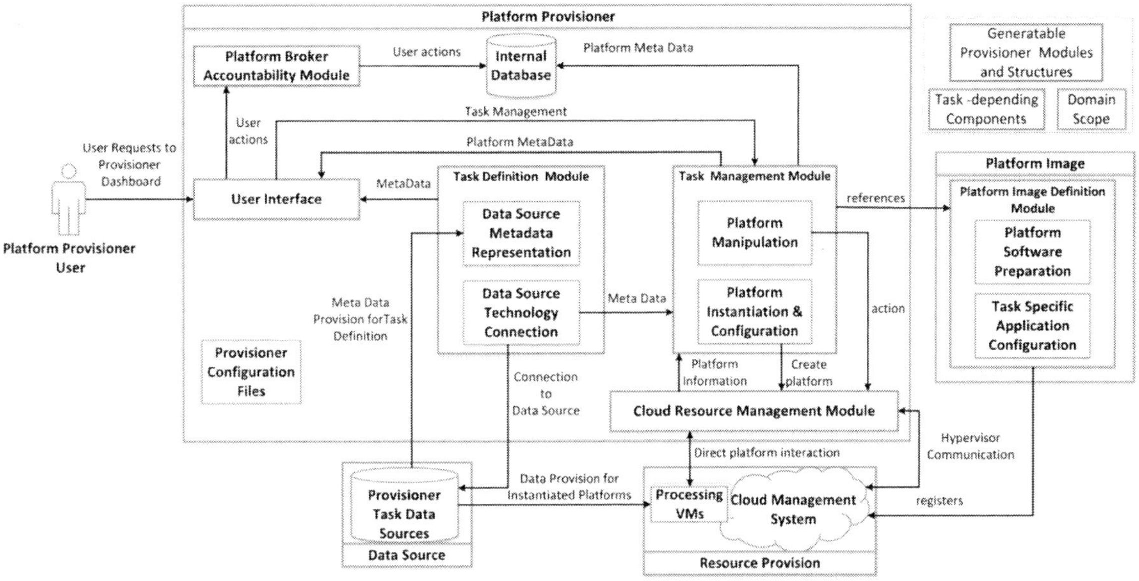

Figure 3. Modules of the generic domain analysis provisioner framework

B. Language independent module implementation

For a programming language independent implementation of the modules mentioned before, the Apache Thrift technology has been used. The definition of the modules, common data structures and provided interfaces is achieved using different Thrift Interface Definition Language (IDL) files that are used to compile it to a language specific implementation. The VMs status server may also be implemented as a Thrift service for transparent function calls using similar procedures as REST. Requirements, such as scalability, versioning or physical distribution of a provisioner are viable using Apache Thrift despite the given complexity of the technology when comparing it to language specific distribution technologies, like *OSGi* or native Remote Procedure Call (RPC).

C. Provisioner module generation

The previously described relations are rich in complexity and dependencies of modules among themselves. With the implementation of a specific application, based on the architecture shown in Figure 3, there are multiple interfaces and data connectors to define, impacting the cumulative provisioner procedure. With respect to the potential intertwined heterogeneous technologies of each sub-module, the necessary domain knowledge further increases the applications complexity. Therefore, a context-free grammar was engineered, enabling the declaration of these coherences as abstract syntax. A model to code transformation enables the translation of a universal domain analysis provisioner framework application model into technology specific skeletons. The creation of structures containing basic logic related to a specific technology supports the efficiency in provisioner task development. Using the *XText* environment, a *Platform*-Domain Specific Language (DSL) was developed, abstracting the architecture's main features and providing input for the code generator. The resulting structures must be enriched with individual module logic.

The *XTend* framework enables parsing previously generated grammar, as well as the utilization of code creation using templates. Implementing a custom template of the DSL, there are no restrictions for web frameworks or technologies respectively. Executing the required shell scripts, source code and technology dependent components the consequent results are placed in a central Dashboard folder. In case of Thrift usage there will be separate IDL files for each action and connector. Due to the freedom of choice regarding programming languages, a pre-filled skeleton for the service implementation containing common logic makes is not feasible. All client-side service calls are formulated inside the user interface structures and a script for creating proper cloud images is prepared. Path definition for processing applications on the local machine, as well as additional software packages, enables the creation of customized platforms.

V. Framework Evaluation

As elaborated in section I the main challenges for a big data analysis frameworks are reusability, scalability, extensibility and maintainability. These important characteristics are presented in the following section.

Reusability: Relies on the separation between general base framework and domain-specific functionalities. Developing and implementing the framework was done focusing on predefined functionalities while providing an intuitive way to integrate domain-specific components. With this approach and the use of common technologies to transfer, process and store large datasets, the framework is able to reduce the required developing time for a new processing task significantly.

Scalability: Processing large or high frequent datasets in a timely manner, requires high scalability. This is achieved by (i) using technologies, which are able to parallelize processing tasks over a large set of individual nodes and (ii) combining the involved components logically to create independent modules, which can be scaled according to the individual load of a processing task. Therefore, the framework is scalable by using multiple modules of the same type or by executing multiple instances of specific components within a module.

Extensibility: Another important aspect of a generic framework is to provide a broad extensibility to include additional functionality or to integrate new technologies.Extensibility is needed to integrate additional functionalities or technologies to face the strongly changing requirements of modern Data applications. The framework has been designed carefully with the focus on defining generic interfaces between the layers and technologies. Therefore, replacing existing components, technologies or complete layers without effecting the remaining parts is possible.

Maintainability: Highly scalable big data frameworks require good component management to reduce the effort and costs.To mitigate this problem a centralized management interface that provides uniform functionalities to configure the nodes, technologies and processing tasks was introduced. For example, this includes adding new nodes, stopping processing tasks or centralized logging for debugging purposes.

Technology Usage for Provisioning: The different parts of the proposed domain analysis provisioner architecture can be implemented in nearly every suitable technology. A template for the provisioner core modules was implemented as a python based Django application. The creation of platform images is realized using *virt-builder*, resulting in *qcow2* images for further registration with different CMS environments. Alternatively, a snapshot of an existing and with the required software assembled VM can be used as platform image. This procedure results in an increased disk allocation and possibly additional network latency for deployment, which can be avoided using *CEPH*. Applying this distributed storage technology, a newly created snapshot only requires the difference between its current size and the size of a previously taken snapshot. Furthermore, this Copy On Write (COW) mechanism increases the speed of a VMs instantiation procedure [13]. The *Cloud Resource Management Module* is adjusted for this CMS. To demonstrate a language independent and distributed setup, all actions and connector modules are implemented as Thrift services. This way, the user interface consolidates the different remote procedures as central contact points, allowing changeability of connectors and action implementations at runtime. The extension of an already active domain analysis provisioner framework with additional tasks may depend on the chosen technology like Django.

VI. Conclusion and Future Work

In this paper we introduced a reusable cloud-based big data framework. The defined preprocessing framework handles communication and transfer of data by providing domain independent and easy adaptable interfaces. This underlying structure stores and processes data. With the help of the configuration layer new analysis tasks for incoming data can be created. Using the application layer, machine-learning tools or other applications can be used in standalone mode or the domain analysis provisioner framework can be deployed inside this layer. The introduced domain analysis provisioner framework provides dynamic modules generated by model-driven software development. The platform gives a ready-to-go definition for platform and resource management while providing interfaces to cloud systems. The domain analysis provisioner framework enables the platform engineer to define a domain specific platform by creating an analysis environment with all required tools and direct access to the stored and preprocessed datasets.

As a next step, we will define data quality properties for the data collection process and implement a domain specific data validation chain using rules and neural-networks to determine the quality of collected datasets in critical environments. Benchmarking and improving scalability and security of the proposed platform, as well as developing machine-learning modules to simplify configuration for preprocessing, are another aspect that will be implemented in the future.

Acknowledgement

This work has received funding from INTERREG Upper Rhine (European Regional Development Fund) and the Ministries for Research of Baden-Wuerttemberg, Rheinland-Pfalz and from the Region Grand Est in the framework of the Science Offensive Upper Rhine.

References

[1] N. Marz and J. Warren, Big Data: Entwicklung und Programmierung von Systemen für große Datenmengen und Einsatz der Lambda-Architektur, ser. mitp Professional. MITP Verlags GmbH, 2016.

[2] D. Namiot and M. Sneps-Sneppe, "On internet of things programming models," in Distributed Computer and Communication Networks: 19th International Conference, DCCN 2016, Moscow, Russia, November 21-25, 2016, Revised Selected Papers. Springer International Publishing, 2016, pp. 13–24.

[3] "NIST special publication 1500-6 nist big data interoperability framework: Volume 6, reference architecture," January 2018. [Online]. Available: http://nvlpubs.nist.gov/nistpubs/SpecialPublications/NIST.SP.1500-6.pdf

[4] F. Rahman, M. Slepian, and A. Mitra, "A novel big-data processing framwork for healthcare applications: Big-data-healthcare-in-a-box," in 2016 IEEE International Conference on Big Data (Big Data), Dec 2016, pp. 3548–3555.

[5] "Cask Data Application Platform (CDAP)," September 2014, [Online] http://customers.cask.co/rs/882-OYR-915/images/CDAP_101.pdf [retrieved: 03-2018].

[6] D. G. Roy, D. De, M. M. Alam, and S. Chattopadhyay, "Multi-cloud scenario based qos enhancing virtual resource brokering," in 2016 3rd International Conference on Recent Advances in Information Technology (RAIT), March 2016, pp. 576–581.

[7] H. Kim, Y. Ha, Y. Kim, K.-N. Joo, and C.-H. Youn, "A vm reservation-based cloud service broker and its performance evaluation." in CloudComp, ser. Lecture Notes of the Institute for Computer Sciences, Social Informatics and Telecommunications Engineering, V. C. M. Leung, R. X. Lai, M. Chen, and J. Wan, Eds., vol. 142. Springer, 2014, pp. 43–52, [Online] http://dblp.uni-trier.de/db/conf/cloudcomp/cloudcomp2014.html [retrieved: 03-2018].

[8] E. Pacini, C. Mateos, and C. G. Garino, "Broker scheduler based on aco for federated cloud-based scientific experiments," in 2016 IEEE Biennial Congress of Argentina (ARGENCON), June 2016, pp. 1–7.

[9] "Cloud security alliance (CSA) big data taxonomy," September 2014, [Online] https://cloudsecurityalliance.org/research/big-data/ [retrieved: 03-2018].

[10] "Nist special publication 1500-3 nist big data interoperability framework: Volume 3, use cases and general requiements," January 2018. [Online]. Available: http://nvlpubs.nist.gov/nistpubs/SpecialPublications/NIST.SP.1500-6.pdf

[11] O. Khedher, Mastering OpenStack. Packt Publishing, 2015, ISBN: 9781784395643.

[12] "Amazon EC2 User Guide," 2017, [Online] http://docs.aws.amazon.com/AWSEC2/latest/UserGuide/user-data.html/ [accessed: 2018-03-16].

[13] W. Kong and Y. Luo, "Multi-level image software assembly technology based on openstack and ceph," in 2016 IEEE Information Technology, Networking, Electronic and Automation Control Conference, May 2016, pp. 307–310.

PKGAWAS: A Knowledge Services and Allergy Early Warning System of Pollinosis Based on Cross-Border Data Integration

Xiaolei Xiu, Sizhu Wu, Jiawei Cui, Xiaokang Sun, Qing Qian*
Institute of Medical Information
Chinese Academy of Medical Sciences & Peking Union Medical College
Beijing, China
e-mail: xiu_xiaolei@163.com; wu.sizhu@imicams.ac.cn; cui.jiawei@imicams.ac.cn; sun.xiaokang@imicams.ac.cn; qian.qing@imicams.ac.cn

Abstract— **In order to meet China's growing demand for knowledge services and allergy early warning of pollinosis, the paper initially explores and develops a system, called "Pollinosis Knowledge Graph and Allergy Warning Analysis System" (PKGAWAS). The system's data comes mainly from professional websites, Chinese Wikipedia and texts, which cover four fields: medicine, agriculture, forestry, and geography. In order to effectively implement multi-source data integration, this paper first uses machine and manual methods to collect data from literature, books, and websites. Then, we store the collected data in a temporary database. After the data is normalized, we store data in different categories, and then integrate the data based on the relationships between entities. Specifically, the paper uses property graph for knowledge representation of the knowledge graph, and other data are analyzed from the three dimensions of space, time, and disease. PKGAWAS not only can provide users with a full range of knowledge services and help, but also has important physical and practical significance for promoting "Healthy China 2030".**

Keywords-PKGAWAS; open data; data integration; knowledge graph; allergy early warning.

I. INTRODUCTION

Pollen allergy first appeared in the 19th century. In 1828, Bostock published its first report on hay fever [1]. Subsequently, in 1873, Blakely proved that pollinosis was caused by pollen from grasses [2]. In the second half of the 20th century, the prevalence of allergic respiratory diseases, such as allergic asthma and allergic rhinitis increased dramatically, affecting millions of people [3]. Pollen allergy is a common disease of allergies, and the incidence rate has increased year by year, seriously affecting human health.

Pollinosis has become a veritable epidemic. It is estimated that due to the increase in urban green areas, more than 50% of the population in industrialized countries will experience hypersensitivity in the next 20 years [4], but it is difficult to cure pollinosis.

In order to effectively reduce the incidence of hay fever, we need to do a good job in prevention [5]. Airborne pollen is routinely monitored in many parts of the world, such as North America and Europe, and the first limited network has also been created for monitoring airborne allergen concentrations [6]. In contrast, the pollen allergy situation in China is grim, but there is no specialized pollinosis knowledge service and allergy early warning website. In China's 18-64 year-old population, the incidence of pollen allergy is 0.5 ~ 1%, and high-risk groups may even reach 5% [7]. However, China only conducted a nationwide survey on the distribution of airborne allergenic pollen in the 1980s. Nearly 30 years later, historical data cannot accurately analyze and predict future pollen concentrations.

But allergic diseases are now receiving the attention of the national government. On October 25, 2016, the CPC Central Committee and the State Council issued and implemented the "Health China 2030" Plan. The purpose of this plan is to promote the construction of a healthy China and improve people's health. During the same year, Beijing Smart Park Summit, Gao Wei, deputy director of the Beijing Municipal Bureau of Landscaping, announced that during the "13th Five-Year Plan" period, Beijing will launch the construction of smart garden system to provide citizens with personalized recommendation services, such as allergens Early warning and others.

In order to meet the growing demand for knowledge services and early warning of pollinosis, this paper attempts to design and develop a system, called Pollinosis Knowledge Graph and Allergy Warning Analysis System (PKGAWAS). The study uses the methods of data integration to secondary develop and utilize of Web data and texts, which span four fields of medicine, meteorology, forestry and geography. Additionally, PKGAWAS can provide users with scientific knowledge of pollen allergy, knowledge graph and allergy early warning, personalized customization services and so on. The development of PKGAWAS is of great theoretical and practical significance for the pollen allergy knowledge service and allergy early warning website construction in China.

The rest of the paper is organized as follows: Section II describes the system architecture. Section III introduces the system data management process, including data source, data collection and preparation, data integration. Section IV presents the system interface. Conclusion and the aspects for future works are provided in Section V.

II. METHODOLOGY

A. *Architecture*

As it has been mentioned in Section I, the main goal of the PKGAWAS-based on Cross-Border Data Integration is to meet the growing demand for knowledge services and allergy early warning of pollinosis. According to this demand, the system needed to fulfill the following main functional requirements:

1) Cross-border data integration: System data come from the fields of medicine, geography, agriculture and history.

2) Multidimensional correlation analysis: It aims to dig deep into the relationship between pollen concentration and space, climate, time and the impact of allergens and regional differences on hay fever.

3) Knowledge organization: Construct a disease-centered dynamic interactive knowledge graph.

4) Allergy early warning.

5) Dynamic interactive visualization.

6) Personalized custom service.

Based on the above functional requirements, the overview of the system architecture of the PKGAWAS are shown in Figure 1. The system mainly has four layers: support layer, data storage layer, functional layer, application layer.

B. System Design

In order to make the website simple and intuitive, the site link level cannot exceed three. The overall structure of the system is shown in Figure 2. PKGAWAS has a total of three layers.

- The first layer is the home page. On the front page, we can see the main functions of PKGAWAS at a glance. In addition, users can not only search for pollen, doctors, hospitals, medicines and pollen allergy related diseases, but also direct access to doctor's database, hospital database, medicine database and Pollen database.
- The second layer is the columns page. This system has five columns page, which are pollen allergy related diseases, knowledge graph, airborne allergenic pollen map, allergy early warning, and about. Pollen allergy related diseases include six diseases, such as pollinosis, allergic rhinitis, bronchial asthma. The system's knowledge graph is dynamically interactive, besides it also has intelligent statistics and related recommended functions. Airborne allergenic pollen map introduces regional, monthly and disease spectrum of pollenfrom a national and local point of view. In the allergy early warning page, PKGAWAS provides users with allergy tracker, future forecast, literature allergy prediction and other services.
- The third layer is the content page.

III. DATA MANAGEMENT

A. Data Source

The data of this study mainly comes from professional websites, Chinese Wikipedia and texts, which cover four fields: medicine, agriculture, forestry, and geography. Professional websites include Clinical Medicine Knowledge Base (CMKB) [8], Beijing Meteorological Service [9], China

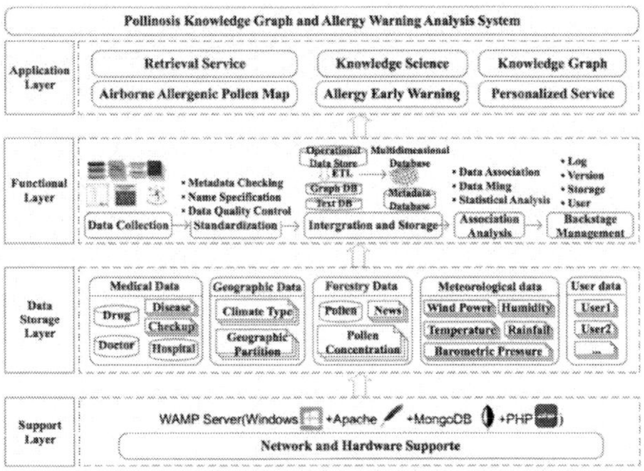

Figure 1. Overview of the system architecture

Weather Network [10], China Food and Drug Administration (CFDA)[11], and Chealth online [12] and so on. The text data refers to literature and a book entitled "Color Atlas of Air-borne Pollens and Plants in China". For literature data, we searched the literature related to pollen allergy from 2000 to 2017 from Wanfang data and the National Knowledge Base Database (CNKI). Chinese Wikipedia refers to Baidu baike and Hudong baike.

B. Data Collection and Preparation

In order to accurately and comprehensively collect data, we must first identify which data to collect and plan the representation of knowledge.

1) Preliminary: The paper adopts the property graph model to perform the knowledge representation of the knowledge graph. The system's property graph is constructed manually and then evaluated by experts. It contains two parts: nodes and relationships, such as Figure 3.

a) Node: Nodes s are the entities in the graph. They can hold any number of attributes (key-value-pairs) called properties. Nodes can be tagged with labels representing their different roles in your domain. In addition to contextualizing node and relationship properties, labels may also serve to attach metadata—index or constraint information—to certain nodes.

b) Relationship: Relationships provide directed, named, semantically relevant connections between two node-entities. A relationship always has a direction, a type, a start node, and an end node. Like nodes, relationships can also have properties [13].

The conceptual layers of the knowledge graph of this system include: diseases, complications, doctors, hospitals, drugs, medical examination methods, and drug companies. For the entities in concepts and concepts in the knowledge graph, the paper uses a top-down and bottom-up approach to construct the knowledge graph. However, the top-down approach is not constructed by building the top relational ontology, but directly by the property and entity-to-entity relationship in the property graph.

2) Data collection: Data collection refers to the process

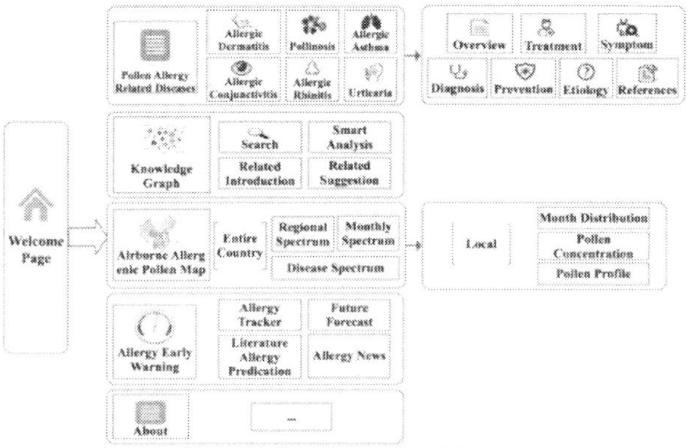

Figure 2. Overall structure of the system

of identifying, selecting, and collecting data from data sources. The data collection method of this study is mainly machine collection, and manual collection of text data is auxiliary.

c) Web Crawler: Using Web crawler technology to crawl entities, property and entity-to-entity relationships from websites, such as the CFDA, Chealth online, CMKB and Chinese Wikipedia and so on. The data obtained using Web crawling techniques is mainly medical data and geographical data.

d) Data interface: We uses the API approach to collect pollen concentration, weather information, such as temperature, humidity, barometric pressure and wind power at the Beijing Meteorological Bureau and China Weather Network.

e) Manual collection: The paper uses manual extraction to extract data from literature and books. This is because the amount of data in the literature is small, and the content required is cluttered. Manual extraction can improve accuracy. Through manual extraction, we collected pollen-related information and medical data.

C. *Data Integration*

This brief data integration process is shown in Figure 4. First, we store the collected data in a temporary database. After data cleansing, conversion, and other normalization processes, we integrate and store the data. In this study, we store data in different categories. The conceptual data and entity data used to construct knowledge graphs are stored and integrated by Neo4j graph database [13]. Then, other pieces of information are stored in a relational database.

The paper integrates the data from three aspects, such as the relationship between entities, different dimensions and application integration.

- The relationship between entities. The paper has constructed a knowledge graph that uses the relationships between entities. Knowledge graph would dynamically present and manage the data that cannot be statically stored and displayed, allowing users to search for the medical information on pollinosis and conduct data mining. There are semantic relationships between diseases, doctors,

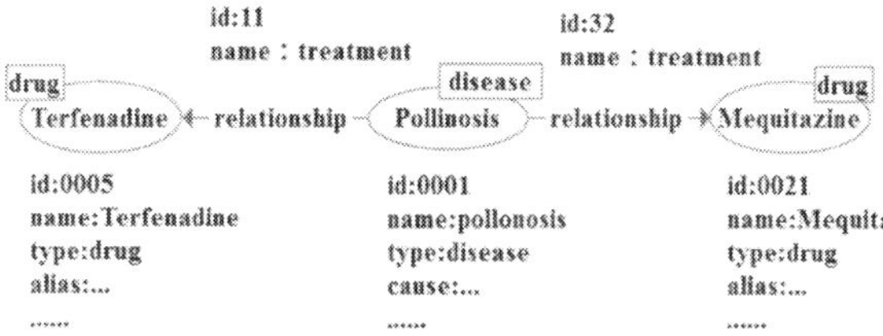

Figure 3. Data Model of Property Graph

  hospitals, medicines, checkups and pharmaceutical companies, such as "belong to", "treat", "examine". The paper first constructs a property graph for knowledge graph to quickly and accurately construct a disease-centered knowledge graph.
- Different dimensions. We analyzed factors affecting pollen concentration from different dimensions, such as space, time and disease. First, the paper conducts a statistical analysis of pollen concentration and geographic partition, climate types, months, related diseases, allergens and other data. Then, an airborne allergenic pollen map including the regional spectrum, the monthly spectrum, and the disease spectrum was constructed. In addition, we displayed in a visual form, such as a nightingale's rose diagram, a doughnut chart, map and so on.
- Application integration. In order to make every page of this system not isolated, this study integrates applications so that they are "alive" and can be associated with other Web pages.

IV. AIRBORNE POLLEN PREDICTION MODEL

There are few studies on airborne pollen prediction model. Several popular algorithm models include neural network models [14][15] and multiple regression algorithms [16][17]. Considering many factors, such as data volume, localization, and authoritativeness, this system adopts the airborne pollen prediction model announced by the Tianjin Meteorological Bureau, which is funded by the China Maritime Affairs Bureau's new technology promotion project "pollen detection and service".

This is a staged prediction model. According to the high, low and stable development trend of pollen concentration, the whole pollen period is divided into 6 stages: In the first stage, the pollen begins to peak in spring; The second stage is the peak period to the spring sub-peak; The third stage the sub-peak to June; From the middle of June to the beginning of August, it is the fourth stage; The fifth stage is from the late August to peak in autumn; after the peak period, when the pollen is over it drops to sixth stage. The multiple regression model is as follows:

$$\Psi_1 = 8565.13 - 0.33H_1 + 0.12H_2 - 0.25H_3 + 3.18T_\alpha^2 - 41.53T_\alpha + 58.77P_3 + 44.61\,T_{min10} - 25.35\,T_{max10} + 17.37V_{\alpha 10} - 8.09P_{10} \quad (1)$$

$$\Psi_2 = -397.84 + 0.14H_1 + 0.13H_2 - 0.16H_3 + 19.716V_{max} + 0.39T_{min8} - 11.29T_{max10} + 5.82T^2_{\alpha 10} - 197.62T_{\alpha 10} + 2.23P_{10} \quad (2)$$

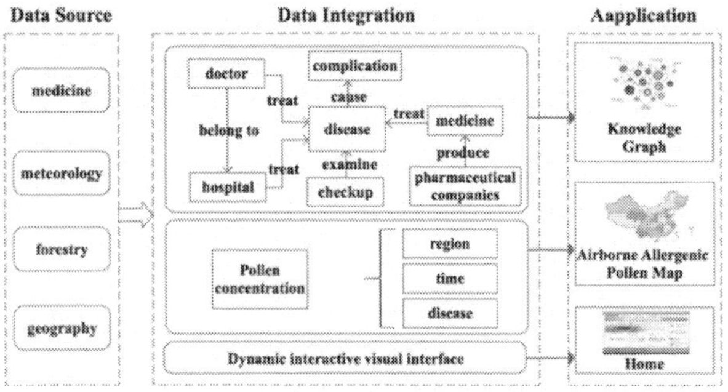

Figure 4. System Data Integration Flow Chart

$$\Psi_3 = 4181.61 - 0.01H_3 - 3.65\Pi + 2.98T_{max3} + 9.35P_8 + 2.84T^2_{min10} - 65.55T_{min10} - 7.1668T_{\alpha 10} - 14.22V_{max10} \quad (3)$$

$$\Psi_4 = -361.40 + 0.06H_2 + 1.67T_\alpha - 0.24f + 0.77T^2_{min10} - 33.72T_{min10} - 0.03T_{max10} - 0.353T_{\alpha 10} + 0.75P_{10} \quad (4)$$

$$\Psi_5 = -4231.271 - 0.337H_1 + 0.137H_2 + 0.39H_3 + 10.26V_{max} - 0.61\ T^2_{\alpha 10} + 32.98T_{\alpha 10} + 0.63P_{10} + 9.84V_{a10} + 3.7292P_{10} \quad (5)$$

$$\Psi_6 = 1183.49 - 0.14H_1 + 0.10H_3 + 0.63T^2_{\alpha 10} - 16.1851T_\alpha - 1.04P_{10} - 0.45f_{10} \quad (6)$$

where Ψ1, Ψ2, ···, Ψ6 are predicted values of pollen concentration. H represents pollen concentration. T_a is average temperature, and T_{min} represents minimum temperature. Maximum temperature is represented by T_{max}. R represents precipitation and P is average pressure. Average relative humidity is represented by f and average wind speed is represented by V_a. V_{max} represents maximum wind speed. Besides, the digital subscript indicates the number of days before the forecast, and T_{min10} indicates the average minimum temperature in the first 10 days of the forecast. If there is no data subscript, it means the next 72 h variable.

V. USE CASE

Our system is implemented and publicly accessible [18]. The home page of the website is shown in Figure 5.

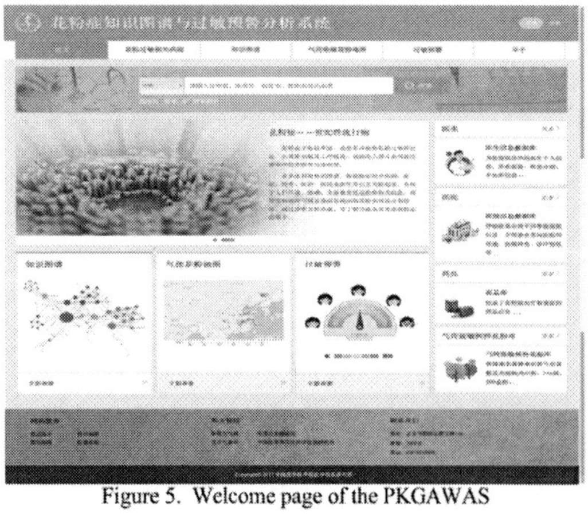

Figure 5. Welcome page of the PKGAWAS

VI. CONCLUSION

Compared with other existing websites, PKGAWAS has the following four aspects of innovation: a) multi-source cross-border data integration; b) multi-dimensional data association analysis; c) dynamic interactive knowledge graph; d) personalized custom service. However, due to the lack of pollen concentration data, there is still much work to be done in the future. First, we will use a crowdsourcing approach to collect pollen concentrations in the country. The second is to seek cooperation from the China meteorological administration to jointly carry out early warning service for pollen allergy.

ACKNOWLEDGMENT

The authors thank Chealth Online for providing medical data. The work of the authors is supported by Institute of Medical Information, Chinese Academy of Medical Sciences & Peking Union Medical College.

REFERENCES

[1] J. Bostock, "Case of a Periodical Affection of the Eyes and Chest, " Annals of Allergy, vol. 18, 1960, pp. 894.

[2] C. H. Blagkley, "Experimental researches on the causes and nature of catarrhus aestivus (hay-fever or hay-asthma)," Blackley, 1959, pp.57.

[3] G. D. Amato and L. Cecchi, "Effects of climate change on environmental factors in respira- tory allergic diseases," Clin Exp Allergy, vol. 38, 2008, pp. 1264–1274.

[4] X. D. Xiao, "Talk about flowers no longer change color," Captial Medicine, vol. 9, 2017, pp. 60–62.

[5] L. P. Dai and C. Lu, "The Pollen and Its Measurement Technique in Spring," Meteorological Monthly, vol. 12, 2000, pp. 49–52.

[6] M. Smith, U. Berger, H. Behrendt and K. C. Bergmann, "Pollen and pollinosis," Chem Immunol Allergy, vol. 100, 2014, pp. 228-233.

[7] Q. Y. Wei, "Diagnosis and Treatment of Pollinosis," Chinese Journal of Practical Internal Medicine, vol. 32, 2015, pp. 89–91.

[8] Institute of Medical Information, Chinese Academy of Medical Sciences, "Clinical Medicine Knowledge Base," 2014, http://www.cmkb.cn.

[9] Beijing Meteorological Bureau, "Beijing Meteorological Service," 2008, http://www.bjmb.gov.cn.

[10] CMA Public Meteorological Service Centre, "China Weather Network," 2008, http://www.weather.com.cn.

[11] China Food and Drug Administration, "China Food and Drug Administration," 2013, http://app1.sfda.gov.cn/datasearch/face3/dir.html.

[12] Institute of Medical Information, Chinese Academy of Medical Sciences, "Chealth", 2014, http://www.chealth.org.cn.

[13] Neo4j, "What is a Graph Database? " 2017, https://neo4j.com/developer/graph-database/.

[14] J. A. Sánchez-Mesa, C. Galan, J. A. Martínezheras and C. Hervásmartínez, "The use of a neural network to forecast daily grass pollen concentration in a Mediterranean region: the southern part of the Iberian Peninsula," Clinical & Experimental Allergy, vol. 32, 2002, pp. 1606–1612.

[15] M. Puc, "Artificial neural network model of the relationship between Betula, pollen and meteorological factors in Szczecin (Poland)," International Journal of Biometeorology, vol. 56, 2012, pp. 395-401.

[16] K. R. Kim et al., "A biology-driven receptor model for daily pollen allergy risk in Korea based on Weibull probability density function," International Journal of Biometeorology, vol. 61, 2016, pp. 1-14.

[17] Z. L. Wu, et at., "Study of Airborne Pollen Prediction Model," Meteorological Science and Technology, vol. 35, 2007, pp. 832-836.

[18] Institute of Medical Information, Chinese Academy of Medical Sciences, "Pollinosis Knowledge Graph and Allergy Warning Analysis System,"2017, http://114.255.123.93:6606/Pollen/.

A Data Clustering Approach for Automated Optical Inspection of Metal Work Pieces

Ruth Tesfaye Zibello, Stephan Trahasch, Tobias Lauer
Department of Electrical Engineering and Information Technology
Offenburg University of Applied Sciences
Offenburg, Germany
e-mail: {ruth.zibello, stephan.trahasch, tobias.lauer}@hs-offenburg.de

Abstract—**This paper describes the use of the single-linkage hierarchical clustering method in outlier detection for manufactured metal work pieces. The main goal of the study is to group defects that occur 5 mm into a work piece from the edge, i.e., the border of the metal work piece. The goal is to remove defects outside the area of interest as outliers. According to the assumptions made for the performance criteria, the single-linkage method has achieved better results compared to other agglomeration methods.**

Keywords-Hierarchical clustering; Outliers; Single-linkage method.

I. INTRODUCTION

Manufacturing processes of metals that end up in different uses involve cutting and shaping of work pieces. During this process, the machine blades that cut or bend such pieces tend to become dull over time, resulting in certain defects, such as dents, scratches, impressions and the like on the work piece.

This work addresses the problem of grouping defects around the border of a metal work piece from the manufacturing process of car body parts. Hence, the objective is to use cluster-based outlier detection in order to realize the clusters that form around the border.

The outcome could help in deciding whether the work piece can be used as is, needs to be polished (reworked) or must be tossed. Furthermore, it can help determine at which point in time the cutting or bending blade requires sharpening or replacement; which falls in the category of *predictive maintenance*.

Cluster analysis, a subfield of unsupervised learning, is used to determine homogeneous subgroups within a larger group of observations. Hierarchical clustering is the approach used to obtain clusters of defects. Variant linkage metrics were sought out during the work. The single-linkage method has turned out to yield the best results.

The remainder of this paper is structured as follows: Section II describes related work and general background. Section III describes the approach and methodology followed during the study. Section IV describes and discusses the results. Finally, in Section V, conclusions and future outlooks are discussed.

II. BACKGROUND

Outliers are observations that deviate from the remainder set of data. Outliers and their detection have been studied in different domains for a variety of applications.

A. *Related Work*

Statistical methods, supervised and unsupervised algorithms are found in literature to conduct outlier detection. These algorithms are further subdivided into *z*-score, classification-based, cluster-based, distance-based etc. to be implemented on univariate or multivariate outlier detection problems.

In [1], distance-based and cluster-based outlier detection algorithms were proposed. The goal was to improve the quality of data preprocessing and capture the underlying patterns using an outlier score for outlier reduction. Distance-based approaches fetch the top r % (percentage recall) of the data based on (dis)similarity measures. While cluster-based approach considers clusters with minimum number of objects as outliers.

The *k*-means algorithm was used for clustering data and Euclidean distance of each object from its corresponding cluster centroid was recorded. Recorded objects were sorted according to their score and those falling below a certain score were eliminated. This work concludes that cluster-based outlier detection outweighs distance-based. It was conducted on three R built-in health care datasets.

In [2], outlier detection based on hierarchical clustering method was conducted to detect erroneous foreign trade transactions in data collected by the Portuguese Institute of Statistics (INE).This work involved statistical performance evaluation according to the criteria specified by the domain experts. Variants of linkage methods presented similar results, but the distance function had major impacts in fulfilling the criteria. The Canberra distance function with a threshold of 5 resulted in performance evaluations of less than 50% of transactions containing at least 90-99 % of the errors, which was better than the desirable target.

This paper reports on an experiment on synthetically generated data that resembles manufactured metal work pieces with defects, using cluster-based outlier detection with hierarchical clustering.

B. *Hierarchical Agglomerative Clustering*

Hierarchical clustering is one type of method that creates a sequence of nested partitions, i.e., a hierarchy of homogeneous groups (clusters). The clusters are visualized in a tree-like structure named dendrogram [3] [4].

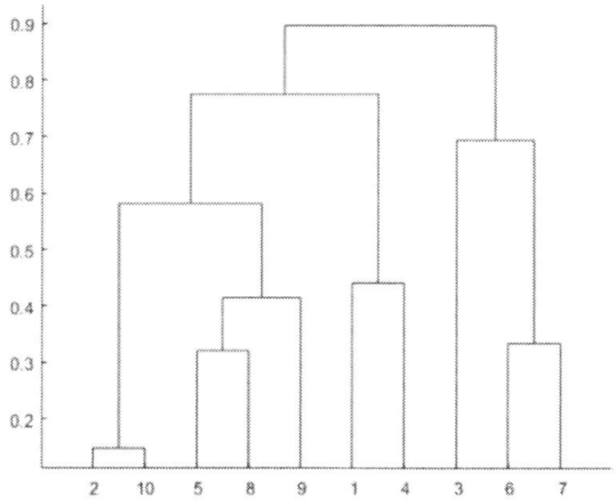

Figure 1. Example of a dendrogram.

The hierarchy ranges from the lowest level (leaf), i.e., each observation in its own cluster, to the highest level (root) consisting of all observations in one cluster. There are two approaches of applying hierarchical clustering: agglomerative and divisive.

Agglomerative clustering works in a bottom-up manner where each object is initially considered as a single-element cluster. Similar pairs of clusters are merged repeatedly until all points are grouped into one root cluster.

The counterpart approach is divisive clustering. It uses a top-down approach; starting from a root cluster and recursively splitting a heterogeneous cluster until each observation is in its own cluster.

Merging and splitting of clusters is performed based on the (dis)similarity measures. The default measure is the Euclidean distance between two observations, whereas the measure between each cluster of observations requires cluster agglomeration (linkage) methods [4].

- Complete: uses the maximum (largest) value of the dissimilarities to link clusters
- Single: opposite to complete, smallest (minimum) value is considered
- Average: as the name describes, it takes the average value of the distance
- Centroid: computes dissimilarity between the centroids of the clusters
- Ward's minimum variance: minimizes the total within cluster variance.

Figure 1 illustrates an example of a dendrogram, where the x-axis shows the observations of the data and the y-axis represents the cophenetic distance (distance between merging/splitting clusters).

Hierarchical clustering method would be more stable approach rather than partitioning clustering techniques because it is not dependent on the initialization of the clusters. The commonly used agglomeration methods are complete, average and ward's minimum variance, these tend to produce balanced trees, whereas, single and centroid tend to produce unbalanced and inversions of clusters respectively.

III. APPROACH

Data used in this work are synthetically generated images resembling a cut part of a car panel (metal work piece) with size 800 mm × 100 mm containing random defects. For this analysis, 25,000 datasets have been generated.

Records in the dataset represent defects that occur during the cutting of the work piece in the production line. Each dataset contains 5 variables and observations in thousands or minimum of hundreds.

Each dataset has the following variables and they are described as follows:

- ID: represents the *i*-th work piece image (0-24999)
- X: horizontal axis of the work piece in mm (0-799)
- Y: Vertical axis of the work piece in mm (0-99)
- D: depth of the defects in μm (micrometers)
- C: category (types) of defects as numbers (1 = dent, 2 = scratch, 3 = pinhole)

Table I shows some rows of data for a randomly chosen workpiece as an example. The variables of interest for clustering are the locations (X and Y) and depth of the defect (D). Data preparation was done by scaling the variables of interest, as they were measured in different units. The variables ID and C were removed as they had no influence in the formation of clusters.

In our approach, agglomerative clustering applying the single linkage method based on Euclidean distance was used to conduct the formation of clusters.

Clusters are identified either by cutting the hierarchy of the resulting dendrogram at a certain height or specified by a domain expert with a predetermined number.

Since each dataset had different records of defects, for the present work the goal was to make the resulting clusters be dependent on the number of observations (n).

The following formula obtained from [2] has been used for the number of clusters.

$$n_c = \max\left(2, \frac{n}{10}\right) \quad (1)$$

It influences the formation of clusters to be dependent on the number of observations within each dataset.

TABLE I: DATA SAMPLE FOR WORKPIECE 13800

ID	X	Y	D	C
13800	0	0	15	3
13800	1	0	15	1
13800	7	35	33	2
13800	40	88	9	3

As performance criteria, assumptions of the production line were made. The first 2000 work pieces will not have any defects as the blade would be new and sharp. Therefore, the first 2000 generated records of data shall just have some generated noises which represent defects with minimum depth. These defects are of no influence in creating a cluster.

In order to satisfy the assumption taken and also realize which synthetic data gave reasonable results, clustering tendency was assessed. Hopkins statistics, a statistical clustering tendency method, was used for assessing whether the data contained inherent grouping structure or random noises [4].

The result value of a Hopkins statistic is a probability which indicates whether the given data $\mathcal{D}$) has non-random or uniformly distributed structure. The following formula shows how clustering tendency using this statistical method is obtained.

$$H = \frac{\sum_{i=1}^{n} y_i}{\sum_{i=1}^{n} x_i + \sum_{i=1}^{n} y_i} \qquad (2)$$

Hopkins statistical probability (H) is the mean of the nearest neighbor distance in a simulated dataset (random $\mathcal{D}$) divided by the sum of the mean nearest neighbor distances in the real ($\mathcal{D}$) and across the simulated dataset. If the value of H > 0.5, then it is concluded that the dataset $\mathcal{D}$ has meaningful clusters [4].

As per the assumptions made for the performance criteria the first 2000 datasets had H < 0.5 and did not contain inherent groups, therefore, no clustering technique was applied to these datasets.

The remaining datasets had H > 0.5. Hence, the next step was to apply hierarchical clustering using the single linkage method based on Euclidean distance and remove outliers.

The approach used in [2] has been adapted to cluster and remove defects outside the border as outliers. The key idea was to use the size of the resulting clusters as indicators of the presence of outliers. In the case of this work, outliers would be those clusters with a number of elements less than some threshold τ.

The threshold used is a fixed number which can be replaced based on the assumptions or a domain expert user sees fit.

This method of outlier detection requires parameters to be specified. The main parameters are the number of clusters n_c and threshold τ. Table II shows the algorithm for outlier detection adapted from [1].

Once the final cluster(s) is/are obtained the further analysis is done in order to determine which cluster(s) has/have defects in the pre-classified range.

IV. RESULTS

The results shown in this section are for the example dataset described in Section 0 (TABLE).

Dataset 13800 contains data about defects present in the 13800th metal work piece manufactured. This dataset contains 1351 observations and 5 variables. The initial clustering determined by (2) ends up with 135 clusters.

TABLE II: ADAPTED ALGORITHM FOR OUTLIER DETECTION USING HIERARCHICAL CLUSTERING [1]

Input :

- Dataset (D) with n observations and k variables
- Standardize variables of interest (X,Y and D)
- Compute H (Hopkins Statistic)
- d: Euclidean distance function
- h: Hierarchical clustering (single-linkage method)
- $n_c = \max\left(2, \frac{n}{10}\right)$
- τ : Threshold = 50 (10 , 20 ….)

Output :

Out: set of outlier observations
If H < 0.5:
    Out → ϕ
If H > 0.5:
    Obtain d from scaled data
    Use algorithm h to grow hierarchy from d
    Group initial clusters with n_c
    For each resulting cluster c Do:
        IF sizeof(c) < τ THEN
        Out → Out U {obs ∈ c}

Figures 2 and 3 show the original dataset and the initial cluster for this specific dataset.

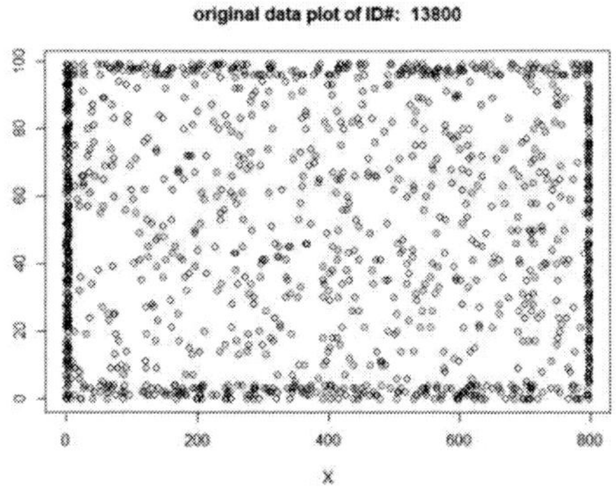

Figure 2. Original data for 13800 work piece.

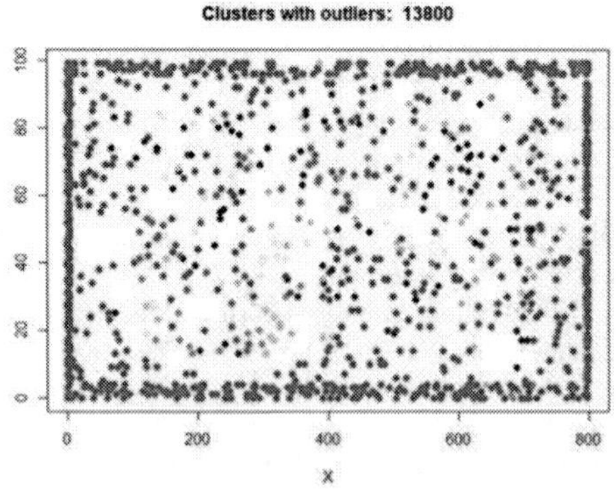

Figure 3. Initial n_c = 135 clusters for 13800 workpiece.

The threshold parameter for this work has been fixed to 50 indicating the minimum number of elements that a cluster should hold. The clusters with number of elements less than the threshold are considered as outliers and removed. The sample dataset ends up having one final cluster, as illustrated in Figure 4.

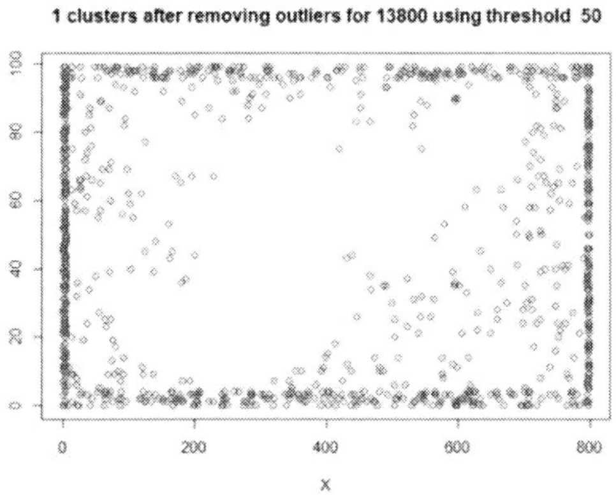

Figure 4. Final cluster for 13800 using single linkage.

Variants of agglomeration techniques were sought before deciding on the single linkage method. The results for the other agglomeration techniques did not fulfill our performance criteria, which aimed to find clusters around the border of the work piece. The other techniques either did not remove clusters, or removed clusters from around the border as a whole. The threshold used for the other agglomeration techniques is less than 50 because they produce balanced trees. The number of elements in all clusters was relatively similar. In contrast, the single linkage produced trees which are unbalanced, i.e., few clusters contained a large number of elements, whereas the rest had a small number of elements and were eliminated as outliers. Figure 5 shows the clusters resulting from different agglomeration techniques with different thresholds for sample work piece 13800.

After having the final clusters, the depth variable is classified into three ranges; 0-9 μm, 10-19 μm and ≥ 20 μm. Figure 6 shows a histogram that illustrates the number of observations in each range within a cluster. This can be helpful to determine whether or not the metal work piece could be of use.

Based on the result depicted above, it could be concluded that the 13800 metal workpiece is of no use as most of the defects have ≥ 20 μm.

It is also of particular interest to follow a series of consecutive work pieces in the production process, in order to see trends and possibly predict – and hence, avoid – machine failures. Figure 7 illustrates how the number of elements within each range of the final cluster(s) changes through time.

This information indicates the growth of defects with high depths in the production process through time which in turn could be used as an indicator when to replace or sharpen the blade in the cutting device. It can be concluded that after manufacturing about 10,000 work pieces, the blade requires sharpening or replacement.

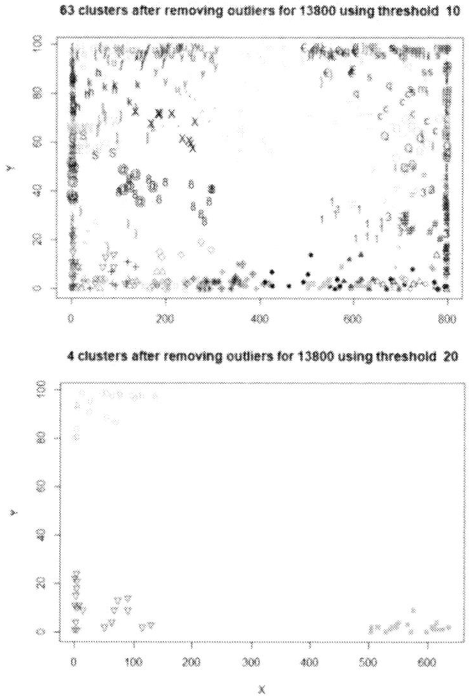

Figure 5. Sample results for 13800 workpiece with complete linkage method.

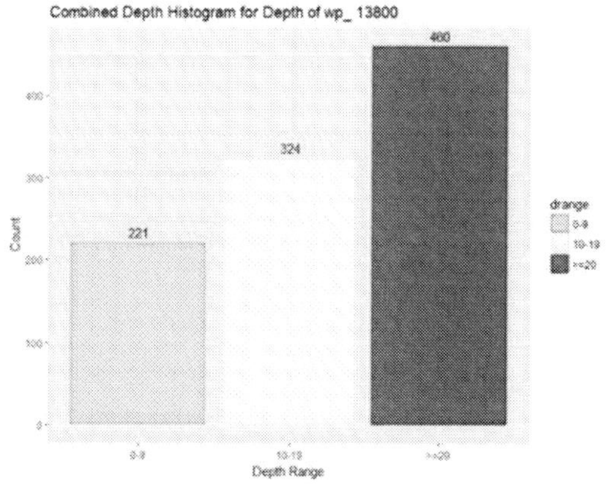

Figure 6. Combined depth histogram of all clusters in 13800.

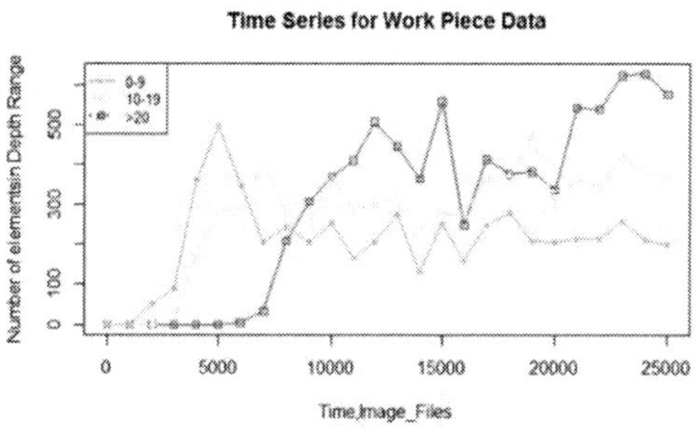

Figure 7: Depth range over time of each cluster for all datasets.

V. CONCLUSION

In this work, hierarchical clustering using the single linkage method has been used to determine clusters of defects around the border of metal work pieces. Clusters with a number of elements less than a fixed threshold are removed as outliers.

Single linkage agglomeration makes up for an ideal choice to be used in outlier identification in comparison to other agglomeration techniques because it tends to produce unbalanced trees where observations are infused one at a time.

Prior to determining clusters within each dataset, the clustering tendency of each dataset is determined.

The results of this work indicate whether the manufactured workpiece could be of use, requires some polishing or is of no use at all. The indicator is for the sharpness of the blade that cuts or bends the workpieces, in order to have less or insignificant defects.

Future outlooks for this work could be to use the obtained results in a classification problem where all datasets contain labels of good, ok and bad work pieces. Based on their labels, work pieces could be intelligently classified.

ACKNOWLEDGMENT

The authors wish to thank Peter Strohm of Jedox AG for his support and valuable input.

REFERENCES

[1] A. Christy, G. Meera Gandhi, and S. Vaithyasubramanian, "Cluster Based Outlier Detection Algorithm For Healthcare Data," *Procedia Computer Science,* no. 50, pp. 209–215, 2015.

[2] A. Loureiro, L. Torgo, and C. Soares, "Outlier Detection Using Clustering Methods: a data cleaning application," Proceedings of KDNet Symposium on Knowledge-based Systems for the Public Sector, 2004.

[3] M. J. Zaki and W. J. Meira, Data Mining and Analysis: Fundamental Concepts and Algorithms, Cambridge University Press, 2014.

[4] A. Kassambra, "STHDA: Statistical Tools For High-Throughput Data Analysis," [Online]. Available from: http://www.sthda.com/english/wiki/print.php?id=234. [retrieved: March 2018]

Optimizing Mixed Fuzzy-Rule Formation by Controlled Evolutionary Strategy

Matthias Lermer, Hendrik Kuijs, Christoph Reich
Institute for Cloud Computing and IT Security
Furtwangen University of Applied Science
Furtwangen, Germany
Email: {matthias.lermer, hendrik.kuijs, christoph.reich}@hs-furtwangen.de

***Abstract*—Machine learning algorithms are heavily applied to address many challenges in various fields. This paper specifically takes a look at use cases from the health sector, as well as the industry 4.0 sector. In both cases, the knowledge about the classification process is as important as the classification itself. One current problem is the disregard of expert knowledge provided by adept human beings. In practice, it is possible and also feasible to learn similar knowledge with machine learning algorithms like artificial neural networks (ANNs) or support vector machines (SVMs). However, time and money could be saved if this expert knowledge was used directly. Right now, this is only possible with more transparent algorithms like rule-based systems or decision trees, where knowledge can be incorporated relatively easily. The approach of this paper shows that rules generated by a mixed fuzzy-rule formation algorithm can be optimized by applying a controlled evolutionary strategy while maintaining the interpretability of the decision-making process. The evaluation is performed by executing the evolutionary strategy proposed in this paper on data from two different industries.**

Keywords–Evolutionary Strategy; Optimization; Fuzzy Logic; Decision support systems; Industry 4.0.

I. Introduction

Nowadays, there is a trend towards using deep learning algorithms, e.g., Deep Neural Networks (DNN), for almost any kind of Machine Learning problem [1]. One of the earlier disadvantages, the slow computation with those kind of algorithms, has been overcome successfully with the help of graphics cards and their optimized cores [2]. Still, one of the big remaining problems is the interpretability of the results when using black box algorithms like DNNs [3][4]. There are many recent approaches to make those results more transparent, but those are still in their infancy [5][6][7]. Other Machine Learning algorithms are more transparent, e.g. Rule-based systems or Decision trees and can provide a human understandable explanation. In practice however, this transparency often comes with the price of worse prediction results.

The approach depends on the use case or the Machine Learning problem itself. Is it more important to absolutely get the best result possible? Or can a weaker result be tolerated if explanations and knowledge about the results origins can be acquired? In case of the two different scenarios evaluated in this paper, the transparent way to the result is as important as the outcome itself.

The remainder of the paper is organized as follows: Section II provides an overview about related work. Section III describes the genetic adaptation of the Mixed Fuzzy-Rule Formation. In Sections IV and V, the evaluations based on two different Use Cases are conducted. Section VI completes the paper by drawing a conclusion and suggesting future work.

II. Related Work

Elsayed et al. [8] combine fuzzy rules and evolutionary algorithms, albeit in a different way than in our approach. In their solution, two algorithms cooperate by using fuzzy rules with complementary characteristics. This results in a higher success rate when applied on different data sets with different optimization problems. Their approach is especially interesting as it can be used to further optimize the method proposed in this paper.

Schaer et al. have shown that the adjustment of established fuzzy rules and fuzzy set functions can lead to better results [9]. Their work was evaluated within an autonomous car racing competition where they could improve the previous score by 0.5 %. The adjustments and optimizations of the fuzzy components were mainly the product of simulation experiments. In the conclusion, they are mentioning that there are plans to use genetic algorithms for the adjustments which is similar to the evolutionary strategy approach proposed in this paper.

Jariyatantiwait and Yen [10] follow the special approach of Differential Evolution (DE). They apply their modification on the ZDT (Zitzler, Deb and Thiele) and DTLZ (Deb, Thiele, Laumanns and Zitzler) test suits [11], which are used for evaluating the optimization of algorithms and map the optimization directly to fuzzy rules. Those rules adapt certain control parameters during the evolution process. Examples are the degree of greediness and exploration. They successfully show that performance metrics can be combined with human understandable knowledge in the form of fuzzy rules. The work conducted in this paper takes a similar approach, but tries to combine classification tasks themselves with fuzzy rules while control parameters like the degree of exploration are defined by hand.

Alcalá-Fdez et al. [12] show that their modification of a evolutionary fuzzy-rule based system leads to an improved performance within monotonic classification problems. In contrast to this paper, the authors used genetic algorithms and concentrated on adjusting crossover mechanisms, including customised incest prevention and restarting processes while the mutation mechanism was kept relatively simple by hardcoding the mutation rate.

The works from various other authors in this section show that evolutionary strategies within classification problems hold a high value, given the good results and the preserved interpretability by humans. This can be observed for many more use cases, e.g., financial market [13] [14], medicine [15], computer science [16], etc. and reinforce the choice to take a deeper look at the two uses cases of this paper. However, a direct comparison to other works with different use cases is very difficult to accomplish and would go beyond the scope of this paper. Furthermore, modifying different parts of the evolution process is still a heavily pursued research topic, regardless of the use case.

III. Preliminary

This work relies on the fuzzy rules generated by the mixed fuzzy-rule formation proposed by Berthold [17]. The decision to use this specific kind of fuzzy logic as a basis for genetic adaptation was based on its ability to cope with high-dimensional data sets while delivering good classification performance. Additionally, the created rules can be interpreted by humans and further expanded on using knowledge engineering. Table I shows a quick and shortened example of a rule.

TABLE I. EXAMPLE RULE

age	*operation year*	*axillary nodes*	*survival*
(24, 48, 60, 64)	(03, 06, 07, 07)	(19, 21, 35, 46)	true

The attributes age, operation year and axillary nodes are described textually in this example. Those 4 values per attribute are to be seen in the usual fuzzy partition context. Looking at the age value, this means that people ranging from 48 - 60 years are members of the complete (survival = true) set, while the rest of the people in ranges from 24-48 and 60-64 years are only partial members of the (survival = true) set. The same applies for the other attributes and the rule is only valid when logically combining all the attributes. The following configuration is used during the fuzzy rule generation with the mixed fuzzy-rule formation algorithm:

- Shrink rules after each commit to reduce conflicting rules
- Use the class with maximum coverage for training
- Min/Max fuzzy norm for the rule activation computation
- Volume Border Based shrink function after the complete rule set has been established to further reduce conflicting rules

Even with shrinking mechanisms in place, many rules are created by the algorithm. It depends on the size of the dataset and its attributes. More data usually results in more created rules when using mixed fuzzy-rule formation. In order to further minimize possible conflicts, only the two rules that represent a class with the highest weight are chosen for the Evolutionary Strategy (ES). This has mainly two reasons.

Firstly, the application of many rules to a big data set can become time consuming, which is still a practical problem. Fernandez et. al show in [18] that solutions for this challenge are still in their infancy. Practical solutions proposed by Rio et al. [19] furthermore show that, depending on the use case, there is always a speed-accuracy trade-off. The second reason is the easier comprehensibility by human experts. To have less, but more robust rules additionally aids in the process of battling over fitting. From a research point of view, this is especially interesting as one of the major problems when implementing predictive maintenance in the context of Industry 4.0 is the ability to generalize the created or extracted knowledge to subsets of machine types, like Computer numerical control (CNC) grinding machines.

A. Workflow

The following list provides a quick overview of the workflow depicted in Figure 1.

1) Split the data into Training/Validation (70%) and Test sets (30%)
2) Create a complete rule-set using the mixed fuzzy-rule formation algorithm
3) Filter the two rules with the highest weight per prediction class
4) Apply the rules to the Test Set
5) Adapt the filtered rules by mutation
6) Compare the results based on F-measure
7) Keep on mutating
8) Stop the iteration after a defined Terminal Condition for Mutation (TC M) has been met. This can take on the form of an interval, result or event
9) Save the adapted rules and results
10) Split the data into training/validation (70%) and test sets (30%) again, but in a different way than before
11) Adapt the mutated rules from the previous iteration
12) Apply the adapted rules to Test Set and save the result
13) Compare the results
14) Stop the iteration after a defined interval, result or event

The algorithm stops the current iteration and starts a new one as soon as a defined terminal condition (TC M) is satisfied. The fitness function used for comparing the results is defined as the classification F-measure, which is selected in order to consider precision, as well as recall. At first, the TC M is called when the algorithm does not improve the F-measure after a certain number of iterations, which could be rather limiting considering that mutations are based on randomness. Another factor was that the mutated rules should never mutate so much that they completely change their meaning. So, a rather low number of maximum 42 mutations per mutation iteration is allowed. When applied to the use cases described in Section V, the final terminal condition is defined as a maximum of 15 mutation iteration rounds. This definition is based on the decision to optimize the existing rules and not to create new ones. In test runs, it was evaluated that with a very high number of mutation rounds, the underlying rule could not be identified any more. To mitigate over fitting, the following two procedures are implemented. Firstly, the first training set in the first mutation round includes data which is held back and used only for validation purposes. Secondly, after each mutation iteration the dataset is split again in a different way based on the pseudo random generator provided by the python random library.

IV. Evolutionary Strategy

The adaptation process concentrates on mutating the generated rules in order to optimize those rules. This procedure pursues a slightly different approach compared to classical genetic algorithms (GAs). Evolutionary Strategy usually does not include a crossover mechanism for the population adaptation.

There are mainly two reasons to concentrate on ES. Firstly, when including crossover mechanisms, the fuzzy rules often drastically change and do not represent their original meaning any more. This stands in opposition to the focus in this paper, which is to optimize existing rules which are built upon

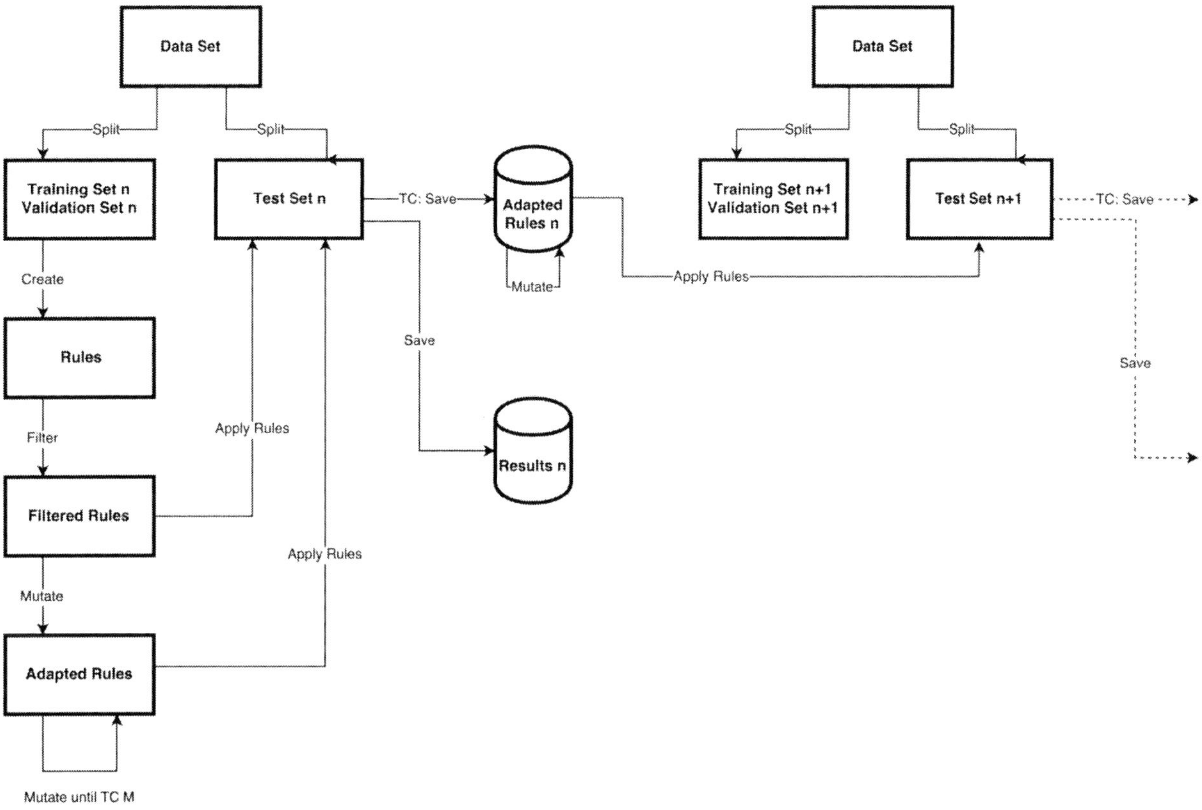

Figure 1. Workflow

specific knowledge. Secondly, when only using mutation, the algorithm can, if needed, dynamically be controlled to a high degree. The first approach was to start with a lower mutation rate (meaning values within the rules were allowed to change up to +-5%) and let the rate steadily increase. The second approach was to start with a higher mutation rate of 40 % and let it steadily decline. In practice however, the best results were achieved using a random mutation rate, confined to a change within -40 % to + 40 %. Surprisingly, this is true for both data sets described in Section V.

V. Evaluation with Use Cases

The following use cases will show the practical applicability of the proposed genetic adaptation. The decision to evaluate with the help of two different data sets is made in order to get a brief look at the generalization potential of the algorithm.

A. Evaluation 1: Health Sector

The 'Haberman's Survival Data' [20] provides information about the survival status of breast cancer patients who underwent surgery. This multivariate dataset contains 306 examples and was gathered by the Billings Hospital in Chicago. The data was provided by the Machine Learning Repository of the University of California, Irvine [21] with the following description of the attributes:

- Age of patient at time of operation (numerical)
- Patient's year of operation (numerical)
- Number of positive axillary nodes detected (numerical)
- Survival Status (binary class attribute)
  - 1 = the patient survived 5 years or longer
  - 2 = the patient died within 5 years

The mutation is performed on the fuzzy rules attributes age, operation year and axillary nodes, shown in Table II. Like previously mentioned, the maximum change of one attribute per mutation lies between -40 % and +40 %. As the data in this use case only consisted of integers, the mutation also delivers only integers. A control mechanism detects if violations of the hard and soft boundaries of the fuzzy rules were the result of a mutation and rolls the fuzzy rule back to the state one step before the violating mutation has occurred. Table II shows one rule created by mixed fuzzy-rule formation and two mutations. Mutation 1 is violating the fuzzy rule in the last value of the attribute age while mutation 2 represents a valid mutation.

TABLE II. MUTATIONS OF AN EXAMPLE RULE

mutation	*age*	*operation year*	*axillary nodes*	*survival*
-	(24, 48, 60, 64)	(03, 06, 07, 07)	(19, 21, 35, 46)	true
1	(24, 48, 60, 59)	(03, 06, 07, 07)	(19, 21, 35, 46)	true
2	(24, 48, 60, 62)	(03, 06, 07, 07)	(19, 21, 35, 46)	true

Figure 2 gives a graphical overview of one part of a rule. The soft limits can clearly be seen in green colour at the operation years 60 and 67 while the hard limits are represented by years 59 and 69.

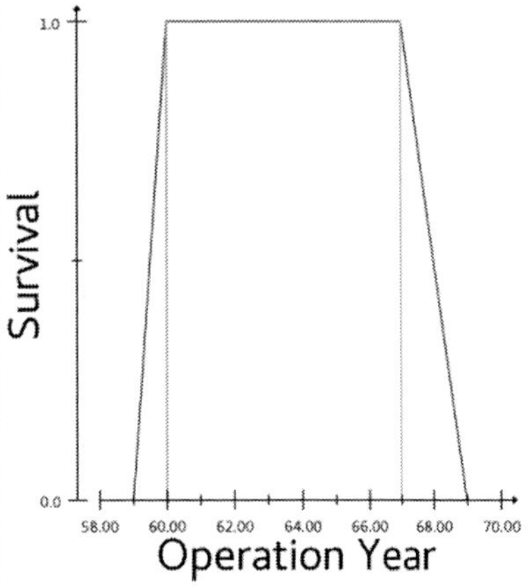

Figure 2. Part of a fuzzy rule

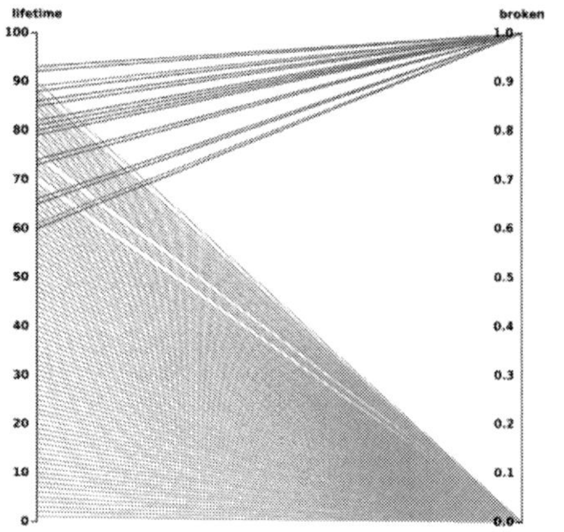

Figure 3. Correlation of lifetime and machine health

TABLE III. SCORING STATISTICS: HEALTH SECTOR

Iteration	Mutations	Rate	F-measure
0	-	-	0.696
1	30	24 %	0.695
2	35	2 %	0.691
3	7	10 %	0.684
4	42	4 %	0.682
5	29	30 %	0.681
6	14	13 %	0.684
7	31	29 %	0.685
8	13	9 %	0.690
9	5	21 %	0.693
10	10	37 %	0.699
11	31	29 %	0.697
12	13	9 %	0.686
13	28	21 %	0.689
14	10	7%	0.693
15 (TC) = 10			0.699

Table III shows the individual iterations of the adaptation process. The number of mutations is listed next to the mutation rate, which represents the average change of the values during that iteration. It can be seen that in iterations 10 and 11 the algorithm leads to a better result. Iteration 15 triggers the terminal condition and iteration 10 is selected, as it improves the F-measure by 0.3 %. Although the improvement may seem small, the new knowledge in form of the mutated fuzzy rules could be evaluated and used by human experts.

B. *Evaluation 2: Industry 4.0*

Industry 4.0 and predictive maintenance is a hot topic in research and business right now. Companies want to precisely predict the date and time a machine needs maintenance in order to produce more efficiently [22]. Often, many sensors are added to machines or along the production line. The data gathered by these sensors is then used to build the predictive models. The dataset used in this evaluation has been provided by Ludovic in [23] and consists of 1001 records. The interesting fact about this dataset is that it also provides additional information like the responsible maintenance team for a certain machine. The following attributes are provided in the data set:

- lifetime of the machine in weeks (numeric)
- pressure (numeric)
- moisture (numeric)
- temperature (numeric)
- provider of the machine (string)
- responsible maintenance team (string)
- status
  - 1 = machine is broken
  - 0 = machine is still working

Another interesting part about this data set is that the information provided is relatively easy to obtain for different kind of machines. Corresponding cost-effective sensors for temperature or moisture measurement can usually be additionally installed, regardless of the age of the machine. In contrast to the first use case, the values of the sensor attributes consist of floating-point numbers. The mutation was performed on the numerical attributes lifetime, pressure, temperature and moisture. It turns out that mutating the string type attributes like provider and maintenance team had a too strong impact on the original fuzzy rule. This makes sense as a slight change in those data types can completely turn a fuzzy rule on its head. Figure 3 shows the correlation of lifetime and health of a machine. Looking at this graph, it makes sense to use a rule-based system to model this correlation and use it for classifications and predictions. However, Figure 4 shows that it is not as easy when looking for correlations of the temperature and the health of a machine as there seems to be a rather equal distribution. Thankfully, fuzzy rule-based systems can cover the correlations between attributes thanks to the soft- and hard boundaries as shown in Table II and, at the same time, retain transparency.

Table IV shows that in this use case, the algorithm improves in iterations 2, 3, 4 and 9 compared to the original fuzzy rule. The F-measure is improved by 0.4 %. This time, the best results are obtained after relatively few iterations.

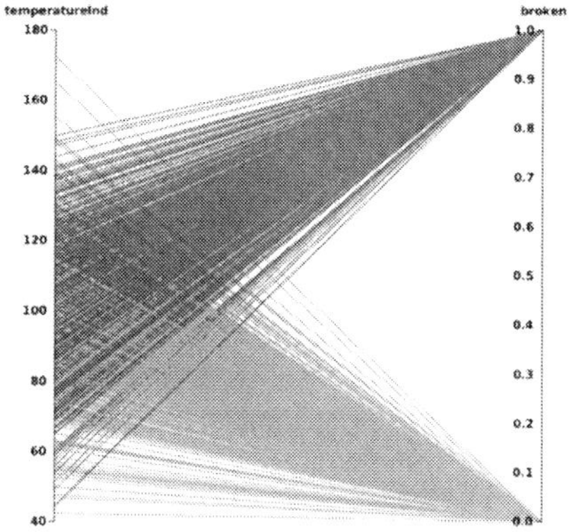

Figure 4. Correlation of temperature and machine health

TABLE IV. SCORING STATISTICS: INDUSTRY 4.0

Iteration	Mutations	Rate	F-measure
0	-	-	0.650
1	3	13 %	0.650
2	23	20 %	0.654
3	30	14 %	0.651
4	1	2 %	0.651
5	13	21 %	0.645
6	16	19 %	0.647
7	25	1 %	0.647
8	40	28 %	0.650
9	31	13 %	0.651
10	27	9 %	0.649
11	9	5 %	0.645
12	22	39 %	0.646
13	8	17 %	0.642
14	20	7 %	0.640
15 (TC) = 2			0.654

VI. CONCLUSION AND FUTURE WORK

The evaluation within two different use cases with different data sets shows that fuzzy rules, generated by mixed fuzzy-rule formation, can be optimized by using the proposed method. The evolutionary strategy is primary based on mutation in order to keep the changes assessable. The implemented control mechanism while mutating ensures that the fuzzy partitioning within the fuzzy rule were not violated. Currently, this optimization is only possible with numerical type attributes within the fuzzy rules.

In the future, it should be evaluated how to deal with string and binary values during the mutation process as one minor change already results in big changes to the fuzzy rule itself. Future work includes the application to bigger data sets with more attributes and records to see if the algorithm can scale accordingly. At the same time, the implications of a bigger data set on the trade of between accuracy and coverage of the data set have to be evaluated. The impact on the computation time has to be analysed as well for those cases. Additionally, it must be evaluated if the algorithm can work for regression problems, too. In general, the algorithm must be tested with more use cases to be able to make comprehensible assumptions about generalisation potential and possibilities. The algorithm will additionally be evaluated with machine data gathered from grinding machines and lathes. This will be a similar use case to the second use case described in this paper. But it should be kept in mind that even simple changes, like slightly different positioned sensors could already complicate the ability to generalize well, even when using the exactly same types of sensors. Furthermore, both use cases should be evaluated in a detailed comparison with other machine learning algorithms, e.g., artificial neural networks.

VII. ACKNOWLEDGEMENT

This work has received funding from INTERREG Upper Rhine (European Regional Development Fund) and the Ministries for Research of Baden-Wuerttemberg, Rheinland-Pfalz and from the Region Grand Est in the framework of the Science Offensive Upper Rhine.

REFERENCES

[1] Statista, "Deep learning market size in U.S. by segment 2014-2025 — Statistic," Available: https://www.statista.com/statistics/779696/united-states-deep-learning-market-size, [retrieved: 03, 2018].

[2] NVIDIA, "Deep Learning & Artificial Intelligence Solutions from NVIDIA," Available: https://www.nvidia.com/en-us/deep-learning-ai, [retrieved: 03, 2018].

[3] S. Shirataki and S. Yamaguchi, "A study on interpretability of decision of machine learning," in 2017 IEEE International Conference on Big Data (Big Data), Dec 2017, pp. 4830–4831.

[4] W. Knight, "The dark secret at the heart of ai," 2017, Available: https://www.technologyreview.com/s/604087/the-dark-secret-at-the-heart-of-ai/, [retrieved: 03, 2018].

[5] G. Montavon, W. Samek, and K.-R. Müller, "Methods for interpreting and understanding deep neural networks," Digital Signal Processing, vol. 73, 2018, pp. 1 – 15.

[6] C. Wu, M. J. F. Gales, A. Ragni, P. Karanasou, and K. C. Sim, "Improving interpretability and regularization in deep learning," IEEE/ACM Transactions on Audio, Speech, and Language Processing, vol. 26, no. 2, Feb 2018, pp. 256–265.

[7] D. Wang, C. Quek, A. H. Tan, C. Miao, G. S. Ng, and Y. Zhou, "Leveraging the trade-off between accuracy and interpretability in a hybrid intelligent system," in 2017 International Conference on Security, Pattern Analysis, and Cybernetics (SPAC), Dec 2017, pp. 55–60.

[8] S. Elsayed, R. Sarker, and C. A. C. Coello, "Fuzzy rule-based design of evolutionary algorithm for optimization," IEEE Transactions on Cybernetics, vol. PP, no. 99, 2017, pp. 1–14.

[9] M. Schaer, M. Brennenstuhl, and R. Dornberger, "Improving the fuzzy logic controller of a car racing competition with adjusted fuzzy sets," in 2016 4th International Symposium on Computational and Business Intelligence (ISCBI), Sept 2016, pp. 118–124.

[10] C. Jariyatantiwait and G. G. Yen, "Fuzzy multiobjective differential evolution using performance metrics feedback," in 2014 IEEE Congress on Evolutionary Computation (CEC), July 2014, pp. 1959–1966.

[11] K. Deb, L. Thiele, M. Laumanns, and E. Zitzler, Scalable Test Problems for Evolutionary Multiobjective Optimization. London: Springer London, 2005, pp. 105–145.

[12] J. Alcalá-Fdez, R. Alcalá, S. González, Y. Nojima, and S. García, "Evolutionary fuzzy rule-based methods for monotonic classification," IEEE Transactions on Fuzzy Systems, vol. 25, no. 6, Dec 2017, pp. 1376–1390.

[13] M. Antonelli, D. Bernardo, H. Hagras, and F. Marcelloni, "Multiobjective evolutionary optimization of type-2 fuzzy rule-based systems for financial data classification," IEEE Transactions on Fuzzy Systems, vol. 25, no. 2, April 2017, pp. 249–264.

[14] J. A. Sanz, D. Bernardo, F. Herrera, H. Bustince, and H. Hagras, "A compact evolutionary interval-valued fuzzy rule-based classification system for the modeling and prediction of real-world financial applications with imbalanced data," IEEE Transactions on Fuzzy Systems, vol. 23, no. 4, Aug 2015, pp. 973–990.

[15] N. L. Tsakiridis, J. B. Theocharis, and G. C. Zalidis, "A fuzzy rule-based system utilizing differential evolution with an application in vis-nir soil spectroscopy," in 2017 IEEE International Conference on Fuzzy Systems (FUZZ-IEEE), July 2017, pp. 1–7.

[16] T. T. Huan, P. D. Huynh, C. V. Kien, and H. P. H. Anh, "Implementation of hybrid adaptive fuzzy sliding model control and evolutionary neural observer for biped robot systems," in 2017 International Conference on System Science and Engineering (ICSSE), July 2017, pp. 77–82.

[17] M. R. Berthold, "Mixed fuzzy rule formation," International Journal of Approximate Reasoning, vol. 32, no. 2, 2003, pp. 67 – 84, soft Computing in Information Mining.

[18] A. Fernandez, C. J. Carmona, M. J. Jesus, and F. Herrera, "A view on fuzzy systems for big data: Progress and opportunities," in International Journal of Computational Intelligence Systems, vol. 9, March 2016, pp. 69–80.

[19] S. del Río, V. Lòpez, J. M. Benítez, and F. Herrera, "A mapreduce approach to address big data classification problems based on the fusion of linguistic fuzzy rules," International Journal of Computational Intelligence Systems, vol. 8, no. 3, 2015, pp. 422–437.

[20] S. J. Haberman, "Generalized residuals for log-linear models," in Proceedings of the 9th International Biometrics Conference, Boston, 1976, pp. 104–122.

[21] M. Lichman, "UCI machine learning repository," 2013, Available: http://archive.ics.uci.edu/ml, [retrieved: 03, 2018].

[22] Roland Berger, "Predictive Maintenance / Servicing tomorrow and where we are really at today," VDMA, Tech. Rep., 2017, Available: https://www.rolandberger.com/de/Publications/pub_predictive_maintenance_2017.html, [retrieved: 03, 2018].

[23] B. Ludovic, "Predictive maintenance," 2018, Available: https://www.kaggle.com/ludobenistant/predictive-maintenance-1/data, [retrieved: 03, 2018].

Wine Critic Scores and Consumer Behavior in a Major USA Metropolitan Market

Andrew P. Snow
School of Information and Telecommunication Systems
Ohio University
Athens, Ohio
e-mail: asnow@ohio.edu

Gary R. Weckman
Department of Industrial and Systems Engineering
Ohio University
Athens, Ohio
e-mail: weckmang@ohio.edu

Abstract— **In this paper, we investigated three questions. First, to what extend do wine critic scores and descriptions influence consumer-buying decisions? Second, to what extent this influence varies with price? Third, how do demographics affect consumer decisions? The experimental design consisted of convenience samples from four different stores in a major United States (US) metropolitan market, with random assignment of consumers to different groups, who completed a total of 240 survey questionnaires. The dependent variable was likelihood to buy wine when presented with varying amount of wine critic information (a control group and three experimental groups with different levels of information). Independent variables included wine price, age, gender, wine interest, store type and location. Major findings include some surprises. For a $20 bottle of wine, the critic information was not a factor on likelihood to purchase, while critic information was a factor for a $50 bottle. These findings varied somewhat based on demographics such as wine club membership, gender, type store, and store location. The findings have implications for wine producer, distributor and retailer marketing methods.**

Keywords-wine critic; consumer behavior; wine marketing; tukey-kramer

I. Introduction

Total world wine production in 2014 was estimated at 271 million hectoliters [1]. The world is producing more wine than ever and Europe is not the only player; new world countries, such as the United States of America (USA), Argentina, Chile, Australia and South Africa are producing large quantities of wine. With China on the horizon, the world production will continue to rise, and there are now thousands of consumer wine choices. Consumers are exposed to a range of wine advertising including magazine ads, emails, website popups and newsletters. Extensive store displays lend perception that wines are of quality and must be purchased. At the end of the day, price range is certainly an important factor consumer wine purchasing decisions. As people only have a certain budget for wine expenditures, a natural question is, how important are wine critic scores in consumer choices?

This is a very important question because of the proliferation of wine ratings in the marketplace. There is evidence to suggest that consumers might be willing to spend a bit more because of a wine critic score. Whether it is a 97-point score from The Wine Advocate or landing in the top 10 of The Wine Spectator's top 100, significant positive attention is great for a wine's image and marketability. Retailers and restaurants may seek the wine and distributors could very well change their purchasing strategy to meet market demand. These scores also affect wineries because higher scores usually lead to higher prices for retailers and direct sales. Also, wine critics are known to have certain specific tastes and it can be argued that if a winery can tailor their wine to that taste and get a high score, perhaps they could increase their price. The purpose of this research is to test how critic's wine scores and descriptions affect consumer behavior in a large USA metropolitan market.

Experimental research in a major USA metropolitan marketplace was conducted to investigate three questions regarding the impact of wine critic information in buying decisions:

R1. How do critic scores and descriptions affect consumer decisions?

R2. If wine critic scores/descriptions do affect consumer decisions, how sensitive are decisions to price?

R3. How do consumer demographics like gender, age and wine club membership affect consumer decisions?

In Section 2, a background on wine assessment and critic scoring. In Section 3, the methodology of the testing is proposed and explained in detail. In Section 4, the results are compared against each other. Finally, in Section 5, the major findings and overall conclusion is stated.

II. Literature Review

Wine is quite arguably the most complex alcoholic beverage in existence. While beer and spirits are produced from grains and vegetables, there are thousands of grape varieties. Beer and spirits can be produced year-round, but for wine production, grapes are only available once a year.

How good a taster is the modern wine critic and what are the necessary qualifications to become a critic? Jancis Robinson is a very influential critic and holds the title of Master of Wine, which is one of the highest accolades attainable in the wine business. Ironically, Robert Parker has no formal wine training or certifications however, for his efforts during his career; he has received the highest honor possible from Italy and France (Commendatore and Knighthood in the Legion of Honor, respectively). Parker has also authored over a dozen books translated into multiple languages. This suggests that a professional certification in wine may not be necessary and experience can be just as valuable as accreditation. Perhaps people would buy a wine highly recommended by a critic because the perception is that the critic knows more about wine than the average person does and have better tastes.

How do people assess wine? There is little evidence to suggest that everyone will enjoy a very expensive wine. A study of 6,000 blind tastings [2] between inexpensive and expensive wine showed that experienced tasters (minority of the population) enjoyed the more expensive wine; however, the inexperienced wine tasters more often enjoyed the less expensive wine.

A test conducted in the USA on how Generation Y buys European wine [3] claims that Generation Y accounts for 72% of food and beverage sales in the USA, and that European wineries should target this group. Their test concluded that when Generation Y purchases European wines, brand familiarity and experience are key factors in the decision process. Interestingly, researchers did not test wine critic reviews for this peer group, and the questionnaire did not ask the subjects if they subscribed to wine publications. Additionally, the test was limited to European.

The problem is that with many more countries producing wine, there are a myriad of choices for consumers. Also, rules regarding labeling vary from country to country (percentage of grape variety/vintage to be used in labeling a wine) which always leads to the infamous traditionalist versus modern debate. A major criticism of European wine labels is that they are hard to understand. Many labels do not have an indication of grape variety and give little clue on the back label as to what is in the bottle. This is confirmed by a survey published in Wines & Vines [4], an organization that compiles wine metrics and information about the wine business. According to a survey conducted in 2005, wine labels confused 36% of USA wine drinkers, 51% of drinkers found imported wine labels very difficult to read/comprehend, and 81% of wine drinkers want labels that are easy to read and understand. Interestingly, 51% of wine drinkers liked humorous wine labels.

It can be argued that the modern labelling simplifies the wine process for the consumer because the labels are easy to understand and indicate grape variety. However, new world labels can be misleading because in the USA, only 75% of a grape variety is required to label that wine as a single variety. Thus, a wine with 76% zinfandel and seven other grapes can be labeled solely as a zinfandel. It could be argued that such labeling is misleading. Either way (traditional or modern), there are many choices, which lead one to question whether consumers are confused. Another study [5] suggests that too many choices can be positive, increasing the likelihood of satisfying customers.

At the top end, there are educated and wealthy connoisseurs who are not afraid to spend for what they know or want. However, sales of Romanée Conti and first growth Bordeaux represent a miniscule amount of wine purchases. At the other end, $10 for a bottle may be too expensive for some people – price is their selection criterion. This leaves a gaping hole of consumers in the middle that are potentially very confused. Consumers may choose to buy a wine for a multitude of reasons (price, prestige, style, country of origin, etc.) and a critic review is something to consider.

A study done in Australia [6] focused on how consumers assess wine. Their report concluded Australian consumers peruse a wine display shelf for one minute. Their research focused on shelf information in front of the bottle (shelf-talker) because although there are many sources of opinion in Australia, there is no major dominating critic influence. Their study concluded that wines with shelf information increased the choice of a particular wine by 7.4%. It is common to find shelf information in the USA; however, the USA is home to some of the world's most influential critics (The Wine Advocate, The Wine Spectator) and their information may be used as well. It is important to note that while the influential critics in the USA taste and rate some of the worlds' most sought-after wines; they also do the same for inexpensive wines. In fact, The Wine Advocate and The Wine Spectator have value reports in their publications that focus on inexpensive/good value wines with good ratings. These publications review many kinds/prices of wine and target professional, collector, intermediate and novice consumers.

Are wine critic reviews always effective? Someone went so far as to say the wine critics are "BS artists" [7]. Quandt bashes critics because scores vary considerably for the same wine, sometimes critics contradict themselves, but most importantly, he attacks the critics for their vocabulary, which no one can understand. What does scorched earth taste like? Or how do zesty minerals differ from minerals – are crushed rocks really delicious? Quant argues that reviews do not tell you much about a wine in terms that an ordinary person can comprehend.

Adding to the argument, tests were conducted by Weil. In one test [8], Weil provided subjects with three wines, of which two were the same. For those who can correctly identify which one is different, they are then presented with the critic review to see if they can match the wine to the verbiage. Only 51% of the subjects could correctly identify the correct review. Weil conducted another test [9] to see if people agree with the wine critic scores. The test was the same, except for those who correctly identify the different one, they were then asked to select which one they prefer. The wines used for the test were from the same producer, one was the entry level, and the other was the reserve. His test concluded that for those who could identify the difference, 52% liked the reserve wine better. Consequently, Weil claims that the average person does not benefit from a critic review because they may not like the same style wine as a critic.

While the previous tests may suggest that wine critic reviews are not effective, there is evidence and reason to suggest that they are perceived to be valuable. The Wine Advocate has at least 40,000 subscribers in every state in the USA and have subscribers in 37 foreign countries [10]. A paper on the impact of wine critics [11] suggest that these reviews can be very valuable for Bordeaux lovers, as wine critics taste almost all Bordeaux wines (at the en priemeur tasting held every April). Most wine consumers cannot attend these events; thus, they may rely on the insight of wine critics. A test was conducted on Bordeaux wines rated by Robert Parker [11] and it was concluded that a "Parker effect" existed and affected pricing for Bordeaux wine by as much as 3 Euro per bottle (highly graded wines were affected most, and the effect diminished for lowly rated wines).

The effectiveness of wine critic scores was tested in the USA in a national grocery chain, targeted in northern California [12]. Over a 2-month period, 32% of all the wines that had ratings were selected for tasting. These wines had critic expert opinions and scores in front of them on the shelves. Using scores from 78 to 89, the test concluded that wines with expert opinion and scores increased demand by 25%, while lower scoring decreased demand. This test may help explain the aforementioned study about consumer confusion because in a grocery store chain, the selections are quite large and within a category, there are dozens of choices within a similar price range. Interestingly, wines that were not selected for testing did not change significantly in sales, illustrating that not everyone may pay attention to reviews or might have already developed brand loyalty before the test was conducted. Although this test was only conducted for two months and in a very small area, it does shed light on the possible effectiveness of wine critic scores.

III. Methodology

In the research presented here, we focused testing in a setting where the sole purpose of the store visit is to buy wine from a wine outlet. We chose to test the effectiveness of wine critic reviews in the Baltimore, Maryland (MD) to Washington District of Columbia (DC) corridor. The stores ranged from small boutique selections to larger stores that cater to everyone in terms of selection and price.

To address the aforementioned research questions, we generated three sets of major null and alternative hypotheses:

Wine Critic Score Influence

- $H1_0$: The WA score has no effect on consumer decisions on selecting wine to buy.
- $H1_a$: The WA score influences consumer decisions on selecting wine to buy.

Wine Critic Descriptions Influence

- $H2_0$: Wine descriptions have no effect on consumer decisions on selecting wine to buy.
- $H2_a$: Wine descriptions influence consumer decisions on selecting wine to buy.

Wine Critic Score versus Description

- $H3_0$: Critic wine scores are given no more weight than wine descriptions by consumers in wine purchasing decisions.
- $H3_a$: Critic wine scores are given more weight than wine descriptions by consumers in wine purchasing decisions.

For the test, we developed a one-page questionnaire for consumers buying wine from wine outlets. Each subject was presented with certain information about two wines. Each subject was asked how likely they would be to buy each wine, by rating on an anchored scale of 1 (lowest) to 7 (highest). Four questionnaires were developed with different information about each wine. All subjects were asked the same questions for each wine, regardless of the experimental group.

Three of these groups were experimental groups and one was a control group. Sampling (store selection) was based on convenience and there was random assignment of subjects to the four different groups.

- Experimental Group A - Subjects were presented with Châteaux, price, critic score and a critic description of the wine.
- Experimental Group B - Subjects were presented with Châteaux, price and critic score, but no critic description of the wine.
- Experimental Group C - Subjects were presented with Châteaux, price and critic description of the wine, but not the critic score.
- Control Group D - Subjects were only presented with Châteaux and the price. This is the control group.

In order to make statistical comparisons, questionnaires were distributed to four retail stores in the greater Washington D.C. and Baltimore area. A total of 240 responses were administered, resulting in 60 responses per experimental group. The stack of questionnaires provided to each store were ordered by group and inconspicuously arranged and labelled (A, B, C, D, A, B, C, D, .. , A, B, C, D) to ensure random subject assignment. Researchers also knew which store questionnaires come from, allowing for additional comparisons as to store type.

Besides demographic information, each questionnaire asked the likelihood of buying two differently priced bottles of wine (no tasting was involved). This allowed testing of whether likelihood to buy was sensitive to price. Subjects were presented with the questionnaire at the cashier during checkout. It was expected that some would choose not to do the survey, but everyone was asked until 60 were completed at each store. Certain demographics were not targeted, e.g., gender, age, as assignment was random and sequential.

As each questionnaire contained different amounts of data, the following legend was used to facilitate an analysis and comparison of the data for groups:

- P – Price
- S – Score
- D – Description

For each questionnaire, châteaux names were provided for each of the two wines. However, for questionnaire A, the châteaux, price, score and description were provided. For questionnaire D, only the châteaux and price were provided. The groups are now referred to as:

- PSD – price/châteaux, score and description (Group A)
- PS – price/châteaux and score (Group B)
- PD – price/châteaux and description (Group C)
- P – price/châteaux (Group D)

To control for possible confounding variables, the following techniques were used:

- Budget - Certain subjects will have more discretionary income than others. Telling everyone that they have a wine budget of $70 for this purchase helped control for this variable.
- Appellations – This was controlled by only using one appellation (Bordeaux).
- Critic – All scores came from one critic source (The Wine Advocate).
- Châteaux name – The name of the two Chateaus were fictional. Real Châteaux names could bias answers if a subject knew of or had tasted these wines.

An example questionnaire is shown in Figure 1 for Group PS (Group B). This questionnaire contains information about several Bordeaux wines. First, assume that you like Bordeaux. Second, assume you have a budget for this purchase of $70. Please indicate how likely you are to purchase a 750ml bottle, based on the information provided. You are not obliged to purchase anything by participating in this survey.

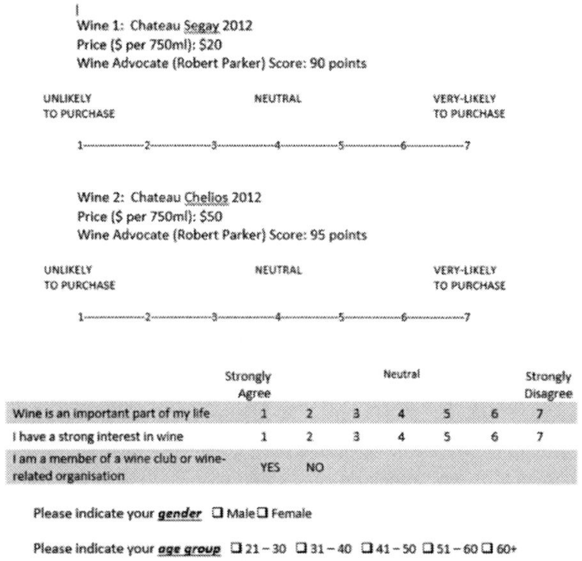
Wine 1: Chateau Segay 2012
Price ($ per 750ml): $20
Wine Advocate (Robert Parker) Score: 90 points

UNLIKELY TO PURCHASE — NEUTRAL — VERY-LIKELY TO PURCHASE

1--------2--------3--------4--------5--------6--------7

Wine 2: Chateau Chelios 2012
Price ($ per 750ml): $50
Wine Advocate (Robert Parker) Score: 95 points

UNLIKELY TO PURCHASE — NEUTRAL — VERY-LIKELY TO PURCHASE

1--------2--------3--------4--------5--------6--------7

	Strongly Agree			Neutral			Strongly Disagree
Wine is an important part of my life	1	2	3	4	5	6	7
I have a strong interest in wine	1	2	3	4	5	6	7
I am a member of a wine club or wine-related organisation	YES	NO					

Please indicate your ***gender*** ❑ Male ❑ Female

Please indicate your ***age group*** ❑ 21 – 30 ❑ 31 – 40 ❑ 41 – 50 ❑ 51 – 60 ❑ 60+

Figure 1. Example of questionaire for Group PS.

The wines selected for the questionnaire were two Bordeaux wines from the 2012 vintage. To eliminate bias during the test, the châteaux names were changed to fictional ones.

- Wine #1 – 2012 Chateau Joanin Becot, Cotes de Castillon ($20)
- Wine #1 pseudonym in the questionnaire – 2012 Chateau Segay
- Wine #2 – 2012 Chateau D'Isaan, Margaux ($50)
- Wine #2 pseudonym in the questionnaire – 2012 Chateau Chelios

Other factors involved were:

- Wine Score – rated by Robert Parker for the 2012 vintage; sourced from his website.
- Wine description – exact wine review from Robert Parker sourced from his website. The reviews were only modified to remove the property name, winemakers/consultants and components of the final assemblage to remove any potential bias.
- Price – the price is the average bottle price in the USA that was sourced from www.wine-searcher.com. This site collects data from wine retailers all over the world.

Based on the factors above, the wines for the questionnaire were chosen:

- Wine Score – a difference of 5 points between the wines was assumed sufficient to clearly distinguish the ratings. The Wine Advocate's rating system says that scores from 90 – 95, "are an outstanding wine of exceptional complexity and character. In short, these are terrific wines" [10]. While both of these wines are in the outstanding category, they fall at opposite ends of the exceptional spectrum. Parker rated the $20 bottle as 90 while the $50 bottle was rated 95.
- Wine Description – Both of the wine descriptions have the classic Parker vocabulary. The wines are described as having plump fruit, intense spices, inky/opaque color and being flashy/opulent. Also, there is mention of the wines being "over achievers" or being underrated.
- Price – Bordeaux can be painfully expensive, so price was a major factor in determining which wines to select. Once above 95 points, the price was too high to use for the test. In fact, we were surprised to find a wine-rated 95 points for $50 because other wines with the same rating score were much more expensive. By having a price difference of $30 between the two wines, the wines were clearly separated from each other.

A. *Hypotheses*

The dependent variable investigated for each experimental group was likelihood to buy the stipulated wine (on a scale of 1 to 7). The expectation regarding the mean dependent variable responses for the groups is given by:

$$\mu_{PSD} > \mu_{PS} > \mu_{PD} > \mu_{P}$$

We expected that consumers, when given all relevant information, will depend heavily on that information, especially the critic score.

After the questionnaires were completed, the likelihoods to buy for each group was compiled and the mean responses for each group compared by the following tests:

- Single Analysis of Variance (ANOVA) test (F-Test) – performed to determine if there was a statistical equivalence of experimental group means, using a critical value of 0.05. If the means were equivalent, no further testing was necessary. If the means were different, further testing was required.
- Tukey-Kramer test – The Single ANOVA test above indicates if at least one on the means is different, but it does not provide the answer as to which means are different. Additionally, some of the means could be

statistically equal and others could be statistically greater/less than each other. The test for this situation is the Tukey-Kramer multiple comparison procedure, also at the 0.05 level of significance. With four control and experimental groups, there are six combinations tested for equivalence.

$$\mu_{PSD} = \mu_{PS} \qquad \mu_{PSD} = \mu_{PD}$$
$$\mu_{PSD} = \mu_{P} \qquad \mu_{PS} = \mu_{PD}$$
$$\mu_{PS} = \mu_{P} \qquad \mu_{PD} = \mu_{P}$$

For the Tukey-Kramer test, the absolute differences in means for each pair were computed and then compared to a critical range, computed by:

$$w_{ij} = Q_{0.05,(k,N-k)}\sqrt{(\frac{1}{n_i} + \frac{1}{n_j})MSW/2} \qquad (1)$$

where Q is the 0.05 critical value of the studentized range distribution, k is the number of groups (in our case 4), n_i, n_j the number of observations in the subpopulations i and j associated with each mean, N is the number of total observations ($n_i + n_j$) and mean-square-within (MSW) is the value from the single factor ANOVA [13].

B. *Statistical Test Hypotheses*

For the tests conducted, all hypotheses were accepted or rejected based on critical value of 0.05. For all tests performed for the \$20 and \$50 bottle, the hypotheses are listed below:

Single ANOVA Test (Means across groups)
H_0: $\mu_{PSD} = \mu_{PS} = \mu_{PD} = \mu_P$
H_a: At least one of the means is unequal.

Tukey-Kramer Test (Pairwise means across groups)
H_0: two means are equal.
H_a: two means are unequal.

T – Test (Means between two sub-demographics)
H_0 – two demographic pairs are equal.
H_a – two 2 demographic pairs are unequal.

IV. Results

A. *Single ANOVA Test*

All the raw data was compiled, and a Single ANOVA Test was performed to determine the mean responses for each of the two bottles of wine. We also conducted ANOVA on different demographic groups. The summary table is listed in Table 1 along with the number of subjects in each demographic.

All colors highlighted orange indicate that there is no statistical difference in the means across the four experimental groups. For the \$20 bottle, all but one category had no statistical differences in the means, thus, we accepted H_0. Although some of the means appear to be different, the critical value of 0.05 was used to determine if statistically significant differences existed. Figure 2 is an example of the Single ANOVA Test performed on the category "Wine Club" for the \$20 bottle.

TABLE I. SINGLE ANOVA TABLE

CATEGORY (n)	\$20				\$50			
	PSD	PS	PD	P	PSD	PS	PD	P
ALL (240)	4.3	4.8	4.1	4.3	3.5	3.4	2.0	1.8
AGE > 40 (79)	4.4	5.0	3.6	3.7	4.4	3.6	2.0	1.4
AGE ≤ 40 (161)	4.3	4.6	4.4	4.6	3.1	3.3	2.1	2.0
WINE CLUB MEMBER (64)	4.8	5.7	5.0	4.6	4.8	4.9	2.6	2.3
NOT CLUB MEMBER (176)	4.0	4.5	3.8	4.2	2.7	3.0	1.8	1.7
BOTIQUE STORE (120)	4.3	4.8	4.4	4.6	3.3	3.0	2.0	1.9
LARGE STORE (120)	4.4	4.7	4.0	4.0	3.8	3.8	2.0	1.7
DC (120)	3.9	4.3	4.4	4.63	3.4	3.0	2.3	2.3
MD (120)	4.8	5.1	4.0	4.0	3.7	3.8	1.7	1.2
MALE (140)	4.4	5.2	4.0	4.4	4.0	3.9	1.7	1.9
FEMALE (100)	4.2	4.1	4.3	4.1	2.9	2.8	2.4	1.5
	Legend for ANOVA Results							
	No Statistical Difference in Means				At Least One Mean Statistically Different			

No difference in the means concludes that a buying decision was indifferent between those presented with all information (Group PSD) and those presented with the least information (Group P). This indicates that perhaps wine critic scores and descriptions are not that relevant for inexpensive Bordeaux. However, a difference was identified for the "Maryland" category. The differences in this category were further tested with the Tukey-Kramer test.

Single ANOVA "Wine Club" (\$20 bottle)

ANOVA: Single Factor

Summary

Groups	Sample size	Sum	Mean	Variance
PSD	24	116.	4.83333	4.23188
PS	13	74.	5.69231	1.73077
PD	16	81.	5.0625	4.4625
P	11	51.	4.63636	4.25455

ANOVA

Source of Variation	SS	df	MS	F	p-level	F crit
Between Groups	8.35198	3	2.78399	0.73396	0.535840232	2.75808
Within Groups	227.58552	60	3.79309			
Total	235.9375	63				

Figure 2. Single ANOVA "Wine Club" (\$20 bottle)

In contrast, for the \$50 bottle, there was a difference in means for all categories except for "Washington DC". To summarize, the Single ANOVA Test only indicated that there is a difference in the means. It does not indicate which of the means are equal, less than or greater than each other. The "Maryland" category for the \$20 bottle, and all categories (except for "Washington D.C.") were further investigated by way of the Tukey-Kramer Test.

B. Tukey-Kramer Test Results

For all differences in means indicated in the Single ANOVA Test, the Tukey-Kramer test was used to investigate the differences. The Single ANOVA only mentions if a difference exists, and the Tukey-Kramer will statistically show which ones are different. For this test, groups are compared to each other (in pairs) to see if the differences were statistically different. A total of 4 groups results in 6 different comparisons. The test was performed for all data for the $50 bottle (only the $20 bottle for Maryland), and was also performed categorically. Figure 3 is the result for the $50 bottle for the category "ALL":

Category "ALL" $50 bottle

ANOVA: Single Factor

SUMMARY

Groups	*Count*	*Sum*	*Average*	*Variance*
PSD	60	212	3.533333333	4.829378531
PS	60	204	3.4	3.73559322
PD	60	121	2.016666667	2.389548023
P	60	106	1.766666667	2.046327684

Tukey-Kramer					
		Total count	240		
		Q	3.74		
		Num df	4	Dem df	234
Comparison	**Abs. Diff.**	**Critical Range**	**Results**		
PSD-PS	0.133	0.870	Not Significantly Different		
PSD-PD	1.517	0.870	Significantly different		
PSD-P	1.767	0.870	Significantly different		
PS-PD	1.383	0.870	Significantly different		
PS-P	1.633	0.870	Significantly different		
PD-P	0.250	0.870	Not Significantly Different		

Figure 3. Tukey-Kramer Test "ALL" $50 bottle

For the Tukey-Kramer test, if the absolute difference of the means was greater than the critical value, H_0 is rejected, noting that the two means are different.

The results are interpreted as follows. For the comparison of "Group PSD" and "Group PS", the absolute value of the difference of means are not higher than the critical range, thus they are not significantly different. That means that if one person was provided with the price, score and description; and the other person was only provided with the price and score, there was no difference in likelihood as to whether they would purchase the wine. This indicates that the description of the wine was less relevant because there was no difference as to the likelihood of making purchase when one group (Group PSD) had more information than another group (Group PS).

The comparison between "Group PD" and "Group P" were also not significantly different. What this means is that the likelihood of purchasing the wine was not influenced by the fact that one group had the price and the description, while the other group was only provided the price. For this comparison, having an additional piece of information (the description) would not influence the purchase decision.

The significant differences lie in the middle (the other 4 comparisons). Comparing "Group PSD" to "Group PD" shows a significant difference. This indicates that the score is a relevant factor when determining the likelihood of a purchase (ANOVA means for PSD is 3.5 and means for PD are 2.0). When looking at the means from the Single ANOVA Test for the means of "Group PSD" are 3.5 and the means for "Group PS" are 3.4, which are statistically equal. This comparison shows that having more information is a relevant factor in determining the likelihood of a purchase.

The absolute difference of the means is the highest for the comparison of "Group PSD" to "Group P" because "Group P" was only provided with the price and Chateau. The significant difference concludes that for this comparison, having all the information versus the least information influences the decision as to the likelihood of making a purchase. The wine critic score appears to be very important as well in the comparison of "Group PS" to "Group "PD". This comparison shows a significant difference; both groups are provided the price, but the likelihood in determining a purchase is statistically different (the ANOVA means for PS 3.4 and the means for PD are 2.0).

Overall, 10 categories were selected for the Tukey-Kramer test for the $50 bottle. Maryland was also tested for the $20 bottle because of differences noted in the Single ANOVA Test. Of the 10 categories, the results of the comparisons were the same for 7 categories, as those noted in the "All" category above, in which "Group PSD" and "Group PS" were not significantly different. Also, "Group PD" and "Group P" were not significantly different. All other comparisons were significantly different. The categories with the same results (which means were equal) are as follows:

- All ($50 bottle)
- > 40 ($50 bottle)
- <= 40 ($50 bottle)
- Maryland ($20 bottle)
- Wine Club ($50 bottle)
- Boutique ($50 bottle)
- Large ($50 bottle)
- Male ($50 bottle)

For these cases, the following is concluded:

$$\mu_{PSD} = \mu_{PS} > \mu_{PD} = \mu_P$$

Other differences were noted than those above in the categories; "No Wine Club", "Marlyand" ($50 bottle) and "Female". Each one will be investigated below.

1) Category "No Wine Club" ($50 bottle)

The differences are almost exactly the same as found in the "All" category above, but there was a significant difference between "Group PSD" and "Group PS. For this comparison, to what extend is the importance of the description? By looking at the means for the two groups from the Single ANOVA, the means for "Group PS" are higher than the means for "Group PSD". This shows that for the $50 bottle, which is a high price point; those not belonging to a wine club are going right to the score. For all other significant differences, price is a major factor. For comparison of "Group PD" and "Group P", there is no significant difference. Here, we conclude:

$$\mu_{PS} > \mu_{PSD} > \mu_{PD} = \mu_P$$

2) *Category "Maryland" ($50 bottle)*

The findings here are mostly consistent with other tables. For comparison of "Group PSD" and Group "PS", there are no differences, highlighting the fact that the description may not be that important. However, there is a significant difference between the comparison of "Group PD" and "Group P". The Single ANOVA means are higher for PD than P, but this shows that for a $50 bottle, description could be a factor in determining the likelihood of a purchase. It is important to note that for the category "Maryland" for the $20, the same comparison of "Group PD" and "Group P" showed no significant difference. There is a price difference of $30 and this finding shows that as the bottle price increases, subjects in Maryland were curious about the description. Here, we conclude:

$$\mu_{PSD} = \mu_{PS} > \mu_{PD} > \mu_P$$

3) *Category "Female" ($50 bottle)*

The results from this category were very interesting because this is the only category where there was a significant difference between "Group PSD" and "Group PD". Although the Single ANOVA means are higher for PSD (2.9) than PD (2.4), those means are far closer to each other than any other category. This shows as the price of the bottle becomes more expensive, women pay attention to the wine description and this can be a factor determining the likelihood of a purchase. This is also true when comparing "Group PS" to "Group PD", as this was the only comparison to be not significantly different amongst the categories. This shows the importance of the wine description to women. This is also true for the "Group PD" and "Group P" comparison. Here, we conclude:

$$\mu_{PSD} = \mu_{PS} \qquad \mu_{PS} = \mu_{PD}$$
$$\mu_{PSD} > \mu_{PD} \qquad \mu_{PD} > \mu_P.$$

C. Equal Variance Pairwise Two-tailed T-Test

The results for the pairwise T-Test are presented in Table 2. Presented with the same information, was the likelihood of purchase different for the $20 and $50 bottle? The statistical difference is based on a 0.05 significance.

In most cases, when presented the same information, price was a factor in determining the likelihood of a purchase. However, there were some instances in which price was not a factor. Most of the instances occurred when the subjects were presented with the most information:

- Age > 40 - to determine the likelihood of a purchase, age was important.
- Wine Club Member – this was the only category that also had a difference when only the score was presented. Maybe these subjects willing to make a high dollar purchase with only the score.
- Large Store – in a large setting, the consumer has many more choices. Perhaps they depend more on critics when there are so many choices.
- Male - little speculation can be offered other than perhaps status of a more expensive highly rated wine?

TABLE 2. UNEQUAL VARIANCE PAIRWISE T-TEST

CATEGORY	Same Subject difference for $20 and $50 Bottle?			
	PSD	PS	PD	P
ALL	0.0113	0.0000	0.0000	0.0000
AGE > 40	0.5000	0.0006	0.0000	0.0001
AGE <= 40	0.0015	0.0000	0.0000	0.0000
WINE CLUB MEMBER	0.5000	0.1050	0.0002	0.0062
NO CLUB MEMBERSHIP	0.0008	0.0000	0.0000	0.0000
BOTIQUE STORE	0.0078	0.0000	0.0000	0.0000
LARGE STORE	0.1457	0.0096	0.0000	0.0000
DC	0.1583	0.0000	0.0000	0.0000
MD	0.0134	0.0012	0.0000	0.0000
MALE	0.2207	0.0004	0.0000	0.0000
FEMALE	0.0022	0.0001	0.0000	0.0000
Statistical Difference Based on T-Test p-Value	No Difference		Difference	

- DC – a small but very affluent city. Also, an international city. Perhaps people in DC are willing to spend more money on wine. City-Data [14] shows that the median household income as of 2013 was about $25,000 higher in Washington DC versus Baltimore.

D. Unequal Variance, Two-Tailed T-Test

Demographic category differences were investigated within the same experimental group. Demographic groups were compared for both $20 and $50 bottles. Statistical differences in Table 3 are based on 0.05 significance. When presented with all relevant information for the $20 bottle, there were only a few instances of demographic differences within the same groups. Most of the differences were between "wine-club versus no-wine-club members" as the information provided decreased (all the way down to price). For each difference (PS, PD and P), the means from the ANOVA table were higher for wine club members, indicating they were more likely to make a purchase. Perhaps the wine club members subscribe to wine publications with ratings? It is also noted that a difference existed between "male versus female" for "Group PS". The likelihood of a purchase, the means were higher for males.

For the $50 bottle, there was a difference as those over 40 were more likely to make a purchase. Just like the $20 bottle, differences were also noted for "wine club versus no wine club" for the $50 bottle. Differences were only noted in "Group PSD and PS" because as price is much higher for a $50 bottle, description and price alone were not enough to make a difference. To note the previous T-Test again, a difference in "Group P" was noted for "DC versus MD", in which the means were higher for DC. This sheds light that perhaps DC is more affluent than MD and those subjects are willing to make a purchase when only provided the price.

TABLE 3. UNEQUAL VARIANCE, TWO-TAILED T-TEST

CATEGORY	Category Difference in Responses?							
	$20				$50			
	PSD	PS	PD	P	PSD	PS	PD	P
AGE > 40 / AGE <= 40	0.826	0.421	0.132	0.156	0.037	0.658	0.8161	0.0831
WINE CLUB MEMBER / NO CLUB MEMBERSHIP	0.124	0.009	0.042	0.002	0.000	0.009	0.1531	0.3920
BOTIQUE STORE / LARGE STORE	0.857	0.824	0.350	0.244	0.415	0.082	0.8046	0.5925
DC / MD	0.103	0.085	0.350	0.244	0.561	0.082	0.1581	0.0038
MALE / FEMALE	0.791	0.015	0.510	0.607	0.056	0.028	0.0951	0.1946
Statistical Difference Based on T-Test p-Value	No Difference				Difference			

For the $50 bottle, there was a difference as those over 40 were more likely to make a purchase. Just like the $20 bottle, differences were also noted for "wine club versus no wine club" for the $50 bottle. Differences were only noted in "Group PSD and PS" because as price is much higher for a $50 bottle, description and price alone were not enough to make a difference. To note the previous T-Test again, a difference in "Group P" was noted for "DC versus MD", in which the means were higher for DC. This sheds light that perhaps DC is more affluent than MD and those subjects are willing to make a purchase when only provided the price.

A very interesting finding is the difference in "male versus female" for "Group PS". This is consistent with the $20 bottle in which the means are higher for the male to make a purchase. The Tukey-Kramer test indicates women regarded the critic description as very important. Only differences existed where the description was not provided, indicating that perhaps males only care about the score.

It is important to also note the comparison of "male versus female" for Group PSD for the $50 bottle. Although the T-Test concluded there was no difference, the results were very close (0.056 with a critical difference value of 0.05). The means for males to purchase for Group PSD were much higher than the means for the female. Although no difference was noted, an opposite conclusion is rationale.

V. MAJOR FINDINGS AND CONCLUSIONS

The likelihood to purchase based on wine critic information was very dependent on price. For a $20 bottle, the critic information was not a factor in consumer decisions. Conversely, for the $50 bottle, the scores and description, or just the score are important.

Demographics definitely play a role. When presented with score and description, the same individual is as likely to buy the $20 bottle as the $50 bottle if they are male, over the age of 40, belong to a wine membership club, shopping in DC, or in a large store. So, gender, age, membership, store location, and type store matter.

When comparing different individuals demographically, wine critic score is more influential for males versus females, and for club membership/no membership, for both the $20 and $50 bottle. In contrast, the wine description matters most to females. The demographic that was most likely to buy wine is club membership, followed by gender, followed by age and location. The type store demographic showed no differences in purchase likelihood.

A. *Research Limitations*

Although random assignment of subjects to groups was used, the four stores were selected using convenience sampling. Existing relationships in the region were exploited to recruit stores for this research.

The questionnaire only focused on one wine region (Bordeaux) in the wine-producing world. Even though the questionnaire asked subjects to assume they like Bordeaux, there could be some bias amongst some subjects if they do not happen to like Bordeaux. Additionally, subjects were asked to assume they had $70 to spend. Some may have had an aversion to buying a $50 bottle of wine.

Another limitation of the questionnaire is that it only had two different bottle prices. Perhaps, more questions could have been asked with different price points.

Lastly, the test results only pertain to a certain geographical area in the U.S. and may not be representative of other countries/regions.

B. *Implications for Producers, Distributors and Retailers*

Wine Producers

According to this research, consumers pay little attention to wine critic scores/information for inexpensive bottles. There are of course other factors -- some producers may be great at making wine, but not so great at marketing. Every wine needs a label; in fact, some anecdotal evidence suggests that for inexpensive imported wines, the label is more important than the wine quality. The literature review concluded customers prefer easy to understand labels.

For those producers in the business of selling expensive wines, this research concludes that wine information is important to consumers likely to buy. As the price rises, those with money and the more educated wine-consumer are likely to seek out additional information about the wine. Strategic positioning is very important as well because this research indicates that those in a very affluent area might make a purchase with little or no information at all. Either way, it would make sense for wine producers to get their wines in front of critics because positive attention never hurts. Of course, the risk is a low rating.

Wine Retailers

For inexpensive wines, retailers should include shelf information to assist consumers. A wine of the month section could be created for those wines a retailer would like to highlight. This research also indicates that in large retail stores, drawing attention to particular wine is good.

It is common for retailers to have a few customers that do not mind spending a lot and if they prefer high scoring wines, retailers should be looking at all wine critic publications and identifying these wines for their customers.

This research indicates that wine club members are more involved customers and are maybe willing to spend a bit more for bottles of wine. Retailers could take advantage of this and create their own wine club for their customers. They could do this with wines of the month and can focus a small part of their business on highly involved wine customers. Certain wines could be selected for this wine group and the purpose is to draw more people to the group. As some consumers are less involved but have interest in wine, belonging to club could potentially make them more involved, and perhaps could lead them into possibly raising their budget for wine over time.

Wine Distributors

Just like wine retailers, distributors need to look at wine critic scores and publications to be aware of what is happening. They also need to be in constant contact with their customers, so they can obtain wines that certain people may be looking for. For expensive wines, it is important for wine sales representatives to transmit wine critic scores to their customers because a retailer might not always have time to be constantly searching for this information.

For inexpensive wines, distributors need to pay attention to market trends and know what their customers are looking for. Distributors need to buy what they know they can sell, but they have to know the trends in the market place as well. A distributor might determine to bring in a new product because the wine label is great, or the wine has a good story. It is common for distributors to have a marketing department, which can prepare shelf information, display signs and anything a retailer might need to help sell the wine. If a distributor does not have this, they should investigate the possibility of doing so.

C. *Future Research*

Analyzing this dataset using more powerful statistical methods could be useful, such as Artificial Neural Network (ANN) approaches or Principal Component Analysis (PCA), to mine more insights.

It would also make sense to replicate this research using more granular pricing to obtain more information on how price influences purchase decisions. For instance -- to fully investigate this question: At what price point would scores and descriptions not be as relevant? Additionally, there are many major metropolitan markets/cities in the USA and if a similar experiment included more cities, more insights could be gained. Likewise, the research could be extended to study international locations and customers.

VI. Acknowledgements

The authors would like to thank Jeffrey Snow, who independently recruited the four stores, conducted the field research, and provided the data. He also provided us his extensive knowledge and expertise regarding wine markets and consumer behavior.

References

[1] OIV. State of the vitiviniculture world market. http://www.oiv.int/oiv/info/en_vins_effer vescents_OIV_2014. Web.

[2] J. Almenberg, et al., "Do More Expensive Wines Taste Better? Evidence from a Large Sample of Blind Tastings", American Association of Wine Economists, Working Paper #16, Print. 2008.

[3] S. Geringer, D. Patterson, and L. Forsythe, "When Generation Y Buys European Wine: A Consumer Decision-Making Model", Academy Of Marketing Studies Journal, vol. 18, no. 1, pp. 167-186, 2014, Business Source Complete, EBSCOhost, viewed 20 January 2015.

[4] Wines & Vines,. 'Designers Take On Label Trends'. N.p., 2015. Web. 9 February. 2015

[5] B. Scheibehenne, R. Greifeneder, and P. Todd, "Can there ever be Too Many Options? A Meta-Analytic Review of Choice" 2010, Business Source Complete, EBSCOhost, viewed 08 Feburary 2015.

[6] L. Francis, L. L. Lockshin, S. Mueller, and P. Osidacz, "How does shelf information influence consumers' wine choices?" Australian and New Zealand Wine Industry Journal Aust. N.Z. Wine Ind. J. vol. 24 no. 3, pp. 50–56, 2009. Print.

[7] R. E. Quandt, "On Wine Bullshit: Some New Software." Journal of Wine Economics vol. 2, no. 2, pp. 129-135, 2007. Print.

[8] R. L. Weil, "Analysis of Reserve and Regular Bottlings: Why Pay for a Difference Only the Critics Claim to Notice?" Chance vol. 18, no. 3, pp. 9-15, 2005. Print.

[9] R. L. Weil, "Debunking Critics' Wine Words: Can Economists Distinguish the Smell of Asphalt from the Taste of Cherries?" Journal of Wine Economics vol. 2, no. 2, pp. 136-144, 2007. Print.

[10] R. Parker, "The Wine Advocate Rating System." Erobertparker.com. https://www.erobertparker.com/info/wstandards.asp.

[11] H. Ali, S. Lecocq, and M. Visser, "The Impact of Gurus: Parker Grades and En Primeur Wine Prices", Economic Journal, vol. 118, no. 529, pp. F158-F173, 2008, Business Source Complete, EBSCOhost, viewed 18 January 2015.

[12] J. Hilger, G. Rafert, and S. Villas-Boas, "Expert Opinion and the Demand for Experience Goods: An Experimental Approach in the Retail Wine Market", Review Of Economics & Statistics, vol. 93, no. 4, pp. 1289-1296, 2011, Business Source Complete, EBSCOhost, viewed 1 February 2015.

[13] J. Hsu, Multiple Comparisons: Theory And Methods. Chapman & Hall/CRC, 1996. Print.

[14] City-data.com,. 'City-Data.Com - Stats About All US Cities - Real Estate, Relocation Info, Crime, House Prices, Cost Of Living, Races, Home Value Estimator, Recent Sales, Income, Photos, Schools, Maps, Weather, Neighborhoods, And More'. N.p., 2015. Web. 8 September. 2015.

On the Number of Conditions in Mining Incomplete Data Sets Using Characteristic Sets and Maximal Consistent Blocks

Patrick G. Clark and Cheng Gao
Department of Electrical Engineering and Computer Science, University of Kansas
Lawrence, KS, USA
Email: patrick.g.clark@gmail.com
cheng.gao@ku.edu

Jerzy W. Grzymala-Busse
Department of Electrical Engineering and Computer Science, University of Kansas, Lawrence, KS, USA
Department of Expert Systems and Artificial Intelligence, University of Information Technology and Management, Rzeszow, Poland
Email: jerzy@ku.edu

Teresa Mroczek
Department of Expert Systems and Artificial Intelligence, University of Information Technology and Management, Rzeszow, Poland
Email: tmroczek@wsiz.rzeszow.pl

***Abstract*—In this paper, we discuss incomplete data sets with two interpretations of missing attribute values, lost values and "do not care" conditions. For such incomplete data sets, we apply data mining based on characteristic sets and maximal consistent blocks. Our previous research shows that an error rate, evaluated by ten-fold cross validation, is sometimes smaller for characteristic sets and sometimes smaller for maximal consistent blocks. Therefore, we are taking the next step, comparing the quality of both approaches to mining incomplete data in terms of complexity of induced rule sets. We show that for data sets with lost values differences are insignificant while for data sets with "do not care" conditions rule sets are the simplest for upper approximations based on characteristic sets or maximal consistent blocks.**

Keywords–Data mining; rough set theory; probabilistic approximations; MLEM2 rule induction algorithm; lost values; "do not care" conditions.

I. Introduction

In this paper, we use two interpretations of a missing attribute value: lost values and "do not care" conditions. Lost values indicate that the original values were erased, and as a result we should use only existing, specified attribute values for rule induction. "Do not care" conditions mean that the missing attribute value may be replaced by any specified attribute value. Additionally, we use for data mining probabilistic approximations, a generalization of the idea of lower and upper approximations known in rough set theory. A probabilistic approximation is associated with a parameter (probability) α, if α = 1, a probabilistic approximation is reduced to the lower approximation; if α is small positive number, e.g., 0.001, a probabilistic approximation becomes the upper approximation. Usually probabilistic approximations are applied to completely specified data sets [1]–[9], such approximations were generalized to incomplete data sets in [10].

Characteristic sets were introduced in [11] for incomplete data sets with any interpretation of missing attribute values. On the other hand, maximal consistent blocks, introduced in [12], were restricted only to data sets with "do not care" conditions, using only lower and upper approximations. Definition of maximal consistent blocks was generalized to cover lost values and probabilistic approximations in [13]. Usefulness of characteristic sets and maximal consistent blocks to mining incomplete data in terms of an error rate was studied in [13]. It was shown that there is a small difference in quality of rule sets induced either way. Therefore, our current objective is to compare characteristic sets with maximal consistent blocks in terms of complexity of induced rule sets. In this paper, we show that for data sets with lost values differences are insignificant while for data sets with "do not care" conditions rule sets are the simplest for upper approximations based on characteristic sets or maximal consistent blocks. The Modified Learning from Examples Module, version 2 (MLEM2) [14] was used for rule induction.

This paper starts with a discussion on incomplete data in Section II where we define attribute-value blocks, characteristic sets and maximal consistent blocks. In Section III, we present probabilistic approximations based on characteristic sets and maximal consistent blocks. Section IV contains the details of our experiments. Finally, conclusions are presented in Section V.

II. Incomplete Data

We assume that the input data sets are presented in the form of a decision table. An example of a decision table is shown in Table I. Rows of the decision table represent cases, while columns are labeled by variables. The set of all cases will be denoted by U. In Table I, U = {1, 2, 3, 4, 5, 6, 7, 8}. Independent variables are called attributes and a dependent variable is called a decision and is denoted by d. The set of all attributes will be denoted by A. In Table I, A = {*Wind*, *Humidity*, *Temperature*}. The value for a case x and an attribute a will be denoted by $a(x)$.

In this paper, we distinguish between two interpretations of missing attribute values: lost values, denoted by "?" and "do not care" conditions, denoted by " ". Table I presents an

TABLE I. A DECISION TABLE

	Attributes			Decision
Case	Wind	Humidity	Temperature	Trip
1	high	low	medium	yes
2	low	*	high	yes
3	*	?	medium	yes
4	low	low	*	yes
5	high	*	*	no
6	low	high	*	no
7	?	high	?	no
8	*	low	medium	no

incomplete data set with both lost values and "do not care" conditions.

The set X of all cases defined by the same value of the decision d is called a *concept*. For example, a concept associated with the value *yes* of the decision *Trip* is the set $\{1, 2, 3, 4\}$.

For a variable a and its value v, (a, v) is called a variable-value pair. A *block* of (a, v), denoted by $[(a, v)]$, is the set $\{x \in U \mid a(x) = v\}$ [15]. For incomplete decision tables, the definition of a block of an attribute-value pair is modified in the following way.

- If for an attribute a and a case x we have $a(x) = ?$, the case x should not be included in any blocks $[(a, v)]$ for all values v of attribute a,
- If for an attribute a and a case x we have $a(x) = *$, the case x should be included in blocks $[(a, v)]$ for all specified values v of attribute a.

For the data set from Table I, the blocks of attribute-value pairs are:

[(Wind, low)] = $\{2, 3, 4, 6, 8\}$,
[(Wind, high)] = $\{1, 3, 5, 8\}$,
[(Humidity, low)] = $\{1, 2, 4, 5, 8\}$,
[(Humidity, high)] = $\{2, 5, 6, 7\}$,
[(Temperature, medium)] = $\{1, 3, 4, 5, 6, 8\}$, and
[(Temperature, high)] = $\{2, 4, 5, 6\}$.

For a case $x \in U$ and $B \subseteq A$, the *characteristic set* $K_B(x)$ is defined as the intersection of the sets $K(x, a)$, for all $a \in B$, where the set $K(x, a)$ is defined in the following way:

- If $a(x)$ is specified, then $K(x, a)$ is the block $[(a, a(x))]$ of attribute a and its value $a(x)$,
- If $a(x) = ?$ or $a(x) = *$, then $K(x, a) = U$.

For Table I and $B = A$,

$K_A(1) = \{1, 5, 8\}$,
$K_A(2) = \{2, 4, 6\}$,
$K_A(3) = \{1, 3, 4, 5, 6, 8\}$,
$K_A(4) = \{2, 4, 8\}$,
$K_A(5) = \{1, 3, 5, 8\}$,
$K_A(6) = \{2, 6\}$,
$K_A(7) = \{2, 5, 6, 7\}$, and
$K_A(8) = \{1, 4, 5, 8\}$.

A binary relation $R(B)$ on U, defined for $x, y \in U$ in the following way

$$(x, y) \in R(B)\ if\ and\ only\ if\ y \in K_B(x) \qquad (1)$$

will be called the *characteristic relation*. In our example, $R(A)$ = {(1, 1), (1, 5), (1, 8), (2, 2), (2, 4), (2, 6), (3, 1), (3, 3), (3, 4), (3, 5), (3, 6), (3, 8), (4, 2), (4, 4), (4, 8), (5, 1), (5, 3), (5, 5), (5, 8), (6, 2), (6, 6), (7, 2), (7, 5), (7, 6), (7, 7), (8, 1), (8, 4), (8, 5), (8, 8)}.

We quote some definitions from [13]. Let X be a subset of U. The set X is *B-consistent* if $(x, y) \in R(B)$ for any $x, y \in X$. If there does not exist a consistent B-subset Y of U such that X is a proper subset of Y, the set X is called a *maximal B-consistent block*. The set of all B-maximal consistent blocks will be denoted by $\mathscr{C}(B)$. In our example, $\mathscr{C}(A)$ = {{1, 5, 8}, {2, 4}, {2, 6}, {3, 5}, {4, 8}, {7}}.

Let $B \subseteq A$ and $Y \in \mathscr{C}(B)$. The set of all maximal B-consistent blocks which include an element x of the set U, i.e. the set

$$\{Y | Y \in \mathscr{C}(B), x \in Y\} \qquad (2)$$

will be denoted by $\mathscr{C}_x(B)$.

For data sets in which all missing attribute values are "do not care" conditions, an idea of a maximal consistent block of B was defined in [16]. Note that in our definition, the maximal consistent blocks of B are defined for arbitrary interpretations of missing attribute values. For Table I, the maximal A-consistent blocks $\mathscr{C}_x(A)$ are

$\mathscr{C}_1(A) = \{\{1, 5, 8\}\}$,
$\mathscr{C}_2(A) = \{\{2, 4\}, \{2, 6\}\}$,
$\mathscr{C}_3(A) = \{\{3, 5\}\}$,
$\mathscr{C}_4(A) = \{\{2, 4\}, \{4, 8\}\}$,
$\mathscr{C}_5(A) = \{\{1, 5, 8\}, \{3, 5\}\}$,
$\mathscr{C}_6(A) = \{\{2, 6\}\}$,
$\mathscr{C}_7(A) = \{\{7\}\}$,
$\mathscr{C}_8(A) = \{\{1, 5, 8\}, \{4, 8\}\}$.

III. PROBABILISTIC APPROXIMATIONS

In this section, we will discuss two types of probabilistic approximations: based on characteristic sets and on maximal consistent blocks.

A. Probabilistic Approximations Based on Characteristic Sets

In general, probabilistic approximations based on characteristic sets may be categorized as singleton, subset and concept [11][17]. In this paper, we restrict our attention only to concept probabilistic approximations, for simplicity calling them probabilistic approximations based on characteristic sets.

A *probabilistic approximation based on characteristic sets* of the set X with the threshold α, $0 < \alpha \leq 1$, denoted by $appr_{\alpha}^{CS}(X)$, is defined as follows

$$\cup\{K_A(x) \mid x \in X,\ Pr(X|K_A(x)) \geq \alpha\}. \qquad (3)$$

For Table I and both concepts $\{1, 2, 3, 4\}$ and $\{5, 6, 7\}$, all distinct probabilistic approximations based on characteristic sets are

$$appr_{0.5}^{CS}(\{1, 2, 3, 4\}) = \{1, 2, 3, 4, 5, 6, 8\},$$

$$appr_{0.667}^{CS}(\{1, 2, 3, 4\}) = \{2, 4, 6, 8\},$$

$$appr_{1}^{CS}(\{1, 2, 3, 4\}) = \emptyset,$$

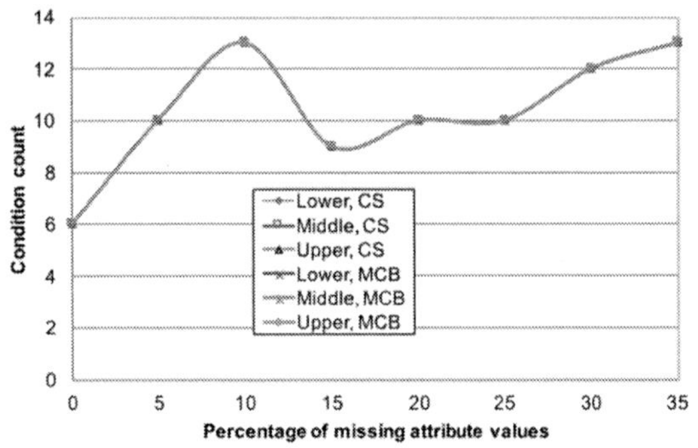

Figure 1. Number of conditions for the *Bankruptcy* data set with lost values

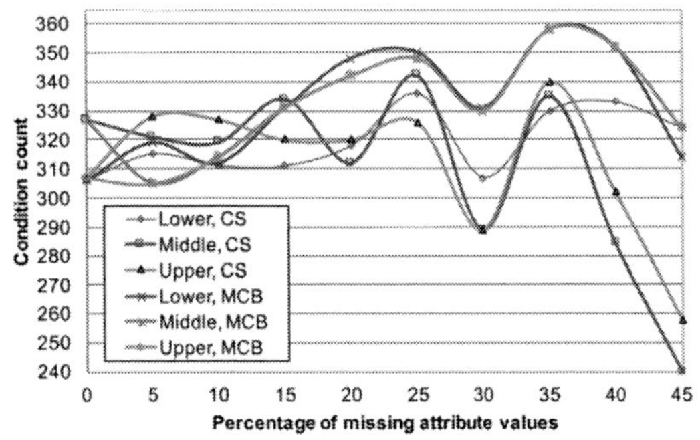

Figure 2. Number of conditions for the *Breast cancer* data set with lost values

$$appr^{CS}_{0.5}(\{5,6,7,8\}) = U,$$

$$appr^{CS}_{0.75}(\{5,6,7,8\}) = \{2,5,6,7\},$$

$$appr^{CS}_{1}(\{5,6,7,8\}) = \emptyset.$$

If for some β, $0 < \beta \leq 1$, a probabilistic approximation $appr^{CS}_{\beta}(X)$ is not listed above, it is equal to the probabilistic approximation $appr^{CS}_{\alpha}(X)$ with the closest α to β, $\alpha \geq \beta$. For example, $appr^{CS}_{0.6}(\{1,2,3,4\}) = appr^{CS}_{0.667}(\{1,2,3,4\})$.

B. Probabilistic Approximations Based on Maximal Consistent Blocks

By analogy with the definition of a probabilistic approximation based on characteristic sets, we may define a probabilistic approximation based on maximal consistent blocks as follows:

A *probabilistic approximation* based on maximal consistent blocks of the set X with the threshold α, $0 < \alpha \leq 1$, and denoted by $appr^{MCB}_{\alpha}(X)$ is defined as follows

$$\cup\{Y \mid Y \in \mathscr{C}_x(A),\ x \in X,\ Pr(X|Y) \geq \alpha\}. \quad (4)$$

All distinct probabilistic approximations based on maximal consistent blocks are

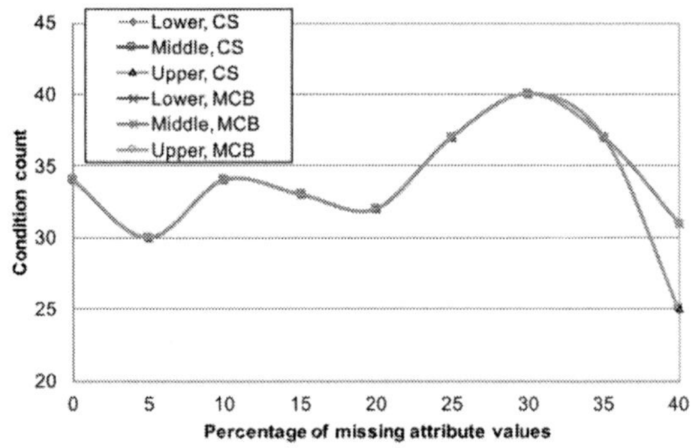

Figure 3. Number of conditions for the *Echocardiogram* data set with lost values

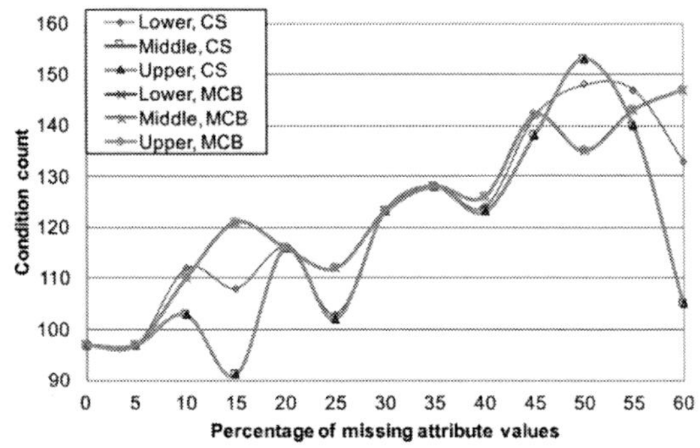

Figure 4. Number of conditions for the *Hepatitis* data set with lost values

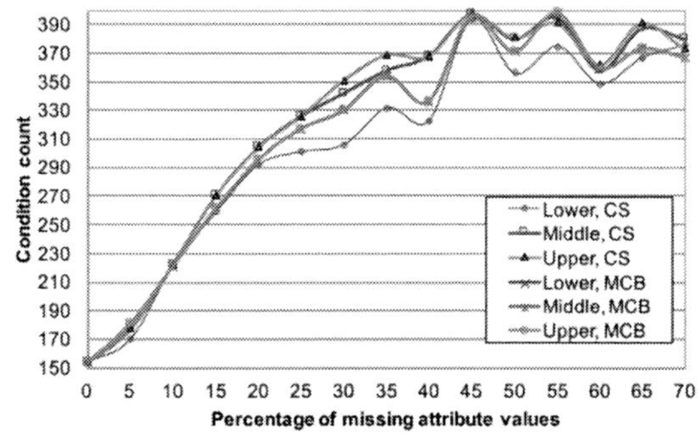

Figure 5. Number of conditions for the *Image segmentation* data set with lost values

$$appr^{MCB}_{0.333}(\{1,2,3,4\}) = \{1,2,3,4,5,6,8\},$$

$$appr^{MCB}_{0.5}(\{1,2,3,4\}) = \{2,3,4,5,6,8\},$$

$$appr^{MCB}_{1}(\{1,2,3,4\}) = \{2,4\},$$

$$appr^{MCB}_{0.5}(\{5,6,7,8\}) = U,$$

$$appr^{MCB}_{0.667}(\{5,6,7,8\}) = \{1,5,7,8\},$$

$$appr^{MCB}_{1}(\{5,6,7,8\}) = \{7\}.$$

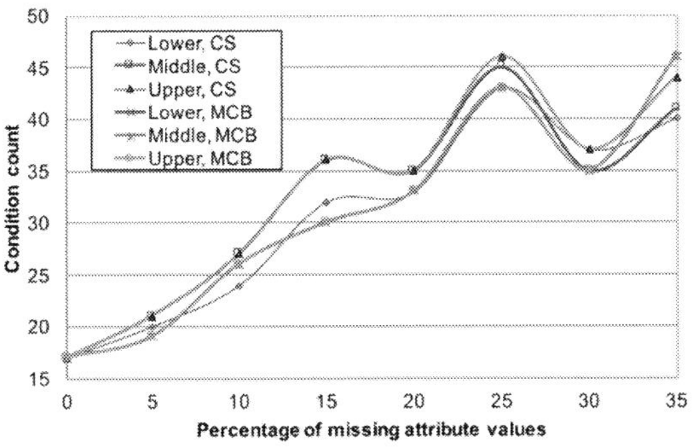

Figure 6. Number of conditions for the *Iris* data set with lost values

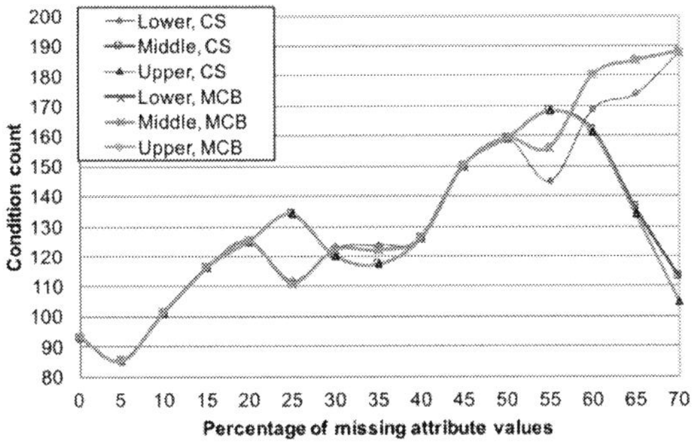

Figure 7. Number of conditions for the *Lymphography* data set with lost values

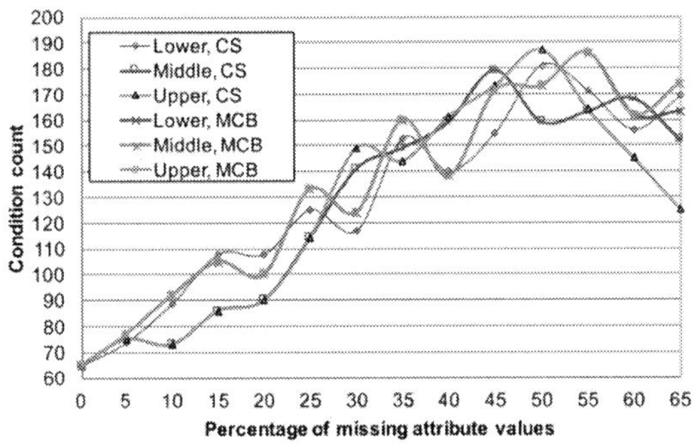

Figure 8. Number of conditions for the *Wine recognition* data set with lost values

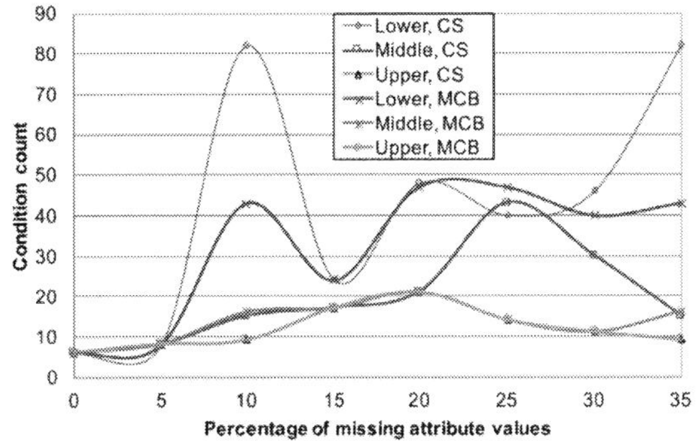

Figure 9. Number of conditions for the *Bankruptcy* data set with "do not care" conditions

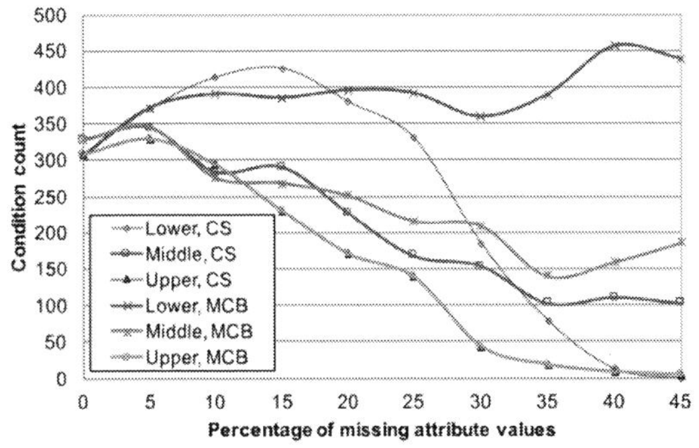

Figure 10. Number of conditions for the *Breast cancer* data set with "do not care" conditions

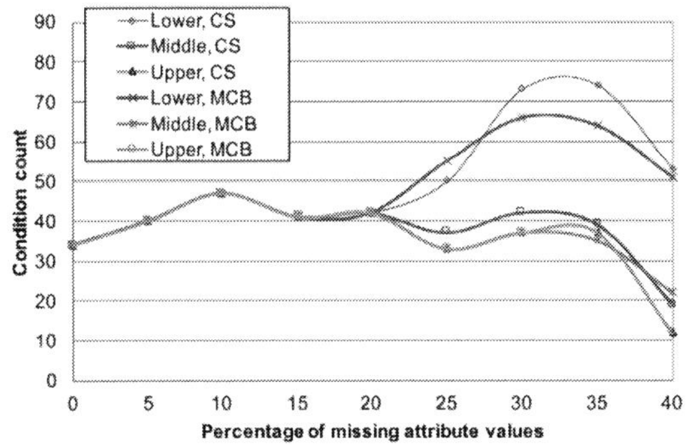

Figure 11. Number of conditions for the *Echocardiogram* data set with "do not care" conditions

IV. EXPERIMENTS

For our experiments, we used eight data sets that are available in the University of California at Irvine *Machine Learning Repository*.

For every data set, a template was created. Such a template was formed by replacing randomly 5% of existing specified attribute values by *lost values*, then adding another 5% of specified values, and so on, until an entire row was full of lost values. The same templates were used for constructing data sets with "do not care" conditions, by replacing "?"s with "*"s.

In our experiments, we used an MLEM2 rule induction algorithm of the Learning from Examples using Rough Sets (LERS) data mining system [18]–[20]. Results of our experiments are presented in Figures 1–16, where "CS" denotes a characteristic set and "MCB" denotes a maximal consistent block. In our experiments, six approaches for mining incomplete data sets were used, since we combined two options: characteristic sets and maximal consistent blocks with three

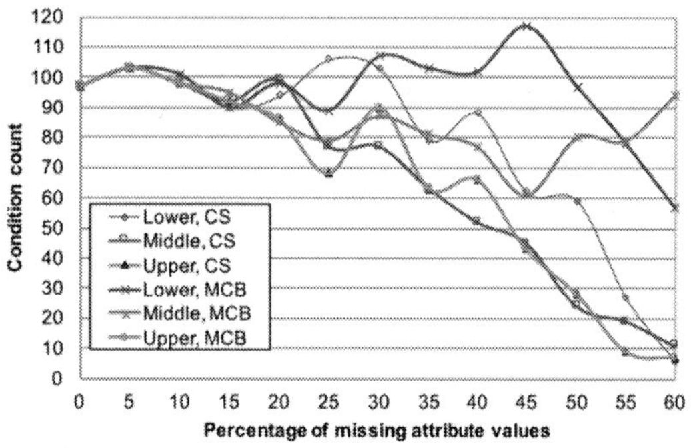

Figure 12. Number of conditions for the *Hepatitis* data set with "do not care" conditions

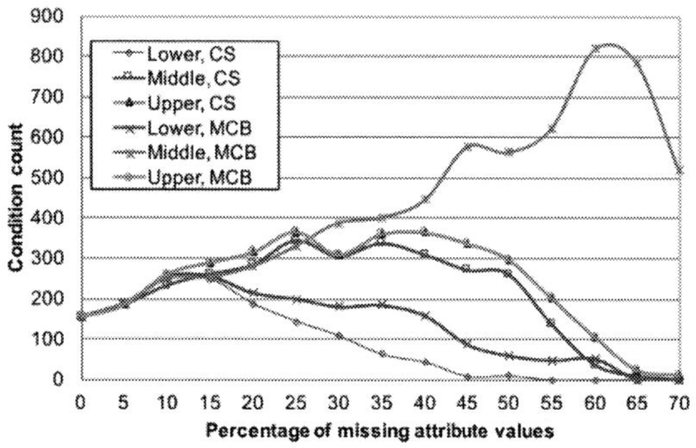

Figure 13. Number of conditions for the *Image segmentation* data set with "do not care" conditions

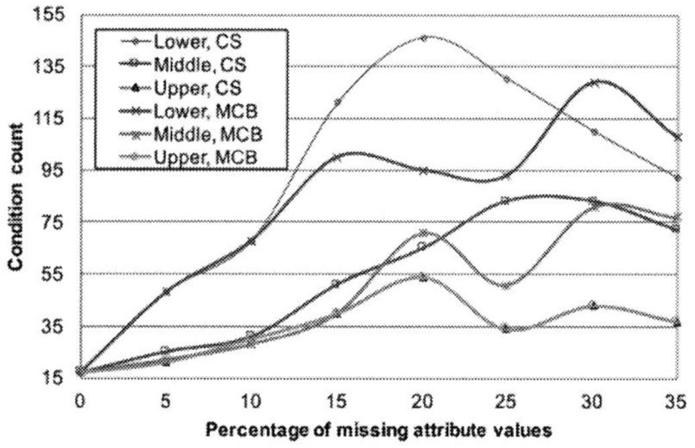

Figure 14. Number of conditions for the *Iris* data set with "do not care" conditions

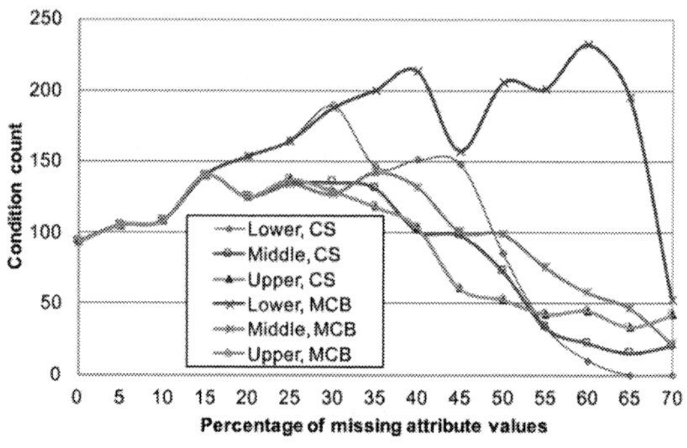

Figure 15. Number of conditions for the *Lymphography* data set with "do not care" conditions

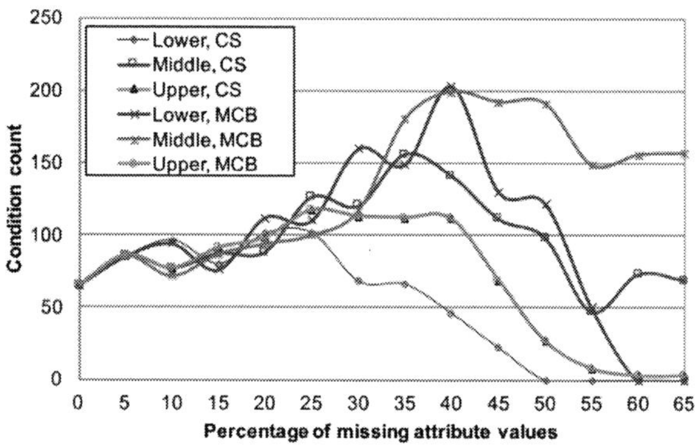

Figure 16. Number of conditions for the *Wine recognition* data set with "do not care" conditions

options of probabilistic approximations: lower (α = 1), middle (α = 0.5) and upper (α = 0.001).

These six approaches were compared by applying the Friedman rank sum test combined with multiple comparisons, with a 5% level of significance. We applied this test to all 16 data sets, eight with lost values and eight with "do not care" conditions.

For eight data sets with lost values, the null hypothesis H_0 of the Friedman test saying that differences between these approaches are insignificant was rejected for *image recognition* as the only data set. However, the post-hoc test (distribution-free multiple comparisons based on the Friedman rank sums) indicated that the differences between all six approaches were statistically insignificant.

For eight data sets with "do not care" conditions, the null hypothesis H_0 of the Friedman test was rejected for all data sets except *wine recognition*. Additionally, for *echocardiogram* data set the post-hoc test shown that the differences between all six approaches were insignificant. Results for the remaining six data sets are presented in Table II. *Image segmentation* data set needs an additional explanation. For all three best approaches (lower approximation based on characteristic sets, lower approximation based on maximal consistent blocks and middle approximation based on characteristic sets) and for large percentages of missing attribute values, lower approximations are reduced to empty sets. This is due to the fact that both characteristic sets and maximal consistent blocks are large, so they cannot be subsets of corresponding concepts. Thus we may as well exclude this data set from further analysis. For remaining five data sets, clean winners are upper approximation based on characteristic sets and maximal consistent blocks. Obviously, for data sets with "do not care" conditions, *concept* upper approximations are identical with upper approximations based on maximal consistent blocks [12].

TABLE II. Results of statistical analysis

Data set	The best approaches	The worst approaches
Bankruptcy	Upper, CS; Upper, MCB	Lower, CS
Breast cancer	Upper, CS; Upper, MCB	Lower, MCB
Hepatitis	Upper, CS; Upper, MCB	Lower, MCB
Image recognition	Lower, CS; Lower, MCB; Middle, CS	Middle, MCB; Upper, CS; Upper, MCB
Iris	Upper, CS; Upper, MCB	Lower, CS; Lower, MCB
Lymphography	Middle, CS; Upper, CS; Upper, MCB	Lower, MCB

V. CONCLUSIONS

In this paper, we compare six approaches for mining incomplete data in terms of complexity of the rule sets. As follows from our experiments, for data sets with lost values, there is not significant difference between all six approaches. For data sets with "do not care" conditions, rule sets induced from upper approximations, based on characteristic sets or maximal consistent blocks, are the simplest in terms of the total number of conditions, in terms of complexity of rule sets.

REFERENCES

[1] J. W. Grzymala-Busse and W. Ziarko, "Data mining based on rough sets," in Data Mining: Opportunities and Challenges, J. Wang, Ed. Hershey, PA: Idea Group Publ., 2003, pp. 142–173.

[2] Z. Pawlak and A. Skowron, "Rough sets: Some extensions," Information Sciences, vol. 177, 2007, pp. 28–40.

[3] Z. Pawlak, S. K. M. Wong, and W. Ziarko, "Rough sets: probabilistic versus deterministic approach," International Journal of Man-Machine Studies, vol. 29, 1988, pp. 81–95.

[4] D. Ślęzak and W. Ziarko, "The investigation of the bayesian rough set model," International Journal of Approximate Reasoning, vol. 40, 2005, pp. 81–91.

[5] S. K. M. Wong and W. Ziarko, "INFER—an adaptive decision support system based on the probabilistic approximate classification," in Proceedings of the 6-th International Workshop on Expert Systems and their Applications, 1986, pp. 713–726.

[6] Y. Y. Yao, "Probabilistic rough set approximations," International Journal of Approximate Reasoning, vol. 49, 2008, pp. 255–271.

[7] Y. Y. Yao and S. K. M. Wong, "A decision theoretic framework for approximate concepts," International Journal of Man-Machine Studies, vol. 37, 1992, pp. 793–809.

[8] W. Ziarko, "Variable precision rough set model," Journal of Computer and System Sciences, vol. 46, no. 1, 1993, pp. 39–59.

[9] ——, "Probabilistic approach to rough sets," International Journal of Approximate Reasoning, vol. 49, 2008, pp. 272–284.

[10] J. W. Grzymala-Busse, "Generalized parameterized approximations," in Proceedings of the 6-th International Conference on Rough Sets and Knowledge Technology, 2011, pp. 136–145.

[11] ——, "Rough set strategies to data with missing attribute values," in Notes of the Workshop on Foundations and New Directions of Data Mining, in conjunction with the Third International Conference on Data Mining, 2003, pp. 56–63.

[12] Y. Leung, W. Wu, and W. Zhang, "Knowledge acquisition in incomplete information systems: A rough set approach," European Journal of Operational Research, vol. 168, 2006, pp. 164–180.

[13] P. G. Clark, C. Gao, J. W. Grzymala-Busse, and T. Mroczek, "Characteristic sets and generalized maximal consistent blocks in mining incomplete data, part i," in Proceedings of the International Joint Conference on Rough Sets, 2017, pp. 477–486.

[14] P. G. Clark and J. W. Grzymala-Busse, "Experiments on rule induction from incomplete data using three probabilistic approximations," in Proceedings of the 2012 IEEE International Conference on Granular Computing, 2012, pp. 90–95.

[15] J. W. Grzymala-Busse, "LERS—a system for learning from examples based on rough sets," in Intelligent Decision Support. Handbook of Applications and Advances of the Rough Set Theory, R. Slowinski, Ed. Dordrecht, Boston, London: Kluwer Academic Publishers, 1992, pp. 3–18.

[16] Y. Leung and D. Li, "Maximal consistent block technique for rule acquisition in incomplete information systems," Information Sciences, vol. 153, 2003, pp. 85–106.

[17] P. G. Clark and J. W. Grzymala-Busse, "Experiments using three probabilistic approximations for rule induction from incomplete data sets," in Proceeedings of the MCCSIS 2012, IADIS European Conference on Data Mining ECDM 2012, 2012, pp. 72–78.

[18] ——, "Experiments on probabilistic approximations," in Proceedings of the 2011 IEEE International Conference on Granular Computing, 2011, pp. 144–149.

[19] J. W. Grzymala-Busse, "A new version of the rule induction system LERS," Fundamenta Informaticae, vol. 31, 1997, pp. 27–39.

[20] ——, "MLEM2: A new algorithm for rule induction from imperfect data," in Proceedings of the 9th International Conference on Information Processing and Management of Uncertainty in Knowledge-Based Systems, 2002, pp. 243–250.